The COVID Chronicles

The COVID Chronicles

*A Journey of
Faith and Hope*

Kimberly Lozada, EdD

LAUREATE
LIFE PRESS

Dallas

Copyright © 2024 by Kimberly Lozada, EdD

Cover photo: Jose Lozada

All rights reserved. Neither this book nor any portion thereof may be reproduced or used in any manner whatsoever without the express written permission of the author, except for the use of brief quotations in a book review.

Printed in the United States of America
First Printing 2024

Publisher: Laureate Life Press, Dallas TX

ISBN: 9798343906790

*To Changing Hearts and Habits
Through Hope and Faith*

introduction

I just decided. It is what I do. Like the day I smoked my last cigarette in 2001. Or the day I decided to give up alcohol in 2019. I just decided.

I peeled off the cellophane wrapper to a brand new, hardcover, lined journal and wrote the date: Friday, March 13, 2020. Friday the 13th.

I decided to chronicle the events that had already begun to unfold overseas and were gaining momentum in the United States, in my state, and in my county. I didn't know what I didn't know, like how long this chronicle project would last, but I was compelled to complete it.

My focus word for 2020 was "commit," so I committed to documenting the events as they played out. Some days were mundane. Some days were magical. I had no idea I would fill *nine* journals over a two-year period documenting the global pandemic, but the daily task of journaling provided a way for me to process this life-altering period in history.

The act of journaling made me hyper aware of each day's events. I processed as I wrote. I looked forward to each new day. I searched for hope and God winks and life lessons.

My story is mostly positive. That is how I approach life most days. For instance, I can focus on the scary horror of tiny particles from an infected person that linger in the air and spread to other people causing illness, or worse, death. Or, I can observe tiny butterflies and hummingbirds that float through my backyard and bring new life through pollination. One approach is stressful; the other, joyful.

A wide range of topics emerge in this chronicle. I quoted Bible verses that were meaningful to me and my personal spiritual journey and reflected exactly what I was feeling and experiencing that day. Was it a coincidence, a fluke, or a God wink?

I referenced news reports and COVID-19 statistics in my journal without including specific citations. I receive my news from a variety of sources each day, including TV stations like ABC, CBS and NBC news affiliates, I subscribe to several online news sources like *The New York Times*, CNN, Fox News and Google News.

I included quotes from my morning Facebook posts that seemed to foreshadow the events which unfolded that day. Some of the events mentioned in *The COVID Chronicles* were historical, while others were hysterical. A fictional horse named Wood Biscuit provided sarcasm and levity during an uncertain time, as well.

The pandemic affected our personal space. We had bubbles, isolation, and quarantine. We stood six feet apart. We developed new relationships with our home space, workspace, outdoors, and nature. Many of us experienced an evolution in education and analyzed our individual political perspectives. Most people experienced challenges and shifts in their mental, physical, and spiritual health. We all shared aspects of this experience.

This is my testimony. I feel vulnerable putting myself "out there" by publishing this book. Why? It is the society we currently live in. I fear criticism and being misunderstood. I fear judgment. I fear having something I wrote being taken out of context. I fear this more than I feared getting COVID or facing breast cancer.

But I also hope. My hope far outweighs my fears. My faith that God guides me through the good and the bad is greater than my fears. I hope the *Chronicles* will serve people to find our commonalities through a shared experience. I believe we have more in common with one another than we are different.

I hope that people can use the *Chronicles* as a starting point for healing. We must face the fallout of the pandemic. One of the saddest consequences of the pandemic is the deep division, isolation, and fear that people still feel. We cannot ignore what happened to us. We cannot bury things and let them fester. We cannot wait for someone else to fix this.

"F.E.A.R. = Forget Everything and Run OR
Face Everything and Rise" —Zig Ziglar

We all want something better for our family, community, nation, and the world. We must start somewhere. What about reading and reflecting on the *Chronicles*? What about answering the reflective questions at the back of this book? What about participating in a one-on-one discussion or a small group book study?

We can begin opening our closed fists and welcoming the possibility of compassion, care, and concern. We can allow empathy to build bridges with our perceived enemies. We can find balance, synergy, and unity from shared lived experiences. Stephen Covey discusses our circle of influence in *The Seven Habits of Highly Effective People*. I am one person, but I have a sphere of influence. I am like a pebble thrown into a pond that creates ripples on the once-still surface. I am like a butterfly who flutters its wings and influences the wind and the climate of the world we live in.

We each have our individual story to tell, but we also have so much in common, including the fact that we all experienced the global pandemic that pervaded our lives between the years 2020 and 2022.

My everyday prayer: *Thank you Lord for this day and the opportunity it brings.*

2019

december

Tues / 2019 Dec 31 / Quote of the Day

New Year's Eve

"The New Year is a painting not yet painted, a path not yet stepped on, a wing not yet taken off. Things haven't happened as of yet. Before the clock strikes twelve, remember that you are blessed with the ability to reshape your life."
Mehmet Murat İldan

The Muddy Creek Trail in the Woodbridge neighborhood where I live in Sachse, Texas has been an important part of my life since I moved into my home twenty years ago. I am married to Jose, and we have two dogs. One is a miniature poodle named Dexter. The other is a standard poodle named Major.

Jose and I walk the trail around Woodbridge Golf Club with the dogs several times a week. It is a special place for us, so we got married on the trail eight years ago on March 12, 2012, at 12:00 p.m. by hole number twelve.

I have three adult stepchildren. Christian is currently in the Air Force stationed in Washington State. Kat is an insurance adjuster and is engaged to Jordan. They are scheduled to elope on March 17th in Colorado. Kyla is finishing chiropractic school at Parker University and is engaged to Taylor.

My immediate family lives in town. Jose's family is in Florida. My ninety-four-year-old grandmother, who I call Mamal, lives an hour away in Arlington.

On December 9, 2019, I created a Facebook group page called 2020

Vision. Every morning, I posted an "Inspirational Quote of the Day" with a pretty picture I colored from the Happy Color app.

The first case of COVID-19 was reported on December 1, 2019.

2020

february

Sun / 2020 Feb 9 / Personal Facebook Page

My focus word for 2020 is "commit." I am committed to seeing my friends. I am committed to a road trip with my cousins and sister. I have committed to two student teachers at Skyline High School through UTeach Dallas. I am committed to my three mentees who are Charles Butt Scholars and are pursuing careers in education.

I am committed to saving money to take Jose on an Alaskan cruise for his 50th birthday in 2021. I am committed to continuing my life of sobriety. Today marks 125 days with no alcohol.

Thurs / 2020 Feb 20 / Cousin Trip

"It takes as much energy to wish as to plan."
Eleanor Roosevelt

My sister, Michelle, my cousins, Jim and Angela, and I, took a cousins' reunion trip to Waco, Texas, for a long weekend. Why Waco? Our grandparents lived there when we were kids, and we had not been back in almost forty years. Our grandparents are gone, and Granddaddy's restaurant, George's Surf and Sirloin, is now a barbecue joint, but we saw lots of sites.

We visited the Schmalz Sandwich Shop, the Cameron Park Zoo, the Waco Suspension Bridges, the Doris Miller Memorial, the Dr. Pepper Museum, and the Texas Ranger Museum.

I found my first painted rock at Lover's Leap which had an angel on it and said, "She believed she could, so she did." We shopped at The Spice Village, and everyone chipped in and bought me a sign that said, "I'm not bossy; I'm motivational."

Mon / 2020 Feb 24 / A Day in Big D

When we returned to Dallas, my husband, Jose, took the day off, and we made a day of touring the local sites. We started at the George W. Bush Library and Museum, then the The Sixth Floor Museum at Dealey Plaza, and finally the Museum of Illusions in downtown Dallas. We stopped at the Leaning Tower of Dallas for funny photos. The Affiliated Computer Services building was dubbed "the Leaning Tower of Dallas" after a failed implosion left it standing at an angle.

march

Fri / 2020 Mar 6 / The Calm Before...

My cousin Angela's company in San Francisco mandated that everyone in the Bay Area work from home until further notice due to the coronavirus.

Thurs / 2020 Mar 12 / ...The Storm

Our 8th wedding anniversary.
"And into the forest I go to lose my mind and find my soul."
John Muir

My plan for the day was to get to work on my step-daughter Kat and her fiancé Jordan's Celebration Luncheon which we planned to host next month after they elope this weekend. My plan included running around town to the post office for stamps, Hobby Lobby for envelope stickers, Walgreens for invitations, Smallcakes to make a cupcake order, Party City for party supplies, and Fisherman's Kitchen to discuss the reservation and menu.

As I dressed for work, the news reported a mandate for no gatherings larger than fifty people due to the coronavirus outbreak. I called Kat. She was disappointed, but she agreed it was best to postpone.

Today was my last day at Richland College prior to spring break. I work part time as the Service Learning Coordinator for Richland Collegiate High School (RCHS). The RCHS service-learning program offers students an opportunity to serve a wide variety of charitable and social agencies including, but not limited to animal shelters, food pantries, senior living facilities, clinics and hospitals, homeless shelters, donation centers, art venues, museums, and libraries. Our students' sixty hours of service learning integrates classroom instruction with real world volunteer service in the community to enhance the students' learning experience. It culminates with a Senior Capstone research paper, infographic, and presentation to a panel of judges.

The news about the coronavirus has increased the likelihood that there will be panic and shut down on the horizon. I took precautions and made sure I had access to my work files by downloading them on a thumb drive before I headed home.

By the time I got home and watched the news, people were starting to panic. I contacted both of my stepdaughters Kat and Kyla. I sent them $100 through a cash app and advised them to get some groceries. Neither felt very concerned, but both promised they would go to the store.

Fri / 2020 Mar 13 / Journal Entry

It's Friday the 13th.

Most school districts have been on spring break this week. News about the coronavirus has prompted districts to announce an extended break. The shelves at Walmart were almost empty. Toilet paper, medicine, water, cleaning supplies, and meat were all gone.

We called the Romantic Riversong Bed and Breakfast in Colorado to check on Kat and Jordan's reservations for their wedding/elopement trip. We had paid for the trip, but we wanted to make sure they could still travel with all the craziness that was unfolding around the coronavirus.

Sun / 2020 Mar 15 / Journal Entry

Social media posts show that people are hoarding supplies, and the stores have empty shelves. Businesses are closing. Schools are closed through the month of April. "Social distancing" is the new normal.

I check on my 94-year-old grandmother, Mamal, daily. Her memory is getting worse. I have tried to get her to make a grocery list for days. My uncle, Michael, should be in town on Monday to stay with her. The news is changing by the hour. The girls reported they went to the store and got groceries. They were surprised the shelves were empty. Kat and Jordan flew out this morning to meet their friends in Denver and to elope.

Mon / 2020 Mar 16 / Journal Entry

"Times of transition are strenuous, but they can be a blessing. They are an opportunity to purge, rethink, prioritize, and be intentional about new habits. We are the architects of our new normal."
Kristen Armstrong

I sent an email to the principal of our school, Craig Hinkle, about suspending service-learning activities at Richland Collegiate High School.

Craig,
I think the service-learning requirement should be a low priority for our students. I think we should put ALL service learning on hold throughout spring break. I am open to any ideas.
Stay safe!

Tues / 2020 Mar 17 / Journal Entry

The news is getting worse. There are no St. Patrick's Day parades. No March Madness games. No concerts. No gatherings of ten or more people. There is a shortage of everything at the grocery stores. We watch President Trump's press conferences every morning around 10:00. Some states, like California and New York, are sheltering in place. All the restaurants are shut down.

Kat and Jordan got married in Colorado. I am worried they may have issues traveling back to Dallas. We are so lucky we did not have to postpone a big wedding and reception. I made calls to check in with all family members, and everyone seems to be okay. My sister's small business has come to a complete halt.

My Facebook Post on the 2020 Vision Group Facebook Page

My focus word for 2020 is "commit." I am committed to this group (2020 Vision) and to this platform. I hope it serves as a bright spot in your day. Despite social distancing, we are a community of amazing people who can encourage and inspire each other. I am committed to celebrating the opportunity to recreate my daily schedule. Cook. Work. Read. Do a puzzle and disconnect from devices. Walk the dog and wave to neighbors. Garden (before it gets too hot). Draw, color, and write. Investigate family history. Organize my photos. Play backgammon. Call friends and family. Be grateful.

Wed / 2020 Mar 18 / Journal Entry

"Just because you got the monkey off your back doesn't mean the circus has left town."
George Carlin

Everything is shut down. We are taking advantage of being stuck at home by sleeping late, catching up on household chores, watching the president on TV, scrolling through Facebook, walking the dogs and watching Netflix. TV is our source of entertainment: *Love is Blind, The Crown, This is Us, Tiger King, The Queen's Gambit,* and *Ozark.*

Thank goodness for my teacher retirement annuity check. Thank goodness Jose can still work from home as a licensed private investigator. Thank goodness we stocked up on groceries and know how to cook, since all the restaurants are shut down. We are in danger of gaining "The Quarantine Fifteen."

Thurs / 2020 Mar 19 / Journal Entry

Day 7, 1 week of coronavirus
"Yes, you can!"
Unknown

I make phone calls to check in on my family. The news is not getting better. Establishing a routine is important. I finished my first jigsaw puzzle, and I baked a cake.

Someone posted on the neighborhood Woodbridge Resident Facebook page encouraging people to post things in their windows to entertain people as they walked around the neighborhood. I participated by posting pictures each day, and I looked for posts as we walked the dogs.

March 17, Shamrocks
March 20, Silly Faces
March 23, Animals
March 26, Encouraging Words
March 29, Flowers
April 1, Jokes
April 4, Easter Eggs

The Facebook posts of people trying to deal with online school are an indication of big changes in education. School districts are offering free Chromebooks and drive-through pickup for free breakfast and lunch meals.

The news reports that the elderly are the most susceptible to the coronavirus. President Trump believes social distancing will end by Easter.

Jose and I set up our home office so we each have a separate workspace.

Craig sent an email.

Good afternoon,
Like you, I have been glued to the news to better understand the impact of the spread of the coronavirus (COVID-19). The future weeks and days will begin to give us more clarity as to how to approach the changes currently taking place—both personally and academically. In the meantime, I thought I would share what I currently know and how to prepare in the near future.

Spring break will be extended for RCHS by one week, through March 29.
Classes will resume on Monday, March 30, online.
Capstone Presentations will be online.
Service Learning has also been suspended until further notice.

One more thought—shared with me by an RCHS Senior. "It's the shared struggle that brings us together." As dark as things may seem, or as uncertain as it may feel, we are all in this together.
Sincerely,
Mr. Hinkle

Fri/ 2020 Mar 20/ Journal Entry

"Be thankful for what you have. Your life is someone else's fairytale."
Wale Ayeni

I placed an online grocery order today. It is not safe to go to the store in person. The supplies at the store have not improved. My online order will not be ready for pickup until Monday afternoon. We had to get Spectrum out to the house to work on our internet. With everyone stuck at home, the internet demands have increased exponentially. Hopefully, we are good to go now.

Sat/ 2020 Mar 21 / Journal Entry

Christian's birthday

"In solitude is healing. Speak to your soul. Listen to your heart. Sometimes in the absence of noise, we find the answers."
Dodinsky

We slept in and made lunch. We decided to make cornbread, coffee cake, and pancake batter before our quart of milk spoils and goes sour. We have had to change our mindset about groceries, supplies, and cooking since we cannot just jump in the car and go to the store or a drive-through. Thank goodness we have food staples. Thank goodness we know how to cook. Thank goodness we have resources. I worry about all the people who do not.

Sun / 2020 Mar 22 / Journal Entry

Dallas County Commissioner, Clay Jenkins, announced "shelter in place/safer at home" for Dallas County for the next twelve days until April 3rd.

We heard honking and saw a car caravan parade. Elementary teachers from the neighborhood elementary school were driving, honking, and waving through the neighborhood streets. It brought tears to my eyes.

Mon / 2020 Mar 23 / Journal Entry

We went to Kroger to pick up the online grocery order I placed last Friday. Only half of the order was filled. Maybe it was due to supply chain issues, or maybe it was because online grocery pick up was new. I picked up an order of brownies and cookies at Tiff's Treats. The store had a line of blue tape three feet from the counter to stand behind.

Jose and I took the dogs on a walk at 11:30 p.m. The neighborhood was eerily quiet. We saw zero people and zero cars. There were zero planes flying overhead.

Tues / 2020 Mar 24 / Journal Entry

I was looking at a paint by number kit that was advertised on my Facebook feed. Kyla sent me a text that she and Taylor ordered one. It must be why it appeared on my feed. Apparently, there is an algorithm Facebook uses to advertise things your friends are interested in. I took advantage of the discount, so I ordered one too.

Wed / 2020 Mar 25 / Journal Entry

My dog, Dexter, was licking and scooting this morning. I did a virtual Vet Chat through my Banfield app. Thank goodness I have doggie health insurance for Dexter and Major. The online vet requested a picture of the infected area. As soon as I texted the picture, he advised me to get Dexter to a vet as soon as possible. I called my veterinarian's office and was told to come right away.

Thank goodness veterinarians are considered "essential services". When I took Dexter into the vet clinic, the vet staff were in hazardous material suits. I had to hand Dexter off and leave. It was eerie, and I got emotional as I walked to my car. I started to cry. Dexter looked miserable, and I started playing "what if" in my mind. What if vets weren't open? What if I didn't have money to get him treatment ($200)? What if this pandemic thing gets worse and one of my humans needs help? It is serious and scary stuff right now.

The vet called for me to pick up Dexter. He had a cone around his neck and medicine for his infection.

I bought chalk so I could do some chalk art on the sidewalk. I felt the need to do something creative. Lots of people were walking. Several made nice comments, and one took a picture of me on the ground. It made me laugh. Our house is on a busy corner, so I chalked messages like:

- If you are here X, you are awesome!
- Today's Special: Eat it or Starve!
- Today is a good day to have a good day!
- When nothing goes right, go left!

Jose made an amazing dinner of pork tenderloin, cherry sauce, mashed potatoes, asparagus, and he managed to create cornbread stuffing from leftovers (cornbread, chicken sausage, celery, onion, red pepper and chicken stock). He is a wonderful cook, and I feel grateful and lucky.

After dinner I saw a post on Facebook. It was a video from Jim Valvano at the 1993 Espy Awards.

"If you laugh, think, and cry every day, you have lived a full day." I needed that! I think I lived a full day today.

Thurs / 2020 Mar 26 / Journal Entry

"But I know, somehow, that only when it is dark enough can you see the stars."
Martin Luther King Jr.

It has been thirteen days since the global pandemic arrived and altered life as we knew it. It has been over ten years since I went to church and thirty plus years since I attended any kind of Sunday School class. I felt a spiritual tug at my heart to revisit my personal relationship with God. My friend and former colleague, Kristi, posted an invitation on Facebook to join her virtual Bible study, and I did.

I downloaded the Bible study app and materials she sent me. I decided to set up a chair in the front lawn under the live oak tree so I could start the Bible study. Each lesson had Bible verses to read from the Read Scripture app and accompanying short YouTube videos from the Bible Project. I found the videos fascinating because they brought the lessons to life, and they made the reading understandable.

Sat / 2020 Mar 28 / Journal Entry

"Yeah, we all shine on. Like the moon and the stars and the sun."
John Lennon

I started the morning with a Google Hangout meeting with my longtime girlfriends, Kristi and Lisa. It was nice to catch up, see their kids and husbands on camera, and hear how everybody was adjusting to shelter in place and online school.

Sun / 2020 Mar 29 / Journal Entry

"I'm the kind of person who would rather rock in my rocking chair when I am old and regret a few things that I did than to sit there and regret that I never tried."
Dolly Parton

We slept later than usual and spent time cuddling with the dogs in the king-sized bed. We are battling boredom with backgammon, beer bread, brownies, and beef ribs. We relearned how to play backgammon by watching a YouTube video. Alexa played classic rock in the background. We watched Dallas Arboretum YouTube videos.

It breaks my heart that people cannot see the beauty of the arboretum right now and that my students cannot do their service learning and volunteer there because of shelter at home. I am grateful for the videos because they are so beautiful to watch instead of the doom and gloom news on television.

We watched another episode of *Ozark* and took the dogs for a walk at 10:00 p.m. We did not see a soul.

A friend of a friend #1 died from the coronavirus.

Mon / 2020 Mar 30 / Journal Entry

"You must do the things you think you cannot do."
Eleanor Roosevelt

I woke up early, put on makeup and jewelry, curled my hair, and sprayed White Diamonds cologne. I put on a real shirt, but I had on yoga pants and house shoes. My laptop camera only shows me from the waist up, so I look professional on camera. I called the campus technology help desk to help me set up Teams, my webcam, and microphone.

Today was the first day RCHS students returned to school—virtually—since the extended Spring Break. I like working in the dining room because there is no television, and I have windows. I can see people walking, biking, and driving. I am glad that I have established some sort of routine. I understand how working from home could be challenging for many people.

A viral video of a Zoom meeting gone bad is circulating today. It showed a work meeting with at least ten employees. One employee can be seen walking through her house while she is on camera. She set the camera down and went to the restroom. It was caught on video, and all her colleagues were trying to signal her and get her attention. Welcome to working from home.

I got two direct deposits from Dallas County Community Colleges and the Teacher Retirement System. I received an email that I am getting paid for the remainder of the semester from UT Dallas even though my field supervisor duties have been suspended due to the coronavirus shutdowns. Again, we are blessed.

I found ski masks I had bought a few years ago, so we can wear them when we leave the house as recommended protection from the virus. I went to Walmart. I think there were more employees than shoppers. I wore gloves while I shopped, again as recommended protection since we don't know how the virus is spread.

Like many others, my fake nail fills are growing out and looking gnarly. All the hair and nail salons are currently closed. The nail supplies were wiped out at Walmart, so I will have to order supplies online to do my nails myself.

My sister sent me a grant application to review. It is for female business owners who have been impacted by COVID-19. Dad told Jose how to apply for a small business loan for $10,000.

A friend of a friend #2 died from the coronavirus.

I had my first virtual Bible study meeting with Kristi. We took turns answering these questions:
- What is your spiritual story?
- What are your hopes and desires for the future?
- What is your experience with God's word?
- What do you expect to get from scripture?

Kristi made an insightful statement, "There is a difference between reading and studying the Bible. If you have a coat and don't wear it, it doesn't transform your life."

Tues / 2020 Mar 31 / Journal Entry

"Sometimes what you are looking for comes when you're not looking at all."
Vi Keeland

We got a pretty good rain shower this morning. The squirrels found the bird feeder, and the dogs saw the squirrels, so when I opened the back door, the dogs rushed, the squirrels scrambled, and the puddles of mud went everywhere.

The barn swallows, Fred and Ethel, appeared a few nights ago. It's been over ten years since they first started to roost on our back door frame each spring. They arrive at sunset and leave at sunrise. They stay for several weeks, then disappear until the next spring. Manny, the male anole lizard, patrols the garden wall and looks for a mate by puffing out his red throat.

I think I could turn and live with the animals, they are so placid and self-contained,
I stand and look at them long and long.
They do not sweat and whine about their condition,
They do not lie awake in the dark and weep for their sins,
They do not make me sick discussing their duty to God,
Not one is dissatisfied, not one is demented with the mania of owning things,
Not one kneels to another, nor to his kind that lived thousands of years ago,
Not one is respectable or unhappy over the whole earth.
(Whitman, Walt, "Song of Myself," Leaves of Grass, *1855)*

Neighbors were walking, waving, noticing the chalk art and window displays. I had a chat with my neighbors, Julia and Courtney, from a distance—six feet away. When they left, another neighbor, Barbara, came over to chat. She stayed ten feet away.

A friend of a friend #3 died from the coronavirus.

COVID-19 Statistics:
- Confirmed cases worldwide: 1,181,825
- Confirmed cases in the United States: 300,915
- Confirmed deaths worldwide: 63,902
- Confirmed deaths in the Unites States: 8,162

april

Wed / 2020 Apr 1 / Journal Entry

"Dearly beloved, we are gathered today to get through this thing called life."
Prince

I had 139 emails from students who were concerned about service learning and graduation. I was assigned twenty-five students who are struggling with various aspects of school. I am responsible for checking in with them via Teams chats or Teams calls. I worked a little and paid bills. I feel blessed on both counts. Many people are unable to go to work because of the governor's order to shelter at home. Dr. Phil, a popular talk show host, used the term "covidiot" to describe people who are not taking this pandemic seriously.

I sent text messages to check in on work friends and my mentees. I called the yearbook sponsor with an idea for the service learning pages in the yearbook. I will offer one hour of service-learning credit to students for submitting a picture of themselves in a mask. The theme of the yearbook page will be "Help yourself, help your neighbor, help your family, help the community, wear a mask!"

The coronavirus has forced parents to become their children's teachers as they finish out the school year at home. It seems that parents have a new appreciation for the work teachers do each day, and this is great news! I only saw one April Fool's joke today. It was a meme from Fox News of Texas Governor Greg Abbott with a caption that read, "Students will have to repeat the 2019-2020 school year." Haha…not funny.

Our family is using the Marco Polo app to post short videos. It is fun to watch them since we cannot see them in person. It is a relief to see them and know they are doing okay.

Jose and I FaceTimed with my nephew, Kevin. His twenty-first birthday was today. Michelle had set up a pub crawl through her house to help him celebrate. Each room had a different theme with drinks or shots. A food truck was scheduled to set up in the neighborhood later in the day.

Facebook is a daily source of entertainment. Today, one post circulated asking people to post a picture based on a color that was assigned to them. It was like "I Spy," only with Facebook photos. The colors included pink, purple, blue, green, yellow, orange, silver, and gold. I was assigned silver, so I posted a picture of a water tower in Gruene, Texas. It was a fun, creative way to spend time posting and scrolling through other people's pictures.

People miss seeing their parents in person, especially if they are elderly. The elderly seem to be the most susceptible to the virus, so nobody visits them. People like my Aunt Lisa, who live in nursing homes, are quarantined and cannot have any visitors. People like Mamal, who live alone and do not know how to use technology, do not get to see other people in person or virtually. Thus, many people have been posting pictures of their moms and dads on social media to celebrate them.

I saw a post on Facebook about people who go to the hospital and are diagnosed with COVID-19. They have to say goodbye to their families in the parking lot or by phone using FaceTime. Families must make end-of-life decisions without ever discussing or knowing their loved one's wishes. It is tragic. It is becoming a common occurrence around the world. I feel blessed that Jose and I have had these end-of-life discussions and made our funeral arrangements three years ago. I pray it is years before we use them.

Thurs / 2020 Apr 2 / Journal Entry

"You can journey to the ends of the earth in search of success, but if you are lucky, you will discover happiness in your own backyard."
Russell Conwell

We took a trip to the gun store to pick up the .380 EZ pistol we ordered a few weeks ago. Our visit was surreal. We wore ski masks and gloves to protect ourselves IN A GUN STORE! We gave our name and phone numbers at the door and waited in the car for enough customers to leave so we could go inside. Due to COVID-19, businesses must limit the number of people allowed inside.

The employees at the gun shop were not wearing masks or gloves. They were not concerned about standing near each other. A police officer was purchasing a gun. He was not wearing gloves or a mask. He was talking about the increase in domestic calls since so many people are stuck at home.

The display cases of guns had "Out of Stock" stickers on every gun. We had to order ammunition for my pistol because they were out of stock on most ammunition, too.

A meme is circulating that says, "I never imagined I would walk into a bank wearing a mask and ask for money." For us, it was walking into a gun store to purchase a gun and ammunition.

Dad placed an alcohol order for home delivery on the new Drizzly app. He placed the order last night. He received an email survey this morning to rate the delivery. He never received the order. Apparently, the driver stole the alcohol he ordered! The driver must have really needed that booze.

We headed to Covington's Nursery and bought hanging baskets, succulents, and new patio door mats. I planted impatiens, petunias, salvia, milkweed, and dianthus in garden pots. I cleaned the patio, watered the plants, cleaned out the fountain, and set up the potted plants to create a lovely Zen zone. The weather was spectacular. Jose and I talked about our day and our blessings.

The first virtual Bible study with Kristi started at the beginning by reading Genesis 1:1-2:3. God wants a relationship with us. I can't stop thinking about the current situation in our world with COVID-19. Is the global pandemic a way for us to get back on track with God?

After a lovely dinner of chicken piccata, Caesar salad, and homemade beer bread, we went on a walk in the dark with the dogs. We can walk in the middle of the street, which is wider and safer than the sidewalks. The streets are empty. The houses are dark. It is very quiet. We talked about our day. With the popularity of the Netflix series *Tiger King*, I suggested we dress up like Joe Exotic and Carol Baskin for Halloween. We can dress the dogs up like tigers. When we got home, it started raining again.

Fri / 2020 Apr 3 / Journal Entry

Week 3, Day 21 at home

"Everybody wants happiness, and nobody wants pain, but you can't have a rainbow without a little rain."
Zion Lee

The dogs barreled out the back door to chase Rocky and Rita, our resident squirrels. The yard had puddles of mud and water due to the incessant rain.

Because Dexter is small, I was able to rinse his feet in the kitchen sink. Major, our standard poodle, is very big at fifty pounds. I dried him at the back door and took him to the guest bathroom. I put him in the tub to rinse his feet and legs. The laundry basket is full of muddy towels again.

I went into the laundry room to start a load of towels in the washing machine, but I got distracted and started organizing the laundry room cabinets. The last time I went to Walmart, I stockpiled cleaning supplies, so they were stacked on top of the washer and dryer and stuffed into the cabinets. The laundry room had to get organized before I could proceed with laundry. It is not unusual for one project to turn into multiple projects with me.

I got laundry started and proceeded to spend the day organizing. I organized the kitchen pantry, dresser drawers, bedroom closets, and bathroom cabinets. I got side-tracked and re-organized two jewelry boxes that belonged to my grandmother, Anna Bell, who lived in Waco.

I have had some sort of jewelry box since I was a kid. My first had a ballet dancer on the inside, and a wind-up knob made her twirl to the music. I started thinking about keepsakes. Why do I have them and keep them?

Besides social media, television is the driving force of entertainment. Now that there are streaming services like Amazon Prime, Hulu, and Netflix, we can watch movies anytime, anywhere, at a price, of course. One of the Facebook posts circulating today is to list your top ten movies. Here is my list of movies that I could watch repeatedly, in no particular order:

1. Singin' in the Rain
2. Steel Magnolias
3. Urban Cowboy
4. Private Benjamin
5. Purple Rain
6. Fried Green Tomatoes
7. Out of Africa
8. Rudy
9. Last of the Mohicans
10. The Shawshank Redemption

Sun / 2020 Apr 5 / Journal Entry

The death toll in the United States is on the rise. There is no sign of flattening the curve. Our numbers in the United States. are surpassing the death tolls in China and Italy. There are at least five states that have not taken steps to shelter in place. Schools will not re-open for in-person classes for the remainder of the school year. Governor Abbott announced new requirements for everyone to start wearing masks in public spaces.

We needed to get out of the house. We donned our homemade bandana masks and headed out with the dogs for a Sunday drive. We encountered minimal traffic. People just are not going anywhere. We could drive slower than the speed limit because there were literally no other cars behind us. We could take our time and look around because we did not have to concentrate on traffic. A few restaurants were open for take-out or drive-through only. Most restaurants were closed. We drove through the grocery store parking lot. It was full. People were walking in and out of the store with no masks or gloves.

It is still difficult to find masks and gloves, but there is a part of the population that does not believe in the dangers of the virus and is refusing to wear them.

The bluebonnets are blooming, and my poor dogs need grooming.

Mon / 2020 Apr 6 / Journal Entry

"You cannot stop the waves, but you can learn to surf."
Jon Kabat-Zinn

Normally, Jose and I would be going and doing. That is one of the best things about retirement. I woke up early thinking we would head out of the house today and drive the Bluebonnet Trail in Ennis, Texas. The past two years I have gone out on my own. I love it. I get to take pictures and enjoy our state flowers blooming in fields and pastures. I thought it would be something we could safely do.

Jose informed me that if we went, I would not be able to get out of the car, even if I had to go to the bathroom. There are too many unknowns about how the coronavirus is spread, and it is not safe. I did not want to argue. I know he loves me and wants what is best for me. We decided not to go to Ennis.

I got dressed anyway. I put on a dress, boots, makeup, and jewelry. It was early, so I went to Walmart to pick up some groceries. It tends to be less crowded early in the morning, especially on a Monday. The store has started funneling people through one entrance. They let one person go into the store when another person comes out. They must monitor how many people are in the store at one time. I wore my bandana mask and shopped. All lanes were self-checkout, so it took much longer to pay for groceries.

Since the coronavirus has put all parties, gatherings, and graduations on hold, people are getting creative for celebrations. Jose and I participated in the drive-by birthday party for our neighbor's daughter. Her guests gathered in their cars at the elementary school up the street to caravan by her house. We made two circles around the block honking and waving, then drove by and dropped off birthday gifts. I gave her a stuffed llama, markers, and a coloring book.

Wed / 2020 Apr 8 / Journal Entry

Dexter had a follow-up visit with the veterinarian. The vet office sent me an email before my visit to download paperwork and add my credit card to the Banfield Hospital app to limit our interaction.

I went out and bought dog grooming clippers, which were picked over, because grooming services are not available due to the coronavirus. Both Dexter and Major are getting shaggy. I watched YouTube videos on how to groom the face, feet, and tails for poodles.

I started with Dexter since he is the smaller of the two. He turned out pretty good. I can see his face and eyes, and his feet and tail area are neat and clean. Major's hair did not cooperate with the clippers. I got three of his four paws trimmed. I got half of his chin. My handsome boy looks like a disaster.

Thurs / 2020 Apr 9 / Journal Entry

I kept myself busy again today. I made banana pumpkin bread and brownies. I made egg salad, tuna salad, chicken salad, and fruit salad for lunch. I mopped the floors and ran the dishwasher. I set out my Easter decorations even though Jose will be the only one to see them.

The mayor of Dallas announced that city parks are closed for the holiday weekend.

Another Facebook challenge posted today was to post ten influential album covers over the next ten days and tag a friend. I have had many albums that influenced me during my life, so I decided to choose albums by female artists. These are my selections:

Day one—Heart, *Little Queen*
Day two—Stevie Nicks, *Bella Donna*
Day three—Linda Ronstadt, *Prisoner in Disguise*
Day four—Madonna, *Madonna*
Day five—Sade, *Diamond Life*
Day six—Laurie Anderson, *Mister Heartbreak*
Day seven—Annie Lennox, *Diva*
Day eight—Janet Jackson, *Control*
Day nine—*Waiting to Exhale*, Soundtrack
Day ten—Cher, *Gypsies, Tramps and Thieves*

We watched a National Geographic 50th Anniversary of Earth Day special. Since people have been sheltered at home, the Earth has started to heal. Pollution is clearing in the air, and waterways all over the world are turning blue from no cruise ships or cargo ships. It would be amazing if enough people took notice and decided to do something to help the environment.

Sun / 2020 Apr 12 / Journal Entry

"Easter is meant to be a symbol of hope, renewal, and new life."
Janine di Giovani

It was another stormy night, but the sun was out this morning. The birds are singing, grass is growing, and flowers are blooming. I made Easter brunch with fresh fruit, banana-pumpkin bread, fried ham, oatmeal, and scrambled eggs. We took the dogs for a long, quiet walk. It was a beautiful, warm, sunny day with no wind.

We watched a live stream of Easter service on Facebook. Many churches are closed for in-person service, while others are still operating as usual. It is difficult for people who are used to worshipping in person, especially during Easter. The pastor said, "Hope endures suffering. It does not escape suffering. Hope is hoping when hope is hopeless. Easter is a do over. It is a rebirth. It is time to begin again."

Jose and I made calls to check in with the kids, our parents, and other family members. We made meatloaf, peas, and mashed potatoes, one of my favorite meals, for Easter dinner. Then we watched *Jesus Christ Superstar Live in Concert* with John Legend and *The Ten Commandments*, which has played on television every Easter weekend since I was a child.

Mon / 2020 Apr 13 / Journal Entry

Dad has been helping us and his other clients navigate the process to get COVID-19 relief money. It is extremely confusing, and Dad lost his temper with me on the phone. He called later to apologize. We laughed and chalked it up to being "covidiots".

Late-night television host Jimmy Fallon has started broadcasting from home. Stephen Colbert is broadcasting alone in a studio. The ladies from *The View* broadcast from a Zoom.

Kyla called to talk about wedding planning. And it begins.

I had another one-on-one virtual Bible study with Kristi today. I was her boss for two years, and now she is leading me. We talked about the blessings that God gave to Israel and to each of us. God gives us what we need to bless others.

Remember this: Whoever sows sparingly will also reap sparingly, and whoever sows generously will also reap generously. Each of you should give what you have decided in your heart to give, not reluctantly or under compulsion, for God loves a cheerful giver. And God is able to bless you abundantly, so that in all things at all times, having all that you need, you will abound in every good work. (NIV. 2 Cor. 9:6-8)

For now, I feel I can use the gifts God has given me to support students and staff at Richland Collegiate High School, to mentor my mentees through Raise Your Hand Texas, to coach my friends through virtual accountability meetings, and to post inspirational quotes and pictures each day through the 2020 Vision page on Facebook.

Tues / 2020 Apr 14 / Journal Entry

"Enjoy the little things in life because one day you'll look back and realize they were the big things."
Kurt Vonnegut

So far, Jose has been able to continue working from home with his private investigation business. However, there are so many unknowns about this pandemic, so we do not know what the future holds for his business. The news reports that money is starting to be dispersed through unemployment checks, small business administration loans, and economic stimulus payments. Dad called and informed us that my sister got a grant and a federal loan for her small business. Her husband got a federal loan for his restaurants. My friend is getting a weekly unemployment check.

After dinner we went to Walmart to get supplies to build belated Easter baskets for our adult daughters. They will do a drive-by tomorrow to pick them up. We bought them breakfast supplies including muffins, sausage, pancake mix, and syrup. We added easy to make dinner ingredients like frozen lasagna, spaghetti and marinara sauce, garlic bread, and salad makings. We added necessities like hand soap, gloves, cleaning supplies, and toilet paper. Jose added his homemade pulled pork and hamburger buns.

I added a jigsaw puzzle, crayons, coloring book, and Trouble!™ board game.

Wed / 2020 Apr 15 / Journal Entry

Kat and Kyla drove over for their "drive-by, curbside pick-up" Easter baskets. They remained in their cars while we handed the Easter goodies to them. There were no hugs, just a short conversation from a distance. Then they took their goodies, waved good-bye, and drove home.

Thurs / 2020 Apr 16 / Journal Entry

People are getting creative. A lady in our neighborhood posted on Facebook that she was doing porch portraits for a donation to a non-profit of your choice. I posed with my dogs and my laptop and mask. It is a picture for the history books. I made a $50 donation to the SPCA.

Fri / 2020 Apr 17 / Journal Entry

Cooking and baking are other shelter-at-home activities that people are doing to keep themselves busy and support their family since restaurants are closed. Thank goodness we both know how to cook and enjoy cooking. Jose made burgers and onion rings and had chili in the Instant Pot. We also made beer bread and snickerdoodle cookies for dessert.

Since 2018, my high school psychology teacher, Dr. Bob Nelson, has hosted a monthly philosophical discussion group. Tonight, we had a Cisco Webex virtual meeting for the Socrates Cafe and transformed the name to Virtual Virtues. It was great to see and hear from everyone, even if it was through a computer screen. It was very interesting to share what we liked about pandemic life: connecting, gardening, walking, meditating, reading, and creating. We also discussed the things we missed, like Thai food, church, haircuts, manicures, pedicures, and hugs.

Sat / 2020 Apr 18 / Journal Entry

"Sometimes I punish myself for having unproductive days, but then I'm reminded that I'm only human and breaks are necessary. Don't feel guilty for putting something on pause temporarily while you reconnect with yourself and find a balance. Remember, your mental health comes first."
Meggan Roxanne

Once again, we put on our homemade bandana masks and took the dogs for a walk. The sky is blue, the sun is shining, and it is 70 degrees. Many people are out doing yard projects today because what else will they do? They can't go anywhere.

I miss going to the local art studio, Pinot's Palette, and painting. I am very happy that we can order paint-at-home kits online from the studio. Each painting, with instructions and supplies, is $25. I ordered all four paintings offered on their website since we have no idea how long this shelter at home will last. I ordered the kits online, and they were delivered to our front porch. Today, Jose and I painted "Day at the Dunes," listened to The Beatles, and worked on our technique.

Sun / 2020 Apr 19 / Journal Entry

Faerie Wisdom: "Pay attention to the feelings in your heart and not the thoughts in your head." Unknown

I am getting used to this new normal. We have found our routine, and it is literally my dream come true—just me, Jose, and the dogs.

I set up the garage like a grooming salon. I set up folding tables to make it easier for me to work on the dogs. I listened to music and pampered the dogs with the garage door open while the rain drizzled and sprinkled. This is my garage playlist:

"Hello"—Adele
"No One"—Alicia Keys
"Giving You the Best That I Got"—Anita Baker
"Precious"—Annie Lennox
"God is a Woman"—Ariana Grande
"When a Man Loves a Woman"—Bette Midler
"Bad Guy"—Billie Eilish
"I Can't Make You Love Me"—Bonnie Raitt
"Piano in the Dark"—Brenda Russell
"If You Love Me"—Brownstone
"True Colors"—Cyndi Lauper
"Sorry Not Sorry"—Demi Lovato
"You Gotta Be"—Des'ree
"I'm Coming Out"—Diana Ross

Kyla and Taylor did a drive-by and dropped off one N-95 surgical mask for us. I gave myself a manicure and pedicure with supplies I ordered online from Amazon. We watched a Dolly Parton biography. My affection for Dolly increases each time I learn more about her.

Mon / 2020 Apr 20 / Journal Entry

Parents have started posting on Facebook about their children who are seniors in high school and are missing out on senior activities due to the coronavirus. They post a senior picture and a description of their accomplishments and goals for the future. People can "Adopt a Senior" and drop off goodie baskets to recognize the student's accomplishments. We adopted two of our friends' kids who are seniors.

I showered, dressed, and went to Walmart to buy supplies for Adopt-a-Senior goodie baskets. Dallas County has issued a mandate to wear masks in public places. Jose and I have been doing this since the beginning of the pandemic -- and wearing gloves. As soon as I got out of my car at Walmart, a woman passed me in the parking lot with no mask. I read reports over the weekend that some stores were not allowing people into the store without a mask. This store, a mile from my house in Dallas County, is in Collin County. Collin County has not made a mask mandate, so she walked right into the store without a mask. I was shocked and disappointed to count six people in the store without a mask, cover, or bandana. On the one hand, it made me mad and sad. On the other hand, people are doing their best to navigate mixed messages about masks, mandates, and how the virus spreads. It is frustrating.

I put on my graduation regalia to deliver our Adopt-a-Senior gifts. We rang the doorbell and dropped off gifts at the doorstep. I stood in the yard in my doctoral regalia, masked, and waved to them when they came out to the porch. It was a small gesture, but it was fun to see the kids feel recognized and their parents' smile.

I had a Facetime call with my friend, Bridget, who is a school administrator. She was working in her car in the school parking lot because she had no internet at her house, and she was able to get a Wi-Fi connection in the school parking lot. Internet connectivity is a huge challenge for people all over the world who are now doing virtual school and working from home. Some people do not have internet services at their residence. Others may have it, but they may not have enough bandwidth for everyone in the family to be on their devices at the same time.

Tues / 2020 Apr 21 / Journal Entry

The governor of each state can determine whether businesses remain closed or may reopen.

There are mixed messages about the use of masks. Some counties have mandates to wear masks in public places, while others do not. Some people are beginning to protest to lift mask restrictions. In addition, many people are debating on social media about which news sources are credible.

Be Kind—copied from a Facebook post by Chris Freytag

As governors are trying to figure out how to ease into a new normal, please remember:
- *Some people don't agree with the state opening…that's okay. Be kind.*
- *Some people are still planning to stay home…that's okay. Be kind.*
- *Some people are still scared of getting the virus and a second wave is coming…that's okay. Be kind.*
- *Some are sighing with relief to go back to work so they don't lose their business or their home…that's okay. Be kind.*
- *Some are thankful they can have the surgery they put off…that's okay. Be kind.*
- *Some will be able to attend interviews after weeks without a job …that's okay. Be kind.*
- *Some will wear masks for weeks…that's okay. Be kind.*
- *Some will rush out to get their hair and nails done…That's okay. Be kind.*

The point is, everyone has a different viewpoint or opinion and that's okay. Be kind. If you have to go out in public, just respect others and be kind. Don't judge fellow humans because you are not in their story. So, remember...be kind.

Thurs / 2020 Apr 23 / Journal Entry

200 days of sobriety, 42 days of shelter at home

The weather is beautiful so people are walking, jogging, and biking. Yard crews are mowing, edging, and blowing. The squirrels and birds are feeding on the bird seed in the bird feeders. All this activity outside of the window is fun to watch, but it makes the dogs go crazy. They bark incessantly, and we yell at them which does not help. Inevitably, this happens during business phone calls and virtual meetings. We must use baby gates to put the dogs in "doggie jail" to reduce the chaos while we work from home.

Walmart and other stores have implemented one-way aisles to help with social distancing. Sign companies are very busy printing signage about wearing masks, sanitizing hands, and standing six feet apart while waiting in line. People are being pretty compliant as a whole.

Fri / 2020 Apr 24 / Journal Entry

"If people sat outside and looked at the stars each night, I'll bet they'd live a lot differently."
Bill Watterston

Jose and I pulled out camping gear from the garage to set up Camp Quarantine in the backyard. We decided to camp out under the stars. I went to Walmart to pick up groceries to cook hamburgers, s'mores, and campfire eggs on the grill.

The aisles are marked one-way, but many people have not noticed the stickers on the floor or the signs on the ends of the aisles. It is one more small behavior to keep people safe from the spread of the virus. As much as I have fussed and fought against self-checkout at the store, I have become pretty good at it.

Jose set up the tent in the backyard for our night of glamping under the stars. We pulled out air mattresses and lanterns from our camping storage boxes. We set up the inside of the tent like a couch with sleeping bags, pillows, and blankets. We put up party patio lights. Jose made burgers on the grill, and we played backgammon on the patio. We listened to classic rock and enjoyed the seventy-degree spring weather.

The flowers and fountain in our backyard created a Zen zone. We made s'mores on the grill. Then, we took the dogs for a long walk at sunset, so it was dark by the time we got back to our glamping site. We watched the HBO documentary on our laptop about Adnan Syed, a young man who was accused of killing his high school girlfriend, and lay on the air mattresses. The dogs were curled up next to us.

Sat / 2020 Apr 25 / Journal Entry

We woke up around 6:45 am. I made breakfast: campfire eggs, sausage, fruit, and biscuits. Jose helped me finish cleaning up Camp Quarantine. Everything is back in its place. The plants are watered, and bird feeders are filled with seed and nectar for the hummingbirds. It is a beautiful Saturday morning. People are jogging and walking. I can hear mowers, edgers, and blowers from the surrounding neighbor's yards.

Sun / 2020 Apr 26 / Journal Entry

The weather is so lovely. I enjoy spending quiet time on the patio, listening to the birds, and looking at the grass and the garden. Jose made brunch, and we had patio painting time while listening to Sade. We painted "Texas Bluebonnets," which is one of the paint-at-home kits we got from Pinot's Palette.

We took the dogs for a walk, and I found a painted rock with a picture of a dandelion painted on it. The seedlings were floating away in the wind. It reminded me of the quote by Kiera Cass, "Some see weeds, others see wishes." I decided to bring it home.

Mon / 2020 Apr 27 / Journal Entry

The groomers are back to work because they are considered essential workers, so I booked an appointment for the dogs for next week.

Wed / 2020 Apr 29 / Journal Entry

"Get outside. Watch the sunrise. Watch the sunset. How does that make you feel? Does it make you feel big or tiny? Because there is something good about feeling both."
Amy Grant

After I finished work for the day I went out to the front yard and did some chalk art on the sidewalk. It is supposed to be sunny for a few days. The creativity was therapeutic. These are some of the messages I wrote:

- Class of 2020—Congrats Grads!
- "Oh, the places you will go!" Dr. Seuss
- Your future is so bright, you have to wear shades.
- Thank you: Doctors, Nurses, Teachers, Grocers, Delivery and Essential Workers!

Thurs / 2020 Apr 30 / Journal Entry

"Be you. Do you. For you."
Vipul Bhave

It is grocery shopping day. Despite a huge sign out front of Walmart, people are still entering the store without a mask or face covering of any kind. Despite the one-way signs on the floor and repeated announcements on the public address system, people are ignoring social distancing rules. Tomorrow, the governor is lifting restrictions for phase I.

I get my news from multiple sources including television, the internet, and social media. Regardless, the news is grim:

COVID-19 Statistics:
- Confirmed cases of COVID-19 worldwide: 3,000,000.
- Confirmed deaths worldwide: 200,000
- Confirmed cases of COVID-19 in the United States: 1,000,000.
- Confirmed deaths in the United States: 53,694
- 3.8 million people in the United States have applied for unemployment.
- Food lines are getting increasingly longer each day.
- 30 million people are out of work.

may

Fri / 2020 May 1 / Journal Entry

"Of course, life is bizarre. The more bizarre it gets, the more interesting it is. The only way to approach it is to make yourself some popcorn and enjoy the show."
David Gerrold

Jose made ribs and wings for Kat and Kyla. They came by for a drive-by pickup of their painting kits, and we surprised them with food. Our neighbor turned forty, so all the neighbors gathered outside for a social distance party. We met some folks I had never even seen before. They live four houses down from us and have lived there for four years. Our yard and plants look better than ever. Life is pretty good. We are blessed.

Sat / 2020 May 2 / Journal Entry

Jose is in the kitchen prepping pork butt for pulled pork, mushrooms and onions for Salisbury steak, and pork tenderloins for meals later this week. I baked two pans of brownies and a cinnamon swirl coffee cake. I found another painted rock with a rainbow on it.

Sun / 2020 May 3 / Journal Entry

"Kindness is always fashionable, and always welcome."
Amelia Barr

Today was a busy, happy day. Jose and I made care packages for an early Mother's Day for my bonus mom Rosie and an early birthday for Michelle. The menu included: pork tenderloin with peach sauce, Brussel sprouts and bacon slaw, Hoppin' John black-eyed peas, roasted corn on the cob, rolls, and brownies.

We drove to Michelle's house first. Jose and I wore our masks when we went inside. Then we drove to Dad and Rosie's house and sat outside on their patio.

Tues / 2020 May 5 / Journal Entry

Jose made me laugh when he came into the office and pretended to be a waiter in a newly opened restaurant and took my dinner order. We enjoyed fajitas, grilled shrimp, guacamole, chips, salsa, queso, beans, and rice for Cinco de Mayo. While we ate, we watched a Facebook live video of mariachis playing music and serenading llamas in sombreros.

Wed / 2020 May 6 / Journal Entry

"Sometimes your joy is the source of your smile, but sometimes your smile can be the source of your joy."
Thich Nhat Hahn

Wednesday is often referred to as "Hump Day," and I feel like I am over it—the hump that is. I am sitting on the patio this morning, and I am in my happy place. It is perfect outside. The neighborhood is quiet. There is no rumble of school buses, and the morning traffic is light. The dogs are lying in the grass and soaking up the sun.

Jose and I drove to the CityLine parking garage to watch the Blue Angels fly over the hospitals to honor health care workers. It was a spectacular day and a special sight to see. There was no wind. It was sunny and seventy degrees with a few clouds in the sky that made a lovely backdrop for the Blue Angels. Pictures and videos flooded the news and social media. We went to Walmart on the way home. The news reported a meat shortage, so we picked up some supplies to make Kat and Kyla another care package with chili dog and Frito Pie fixings.

My cousin, Angela, posted about a new tradition in Marin County, California, of people howling at 8:00 p.m. each night. In some cities, like New York, people bang pots and pans on their balconies each night to honor the health care workers and to know other people are out there, while everyone stays sheltered at home.

Thurs / 2020 May 7 / Journal Entry

"Face your fears and doubts, and new worlds will open to you."
Robert Kiyosaki

I dropped the dogs off at the groomer this morning. Finally! I took the groomers cookies. I am so glad they are back to work.

I received an email from Dallas County Community College that they have already decided that fall semester classes will be online.

Dear DCCCD Employees,

While we remain in a public health crisis, the health and safety of our students and employees, along with the learning environment we provide, are our primary considerations. Based on the Board's input and continued guidance from our local health professionals, we have decided to continue offering online learning for classes through the fall.

Across the district's seven campuses, there are normally 40,000 students and employees on site any given day. To provide a safe instructional environment in the midst of COVID-19, we would have to individually screen every one of these students and employees upon entering our campuses each day. It is simply not feasible to accommodate this volume of daily temperature taking and health monitoring.

Additionally, we have several task forces working to determine how these changes will impact employees as we return to limited campus operations in a phased approach. There are a number of issues to consider, including the use of personal protective equipment (PPE), controlling the number of people who enter and occupy a building at one time, temperature checks, staggered work schedules, continued deep cleaning of all facilities and of course, ensuring that those who are in a building are adhering to social distancing guidelines.

Many of you have also expressed interest in continuing to work remotely, so we are also examining our telecommuting policies to determine if some roles may continue to do so, especially for those employees who fall into vulnerable groups.

Our Board of Trustees recognizes our concerns and efforts to safely and responsibly support our students and employees during this challenging time. Those employees who under district policy would otherwise be scheduled to work or teach will continue to be paid through the fiscal year ending August 31. The Board has also directed us to find ways to continue to engage employees during this difficult time of working remotely. Look for details around these opportunities soon.

The decision to remain online for the fall semester is a difficult one because we know that this "new normal" is not easy on any of us. Despite our challenges, you've remained focused on our students' success. Thank you for continuing to exhibit the empathy, resiliency, and innovation that exemplify the DCCCD way.

Stay well,
Joe May
Chancellor

Fri / 2020 May 8 / Journal Entry

I check my Facebook when I wake up. Memories from previous years on this day are the first things that pop up on my timeline. I have always chosen to post positive things on Facebook, so it is a good way to start each day. Today a picture of my mom came up from an old Mother's Day post. She passed away in 2002 from colon cancer at the age of fify-four.

Michelle's birthday is tomorrow, and Cousin Jim's is coming up, so we will leave Marco Polo birthday messages tomorrow. My neighbor brought moms on the block and me red roses in a bud vase for Mother's Day. There was another drive-by graduation parade for a graduating senior down the street. Yard signs are a new, booming business for life events. It was a great day. I live in a great neighborhood.

Sat / 2020 May 9 / Journal Entry

"It's a helluva start, being able to recognize what makes you happy."
Lucille Ball

The weather is absolutely gorgeous. I took the dogs for a long walk around the neighborhood trail. There were faerie doors all along the trail made mostly from popsicle sticks. Each one was painted and decorated in a unique way. They were attached to the trees, some high and some low. It was an unexpected way to start my day. I found another painted rock which said, "You will never get COVID-19."

I watered the plants. We sat on the back patio and enjoyed the weather and nature. The doves, bluejays, cardinals, barn swallows, and lizards all made appearances. I spotted our first hummingbird feeding on our salvia plants. A new little squirrel has joined the critter crew. We named him Rudy.

The girls came by for a curbside pickup of groceries: hamburger meat, hot dogs, buns, cornbread mix, cheese, and Wick Fowler's Chili Kit.

Jose made burgers, fries, and onion rings for lunch. I heard Hawaiian music outside, and the Kona Snow Cone Truck was at a neighbor's house. I bought two snow cones. It was a great day. I have a great family.

Sun / 2020 May 10 / Journal Entry

Mother's Day. We went for a walk today on the trail and never passed a soul. It was perfect weather. I sat on the patio and read *Elle Decor* and *Harper's Bazaar* magazines. Alexa played the 80's Chill playlist in the background. It was a lovely, leisurely way to spend Mother's Day during a pandemic.

Mon / 2020 May 11 / Journal Entry

Day 60 of shelter at home.
Day 217 of sobriety.

Mundane tasks were on the agenda today. Grocery shopping took two and a half hours to keep six feet apart, go one-way down the aisles, unload the groceries to scan, self-checkout, re-load the cart, unload the cart into the car, drive home, unload the car, and put away the groceries.

Tues / 2020 May 12 / Journal Entry

"Sometimes you have to look back to understand what lies ahead."
Yvonne Woon

I finally got my nails done today. Nail shops have reopened with safety protocols. They are limited to twenty-five percent occupancy, and everyone must wear a mask. To keep as much space as possible between people, they have installed plexiglass windows with a slot to put your hands through so there is a barrier between the customer and the nail technician.

I went to Walmart to return some sandals I bought for Jose, and I got super pissed off. As I approached the customer service desk to make my return, a woman jumped in front of me. She did not have a mask. The transaction took forever. The slowest worker on the planet was trying to help her. The longer I waited, the more upset I got. I was cursing behind my mask, and my blood pressure was raging! When I finally got up to the counter to return the sandals that had never been worn, the clerk told me she could not return the sandals due to COVID-19. I thought my head exploded. On top of everything else, I was hangry (hungry + angry).

As I walked to my car, I had to tell myself that if this is the worst thing that has happened to me in the past sixty days, I am blessed. My body was having a physical reaction to the anger, and my mind was trying to calm down.

I had to pause and think about people with REAL problems. For instance, the news reported that the police found a little boy tied up in a shed behind his house yesterday. He had been in the shed for two weeks. I am confused as to why I went crazy today.

Wed / 2020 May 13 / Journal Entry

I feel depressed. The spring semester is officially over with no celebration of any kind. Today was supposed to be graduation for the RCHS students in the class of 2020.

Dad called, which was nice. I received a belated Mother's Day gift from Christian. He sent me a COVID-19 Christmas ornament. It was a wooden roll of toilet paper that said "I love you more than toilet paper. COVID 2020."

Fri / 2020 May 15 / Journal Entry

"Science will get us out of this, but art will get us through it."
Mo Willems

I feel blue. There are heated debates on whether to wear masks. I do not understand why people won't just simply do it. A Facebook post stated, "Remember 'Click it or ticket'? Maybe we'll start 'Mask it or casket' for the same reason." Masks are precautionary, like sunscreen. I just don't get it. It is all weird and hard to understand. I need to get my groove back!

After lunch we listened to classic rock and painted "Freshly Picked Roses" from one of the paint kits we had delivered a few weeks ago. I love it when Jose paints with me.

Sat / 2020 May 16 / Journal Entry

"#2 pencils and a dream can take you anywhere."
Joyce Meyers

Pancakes, prayer, and painting were on the agenda today. It was raining. I wanted to paint my own rocks that I ordered from Amazon, but I wasn't really sure how to go about it so I searched Google and YouTube. I painted twenty-seven rocks. The garage door was open, and the rain was steady. I listened to a playlist I created called "Girlz."

"Manic Monday," The Bangles
"Don't Make Me Over," Candice Glover
"Firework," Katy Perry
"Excellent Birds," Laurie Anderson
"Down So Low," Linda Ronstadt
"Love Don't Cost a Thing," Jennifer Lopez
"You Haven't Seen the Last of Me," Cher
"Express," Christina Aguilera
"IDGAF," Dua Lipa
"Lights," Ellie Goulding
"Style," Taylor Swift
"Girl Crush," Little Big Town
"Malibu," Miley Cyrus
"Sorry Not Sorry," Demi Lovato
"Havana," Camila Cabello
"Wolves," Selena Gomez
"One Last Time," Ariana Grande
"Heartbeat Song," Kelly Clarkson
"Me Too," Meaghan Trainor
"Finally," CeCe Peniston
"Applause," Lady Gaga
"Brave," Sara Bareilles
"Fancy," Iggy Azalea
"Chandelier," Sia

At 1:30 p.m. today, a police-escorted parade of Wylie East graduates drove honking down Creek Crossing Lane. I stood on the corner under an umbrella because it was raining hard. I waved and gave thumbs up to each car. Parents were driving their high school students who sat in the back seats with their graduation regalia on and waved as they went by. Some of the cars were decorated. It was raining, but it didn't matter. It was a celebration. I got teary eyed thinking about canceled graduation ceremonies. A few of the neighbors came out and stood on their front porches when they heard the horns honking.

Jose made another delicious dinner, and we watched Graduate Together, a tribute to the 2020 graduates, and listened to Barack Obama give the commencement speech:

Hi, everybody,

I couldn't be prouder of all of you in the graduating Class of 2020—as well as the teachers and the coaches, and most of all, parents and family who guided you along the way.

Now graduating is a big achievement under any circumstances. Some of you have had to overcome serious obstacles along the way, whether it was an illness, or a parent losing a job, or living in a neighborhood where people too often count you out. Along with the usual challenges of growing up, all of you have had to deal with the added pressures of social media, reports of school shootings, and the specter of climate change.

Now I'll be honest with you—the disappointments of missing a live graduation, those will pass pretty quickly. I don't remember much from my own high school graduation. But what remains true is that your graduation marks your passage into adulthood—the time when you begin to take charge of your own life. It's when you get to decide what's important to you: The kind of career you want to pursue. Who you want to build a family with. The values you want to live by. And given the current state of the world, that may be kind of scary.

If you'd planned on going away for college, getting dropped off at campus in the fall—that's no longer a given. If you were planning to work while going to school, finding that first job is going to be tougher. Even families that are relatively well-off are dealing with massive uncertainty. Those who were struggling before—they're hanging on by a thread.

All of which means you'll have to grow up faster than some generations. This pandemic has shaken up the status quo and laid bare a lot of our country's deep-seated problems -- from massive economic inequality to ongoing racial disparities to a lack of basic health care for people who need it. It's woken a lot of young people to the fact that the old ways of doing things just don't work; that it doesn't matter how much money you make if everyone around you is hungry and sick; and that our society and our democracy only work when we think not just about ourselves, but about each other.

That realization may be kind of intimidating. But I hope it's also inspiring. With all the challenges this country faces right now, nobody can tell you "No, you're too young to understand" or "This is how it's always been done." Because with so much uncertainty, with everything suddenly up for grabs, this is your generation's world to shape.
I'll leave you with three quick pieces of advice.

First, don't be afraid. America's gone through tough times before—slavery and civil war, famine and disease, the Great Depression and 9/11. And each time we came out stronger, usually because a new generation, young people like you, learned from past mistakes and figured out how to make things better.

Second, do what you think is right. Doing what feels good, what's convenient, what's easy—that's how little kids think. I hope that instead, you decide to ground yourself in values that last, like honesty, hard work, responsibility, fairness, generosity, respect for others. You won't get it right every time; you'll make mistakes like we all do. But if you listen to the truth that's inside yourself, even when it's hard, even when it's inconvenient, people will notice. They'll gravitate towards you. And you'll be part of the solution instead of part of the problem.

And finally, build a community. No one does big things by themselves. Right now, when people are scared, it's easy to be cynical and say let me just look out for myself, or my family, or people who look or think or pray like me. But if we're going to get through these difficult times; if we're going to create a world where everybody has the opportunity to find a job and afford college; if we're going to save the environment and defeat future pandemics, then we're going to have to do it together. Stand up for one another's rights. Leave behind all the old ways of thinking that divide us -- sexism, racial prejudice, status, greed -- and set the world on a different path.

But the truth is that you don't need us to tell you what to do. Because in so many ways, you've already started to lead.

Congratulations, class of 2020. Keep making us proud.

Sun / 2020 May 17 / Journal Entry

Day 65 of safer at home.

We watched a movie called *Five Feet Apart* which was released a few years ago. It is about a kid with cystic fibrosis who must wear a mask to stay healthy. It was surreal.

Mon / 2020 May 18 / Journal Entry

I received an email that I was allowed to return to campus to retrieve items from my office so I could work from home. Traffic was light. All but one entrance to the campus was closed. I had to show my badge to get access at an assigned time to be on campus. I had to park on the opposite side of the campus from my office, which is across the pond.

I had a dolly and two boxes and navigated around empty buildings and handicapped ramps to get to my office in the Kiowa building. It was hot and humid. The way I normally would have traveled across campus was through underground hallways, but the buildings were not open, so it was not an option.

When I got to my office in Kiowa, the building was locked. While I waited for the campus police to unlock it, I snapped pictures of the desolate campus and empty parking lot. There was no sign of life, no cars, no humans, no geese or ducks. It was an eerie, sad, and historic moment. The campus was a ghost town. The bushes were overgrown, and the weeds and grass were tall.

Once inside the building, I was all alone. Again, I snapped some pictures of the lobby which was empty and quiet. Normally it would be full of students talking, eating, studying, laughing, and sleeping. Everything had been removed from the top of my desk.

At the beginning of the pandemic the custodial staff had done a deep clean of all surfaces in anticipation of our return after spring break. That was months ago.

I decided to take all my belongings home with me. I packed files, office supplies, and personal items. Who knows when and if I will be back. I loaded the boxes, piled them on the dolly, and wrote notes to my four office mates. "Hi! I miss you! 2020."

I snapped more pictures of the office, hallways, bathrooms, and calendars. It was apocalyptic. All the calendars were still in March. As I set off back to my car, I had to travel slowly so my boxes wouldn't topple over. I took more pictures of buildings, passageways, and gathering spots that were still silent and empty. The student newspaper, *The Richland Chronicle*, sat stacked in the newsstand, stuck in time. The March 3rd edition's front cover featured a story titled, "COVID- 19 Goes Global." It also had a picture of the Leaning Tower of Dallas. The back page showed the school mascot, a Thunderduck, with sunglasses on and a caption, "Enjoy Spring Break!"

Who would have guessed that two weeks later we would be sheltering at home?

One of the things I retrieved from my office today was a painted rock I found at Lover's Leap in Waco on the Cousin's Trip back in February. I had it on my desk and brought it home and put it in the raised garden with the flowers I planted from seeds. The rock says, "She believed she could, so she did." Damn right!

Tues / 2020 May 19 / Journal Entry

"In three words I can sum up everything I've learned about life. It goes on."
Robert Frost

Our neighbors had a baby girl yesterday. Her name is Miss Josie Pearl.

I called Mamal and Uncle Michael to check in. Mamal answered the phone out of breath, and she was rambling. I couldn't understand what she was trying to tell me. "Michael has the virus!" I told her to put him on the phone. He was in his room. He stated he thought he might have coronavirus, but he downplayed it. He said he was not going to take a test. He was not going to go to the doctor. He was going to stay in his room and wear a mask. All I can do is pray and check on them tomorrow.

Wed / 2020 May 20 / Journal Entry

"Life is amazing! And then it's awful. And then it's amazing again. And in between the amazing and awful it's ordinary and mundane and routine."
L. R. Knost

Jose bought an ultraviolet sanitizer from Amazon, so anything that can fit into it (keys, remote controls, phones, pens) goes in for eighteen minutes. The best part of the purchase was a packet of stickers. How fun is that? The packet contained a whale, llama, peace sign, hot air balloon, and flower stickers. There were also stickers that said, "Ugh," "Mental Health Matters," "Don't Worry Be Happy," "Today We Fight," "Mermaid Macchiato," and "Radiate Positivity."

I have had doubts and anxiety about my future as a part-time employee during the pandemic. The principal called this morning and offered me a project to work on—giving access codes to students for free online SAT prep classes this summer. It made my doubts and anxiety subside.

I checked in on Uncle Michael and Mamal. He said he felt better, and he ran errands today. We watched the Wonderful World of Disney movie, *Moana*. One of my favorite quotes from the movie is: *"There comes a day when you're gonna look around and realize happiness is where you are."*

Thurs / 2020 May 21 / Journal Entry

"If you're not making mistakes, you're not making decisions."
Catherine Cook

If COVID-19 had not happened, today would have been the beginning of a four-day holiday weekend for many people. It would have been the end of the school year and the beginning of summer. There would be cook-outs and graduation parties and family outings.

Today was a big step or leap of faith. I met my friend Chris for lunch at Gloria's. Restaurants are currently limited to twenty-five percent capacity. We were the first guests to arrive. The staff was wearing masks and gloves. We were given a touchless menu with a QR code. I used my phone to scan the QR code so I could access the online menu. We sat outdoors on the patio. As we ate our lunch, more diners came in. The host spaced each party apart from each other. Tomorrow restaurants will be able to open to fifty percent capacity.

After lunch, Chris and I took separate cars to our former colleagues' visitation service. We did not know what to expect. We were among the first visitors. We wore masks and used our own pens to sign the guest book. We paid our respects, from a distance, to his wife and daughter who also wore masks. There were five or six other men, tall men, probably his former basketball teammates, standing on the other side of the room. They had masks, too. We were the only people there. I could not help but wonder if it was due to the coronavirus. I was sad that we did not see more people, but I was happy that we were able to pay our respects without compromising our safety bubble.

Fri / 2020 May 22 / Journal Entry

We ordered Whataburger online for lunch. We customized our order online, paid online, and all I had to do when I got there was pull into a designated parking space, text a number that indicated I had arrived, and wait for a masked worker to bring out our food. The double drive-through lanes were wrapped around the building.

The Residents of Woodbridge Facebook page has been flooded with posts about the neighborhood pools reopening. Currently, they are all closed. Some residents are in favor of the pools staying closed due to the pandemic. There are debates about how to re-open the pools safely. There are residents who think we should get refunds for our homeowner's association dues if the pools stay closed.

Wood Biscuit Post on the Woodbridge Residents Facebook page:

Wood Biscuit is a fictional Facebook character created by one of the Woodbridge residents, Kenny Newell. Wood Biscuit is a horse.

[The post started with a photo of a horse stepping into an inflatable pool.]

Please sign the petition to quit posting about pools and beating a dead horse. Keep the pools closed. [Then came four emojis.] Crying emoji, horse emoji, horse emoji, crying emoji.

Even the stick is tired of beating this majestic dead beast. #1stWorldProblems, #NoHatersOrSwimmers

We had a socially distant Holly Hills Hangout with the neighbors.

Jose received an email notification that he was approved for a COVID-19 Economic Injury Disaster Loan for his small business.

Mon / 2020 May 25 / Journal Entry

Memorial Day and Murder of George Floyd

"Home of the free because of the brave."
Unknown

We woke up early to go to the Carry the Load drive-through, a parade in Turtle Creek near downtown Dallas. Carry the Load is a non-profit that celebrates our heroes and educates the community on how to celebrate Memorial Day. It was raining, and we drove along the two-mile route twice. It is a shame the walk was canceled due to COVID-19, but it was nice that the drive-through was available as a good alternative. It is important for people to remember why Memorial Day exists.

We decided to take a leap of faith and go out to eat at a restaurant. We chose Pappasito's Mexican Cantina. It was the first day to open their dining room. They had removed over half of their tables to comply with the fifty percent occupancy and social distancing requirements. It was the first time Jose and I ate in a restaurant together since the pandemic started in March.

Tues / 2020 May 26 / Journal Entry

"Courage is being scared to death...and saddling up anyway."
John Wayne

I worked in person at Richland today. It has been seventy-five days since the last day I worked on campus on March 12th. When I drove into the parking lot there was a rainbow over the campus.

We had a textbook-and-laptop-return event. It was a drive-through process. The students had scheduled time slots to arrive on campus. They were required to wear masks or some sort of face covering. The campus police monitored who entered the campus. The staff working at the event wore masks and stayed at least six feet apart under tents that were set up outside in the parking lot.

As students drove up, we directed them when to exit their car, sanitize their hands, place their books and laptops in a clear plastic bag, label the bag with an index card, seal the bag, leave the bag on the table, sanitize their hands again, and return to their car. Staff members with gloves would transfer the bag of books and laptops to carts where they were moved into the building to "quarantine" for two weeks. Other staff members, like me, directed traffic in the parking lot. The event was very well organized. It was nice to see my co-workers in person. The forecast had predicted rain all day, but it was cloudy, breezy and seventy-five degrees. We could not have asked for nicer weather to work outside all day.

Wood Biscuit Post
{Picture of Wood Biscuit in a canoe with a turtle shell photoshopped on his back.}

Fake Neighborhood update: Oh, how the world can turn on a dime. Turtle Gangs. You heard me right. A request has been made to round up the turtles in the ponds because they are interfering with fishing. Don't fear...Wood Biscuit is on the job. We quickly headed over to the pond in disguise to investigate these web-footed miscreants. After an exhaustive investigation...guess what we found? ...wait for it.... Turtles being turtles. It wasn't a crisis at all. [Sad emoji face.]

Wed / 2020 May 27 / Journal Entry

Today was day two of the textbook-and-laptop-return event at RCHS. We have been very diligent and consistent with our safety protocols for students and staff. It was hot and sunny today. I am wiped out!

Thurs / 2020 May 28 / Journal Entry

"Adventure is worthwhile."
Aesop

Today was day three of directing traffic at RCHS. I am getting a lovely farmer's tan on my arms, striped tan lines from my sandals on my feet, and a weird mask tan on my face.

I got an email from the college that my supervisor considers me an "essential worker" during COVID-19:

"Your supervisor submitted a request on your behalf for access to Richland college as an essential employee. This request has been approved. Essential Employees are required to wear masks while on campus. Employees can cover their mouths and noses with a personal mask or a piece of cloth such as a scarf, bandanna, or handkerchief."

Fri / 2020 May 29 / Journal Entry

George Floyd's senseless death is all over the news and social media. The video of a police officer with his knee on George Floyd's neck for eight minutes is disturbing. You can hear George Floyd say, "I can't breathe," over and over again. He even cries out for his mother. The city of Minneapolis is erupting in protests and riots.

There is a curfew in the City of Dallas due to protests.

Wood Biscuit Post

[Picture of a man sitting on a hill looking over a neighborhood. There is a horse sitting on the ground next to him.]

Unofficial Weekend Musing: Wow...what a busy week. It was filled with pool petitions and gangs of turtles. Wood Biscuit and I decided to walk up a nearby hill and look at Woodbridge from above. While on the walk I asked, "Did we do some good this week?"

Wood Biscuit replied, "I think so. We probably made a few people smile while reading our posts. I think we also changed the tone of the conversation. People seem to be complaining less and taking the hard times in stride. Hopefully, they are more thankful for the blessed lives that they have living here in Woodbridge. There are many that have nothing. They have lost everything, not just access to a pool."

I shrugged and thought for a moment. Then I replied, "I guess you're right. I guess we all need to be more active in changing the world. Maybe we should give people a chance to give more and gripe less." We both smiled and looked down at the houses. We both wondered if the people had it in them to give to those less fortunate. As we parted near the Highlands pool, I turned and said, "Will I see you again next week?" Wood Biscuit smiled and replied, "My saddle is always near if I'm needed."

Attached to this post is a link to donate to the North Texas Food Bank. Give a couple of dollars if you smiled this week. Smile emoji, #ThanksForReading"

I also received the yard sign I ordered from a friend who was selling things on Facebook:
Love your neighbor who doesn't:
Look like you
Think like you
Love like you
Speak like you

Pray like you
Vote like you.
Love your neighbor. No exceptions!

Sat / 2020 May 30 / Journal Entry

"When I was a boy and I would see scary things in the news, my mother would say to me, 'Look for the helpers. You will always find people who are helping.'"
Fred Rogers

Jose set up the inflatable Walmart pool on the patio. I took my lunch outside to eat, and Rudy the squirrel was in the pool. He was swimming and desperately trying to get out. I have no idea how he got into the pool or how long he had been in the water. I yelled for Jose to bring a big baking sheet from the kitchen. I scooped Rudy out of the water. The poor guy was exhausted. I set the tray on a chair, and Rudy just laid on it, motionless, for about ten minutes. It seemed like an eternity. Jose and I kept our distance while he recovered. He finally got up and scampered behind the bushes. He had to rest again before he could climb the fence to safety.

I couldn't help but think about my instinct as a human to help a poor, defenseless animal. I cannot comprehend what happened to George Floyd. I reflected on how long the squirrel laid motionless—ten minutes. I thought about George Floyd lying on the pavement, motionless, with a knee on his neck for over eight minutes. Rudy got away. A few hours later, he was back at the bird feeder filling his belly. George Floyd was not so lucky.

Wood Biscuit Post

[Picture of Wood Biscuit in space.]

Unofficial Neighborhood Update: Saturday was a day of numbers. Even though Wood Biscuit has no fingers to count with, it was easy for him to do the math. The important numbers were 2,415, two, and one. Late this evening my phone dinged indicating that I had a message. Wood

Biscuit sent me a text. It read, "The residents of Woodbridge have already donated enough money to the North Texas Food Bank to provide 2,415 meals for needy families." "That is unbelievable," I said, "That is the same number of turtles in the Highlands Turtle Pond Gang." Coincidence? I think not.

"Don't be silly!" Wood Biscuit snorted. "There are good numbers everywhere. You just have to look for them each day. Like two. We sent two people to space successfully today. It was a beautiful launch, and they will arrive at the space station in the morning. Two miracles orbiting the earth." I shrugged and said, "I was thinking about the two people banned from making comments in the Woodbridge forum this week. I guess it's all what you decide to focus on."

We both paused for a second, and I tried to think of a good number. "One…yes…one is a good number. When we all come together for one cause, we can make a bigger impact. We feed others…we send people to space. We make the world a better place. It sounds like a good number to me." I hung up the phone and walked outside. I thought, "How does a horse hold an iPhone?"

Thanks to everyone who gave to the North Texas Food Bank after reading these silly unofficial fake stories about a horse. I'm humbled by your generosity. [Smile emoji]

I love the Woodbridge Facebook posts featuring Wood Biscuit, the resident Fake News horse, who patrols the swimming pools and turtle gangs in the neighborhood.

Sun / 2020 May 31 / Journal Entry

I woke up to a beautiful morning. While I was tending to the patio, Jose made breakfast. I decided to trim the bushes. The dogs were "helping" by dozing in the grass and soaking up the sun. The Walmart pool was ready, and I could not wait to get in it.

I stared at the clouds in the sky for a long time. I laid back and enjoyed the day. Jose brought me lunch and joined me in the pool.

The sun wiped me out. I fell asleep for a while. The neighborhood is quiet, unlike the protesting and rioting world around us.

I wonder if the events of the last few days are related. It's things like this that make me go hmmmm. (God wink before I had a word for it).

It has been a couple of weeks since the popsicle stick faerie doors first appeared attached to trees on the neighborhood walking trail. Now it had evolved into a full blown faerie village with faerie houses, gnomes, a toy store, coffee shop, and hotel. We saw two faerie godmothers on a ladder hanging a faerie rocket house. I love discovering painted rocks with encouraging messages like, "In God We Trust", "Prove Them Wrong" and "Believe". I spotted a Puerto Rican flag rock for Jose! I spotted a painted rock that said, "Hope." That was a real treasure.

The past few weeks we have seen lots of families walking, fishing, and riding bikes together. In twenty years, I have never seen so much family activity in the neighborhood. I really love the painted rocks and faerie houses. I also love the efforts of people trying to make the world a better place despite the present circumstances.

Wood Biscuit Post

Picture of a white woman with a face mask looking out her window. There is a reflection of Wood Biscuit in the window.

Unofficial Fake Neighborhood Update: "It's easy to get caught up in all of the worry when the news on TV is bad every night." Those were the words from a local resident today after making a mistake.

Local resident Karen mistook today's 2020 Senior Parade for a slow speed police chase in the neighborhood. She was simply making a tuna sandwich and ran to the windows when she heard the sirens.

"First, I saw a fire truck, then another fire truck, then a police car, then another police car. In front of them were a bunch of kids with streamers

and balloons. Their bodies were sticking out of cars. Right then, I knew something was sour. I dialed a nine and a one...then I waited with my finger on the one. That's when my dog Pookie barked and scared me. The sound frightened me, and I hit the last one by accident."

Some residents question the validity of Karen's story because of her numerous calls in the past. The previous reports were mostly gunshots on the 4th of July and one call because kids were wearing down the sidewalk from riding their bikes too much. #Congrats2020Seniors

COVID-19 Statistics:
Confirmed cases worldwide: 6,034,983
Confirmed deaths worldwide: 376,497
Confirmed cases in the United States: 1,716,638
Confirmed deaths in the United States: 106,000

june

Mon / 2020 June 1 / Journal Entry

Day 90—Safer at Home

"Change will not come if we wait for some other person, or if we wait for some other time. We are the ones we've been waiting for. We are the change we seek."
Barack Obama

George Floyd's brother is calling for peace. The news is covering the looting, arrests, and police officers who are kneeling and marching with the protestors. Facebook is flooded with posts about the unrest. The news is also reporting concerns that COVID-19 may continue to spread due to the protests.

Wood Biscuit Post

[Picture of a yard with a sculpture of dog poo. Wood Biscuit is in the corner with a French beret on his head.]

Unofficial Social Committee Update: In times of social distancing, it's really hard to be on a social committee. Great ideas are rare. You have to think outside the box. Thank the Lord we are blessed with a forward thinking and creative group of people. In an effort to make a negative into a positive, the committee announced that they will be gathering all the dog poop left on sidewalks by lazy residents over the next month. They have named the initiative, "Poo unto others as they poo unto you."

The poo will then be sculpted into art and left on the lawn of one lucky offender. French artist Woodrow Bisquet will be in charge of making the modern art sculpture. Woodrow has worked in many mediums such as marble, glass, and wood. This will be his first attempt at sculpting the bad manners of others.

The fake committee chairperson was quoted as saying, "It's our way of giving back to those that gave to us." #GiveACrap, #DooDooYourPart

Tues / 2020 June 2 / Journal Entry

Blackout Tuesday to protest the murder of George Floyd.

I woke up at 4:30 a.m. and could not sleep. I was thinking, "What can I do to change this?" I am deeply troubled. I am struggling to find the words to pray because I am overwhelmed with how much there is to pray about.

Facebook profile pictures are going black. The radio station had a moment of silence. Twitter changed its logo. Businesses that normally send daily email advertisements are sending emails in response to the civic unrest.

I went to my nail appointment. I had to fill out a COVID-19 questionnaire and get my temperature taken. I enjoyed a quiet salon and spa experience.

As I was waiting for my nails to dry, a woman came in without a mask. She fussed about how it made her have headaches. Then she said she did not have a mask. Then she said her mask was dirty. Then she said masks do not do anything. The spa manager was very nice but told her she had to have one, and she had to wear it. Miraculously, she put one on.

I went through the Chick-Fil-A drive-through to pick up lunch and a dinner meal kit. They have double lanes for ordering, paying, and picking up. It is extremely efficient and super busy. It is a phenomenon of fast food. Today they messed up my order. It caused a small back up. The man behind me was losing his mind. He was yelling at me and hanging out of his window. He was yelling at the workers.

He started getting out of his truck to yell at me to get out of his way so he could go on with his day. I was fuming.

Today, I witnessed two white people acting like white people with privilege. I am disgusted and embarrassed. As I replayed my story to Jose, he told me he went into a 7-11 while he was out today. He was the only person wearing a mask. He said everyone was looking at him like he was the crazy one. It frightens me. We are in the middle of a global pandemic which has taken a back seat to the riot news. New cases have been reported today. New deaths have been reported today.

I am worried about my brown husband and my multiracial kids.

I am glad I had a virtual Bible study with Kristi today. I needed to refocus my frustration with people and focus on being right with God. Kristi and I have studied together for nine weeks. I appreciated her spiritual guidance. This was the challenge at the end of our lesson: "As this study comes to a close, it's imperative that you allow God to turn your focus outward and begin seeking those He wants to impact through you."

I am so blessed that Jose is levelheaded and even tempered. I spent the better part of our walk tonight venting and fussing about the day's events. He just listened. I appreciate him so much. I love him so much. I pray for him. I often wonder how I ever got so lucky to be with him all these years. We spent part of our walk reminiscing that one year ago we were in Costa Maya with parrots on our heads in the aviary overlooking a lovely Mexican beach.

The Chancellor of the Dallas County Community College District sent an email:

The COVID-19 pandemic, combined with the tragic events in Minneapolis resulting in protests in Dallas and across the nation, has been unlike anything we've ever experienced.

As we grapple with the senseless death of Mr. George Floyd in Minne-

apolis and the actions of the police officers involved, I acknowledge the challenges many within our communities face, including the all too familiar reminders of the systemic racial injustice that continues to exist in this country. While I don't have all the answers, I recognize the hope and strength we see in our students and employees every day is why we must move forward with a deeper love and respect for each other, increased equity in action, and learning and growing from this truly devastating situation so we can emerge stronger.

We knew the day would come when we would need to reopen our campuses and carry out our mission to serve students. To do this, we are taking a very careful, tempered approach to coming back, evaluating each phase daily to ensure that our employees and students remain safe. And even as we phase in our re-entry, we will all need to remain agile, understanding that this is a fluid environment that could change very rapidly.

There are no plans for an immediate return of all employees to our locations at this point, driven in part by state orders regarding that office capacity not exceed fifty percent. But of even higher importance is ensuring that we meet CDC guidelines regarding social distance and safe workplace protocols. It would be impossible to meet those guidelines if all our employees returned at once. Employees who have not been notified directly by their supervisor to return to campus will continue to work remotely.

I am confident that this plan will effectively balance our responsibility to serve students, while ensuring the safety of our entire DCCCD community. As I've said before, you are the backbone of this district, and our many successes would not be possible without you. When the history books are written about this critical time, our efforts to overcome all our challenges will be listed as one of our finest moments. Upon beginning this new journey, I encourage you to maintain your positive, tenacious spirit as we go about the business of educating our students and creating a safer, more just, and equitable society for all.

Stay well,
Joe May

When Jose and I took our evening walk we spotted thirteen rabbits. We noticed the vitex trees and hydrangeas were blooming beautifully all around the neighborhood.

We discovered new additions to the Faerie Village including a sign that said, "Stella Springs Faerie Community." There were new faerie houses of metal and wood which have replaced most of the popsicle stick faerie doors. We found a log cabin, faerie condominium, townhome, and high rise. The community had expanded to include a faerie nursery, a faerie ice cream cart, a faerie trading post, and a faerie/alien Area 51. The fairies have stepped up their game.

There were painted rocks that said, "Joy", "Stay Safe", and "Be Kind, Be Strong, Be You!" These were all timely messages for me.

Wed / 2020 June 3 / Journal Entry

"If you walk in the footsteps of a stranger, you'll learn things you never knew you never knew." Disney's Pocahontas

The fact that I cannot sleep is nothing compared to a person begging for his mother because he can't breathe.

The news reports 9,300 arrests related to protests. We are amid a global pandemic, a cultural pandemic, and a spiritual pandemic. I usually do not post anything on Facebook that is remotely political in nature for two reasons: (1) I was taught that it was impolite to talk about politics in public, and (2) I do not want a slew of hateful comments in my Facebook feed. But today I am not afraid. I posted several video clips that I personally found thought provoking and caused me, a white woman, to reflect on my white privilege.

I am responsible for educating myself to know better and to do better. It is what I would want people to do if something unimaginable had happened to me or to one of my family members due to their race. I want to be part of the solution, not part of the problem. I asked the question of students and staff for years as a public-school administrator, "Are you part of the problem or part of the solution?"

This is a list of things I researched today to help me evaluate my own behavior towards people of different races:
- Jane Elliott's "Blue Eyes/Brown Eyes" experiment on YouTube. She was a third-grade teacher who conducted the experiment in her class on April 5, 1968, the day after the assassination of Martin Luther King, Jr.
- Emmanuel Acho's *Uncomfortable Conversations with a Black Man* series on YouTube: "You cannot fix a problem you do not know you have."
- Audiobook by Robin DiAngelo *White Fragility: Why It Is So Hard for White People to Talk About Racism*
- Martin Luther King, Jr.'s, thekingcenter.org, "The Triple Evils (Poverty, Racism, Militarism)," "Six Steps of Nonviolent Social Change," "Six Principles of Nonviolence," and "The Beloved Community"

These were some notes I scribbled:
- There is a difference between indoctrinated and educated.
- Whiteness is not rightness.
- We are a salad bowl more than a melting pot.
- What would you like to do with "them?"
- Should the color of someone's eyes have anything to do with how you treat them?
- Fill out your census.
- Vote!

Thurs / 2020 June 4 / Journal Entry

I had a quiet conversation with Jose this morning. I asked how he was feeling about everything. He doesn't share. He doesn't complain. He doesn't show his emotions, but that doesn't mean he doesn't think and feel. He says, in a joking manner, that he is like a ninja or "karate man." He has bruises on the inside. (This is a reference to a line in *Trading Places* with Eddie Murphy).

I expressed my sadness for our multiracial family, our police family, our military family, our community, and my whiteness. He suggested I take a break from social media and the news, but it is important to me to be informed.

We got up late and went out to pick up lunch. We watched the hummingbirds while we ate on the patio. This morning Major stood on the patio and a hummingbird circled the top knot on his head for about thirty seconds. Major saw the bird, but he didn't move. The bird looked like he wanted to land on Major's head, like it was a nest, or pollinate it, like it was a flower.

Kat posted a powerful video about running an unfair race. It made me proud of her. It is a YouTube video called "Privilege/Class/Social Inequalities Explained in a Race for $100."

George Floyd's memorial service was on television today. The protests continued.

Jose and I make a conscious effort to periodically check in, especially with family, and often with friends. Today Dad sent a "checking in" text to Michelle and me.

Dad: "I'm just checking in. We're still okay. How about you?"
Michelle: "Good here"
Me: "Just trying to process George Floyd's death, protests, my multiracial family, my cop family, my military family, my whiteness, my Christianity...it's a lot. Just say a prayer for us please. AND day 241 of no alcohol!"
Michelle: "It is a lot."
Dad: "Yes, it is. Count our blessings. We're all okay."

Wood Biscuit Post [Pictures of faerie houses.]

Unofficial Fake Neighborhood Update: The walking paths have seen a significant improvement lately. If you have taken a stroll, you may have seen the new Stella Springs expansion in Woodbridge. Great landscaping, rope ladders, and wood fences are just a few of the highlights. The new house also brings with it something different— gnomes.

In a wooded area that has always been dominated by faerie houses, this is the first family of gnomes. Why is this important, you ask? Because traditionally faerie houses are single doors leading into trees. Sure, some have been in logs and other wooded objects, but those are the exceptions.

This is relevant because the gnomes built their house on the open ground, causing some raised eyebrows in the faerie community.

As we all know, fairies are known to be generally good, but at times resistant to change. So, we went to ask them about the new gnomes after meeting them at a weekend cookout. Jerry Faerie was the first to tell us about meeting them. "At first, I admit I was worried because they didn't look like me, no wings, odd hats, and colorful pants. Then I realized that the hats were to hide a receding hairline. So, I got one for myself. I think I'm looking pretty good. I even canceled my subscription to the Hair Club for Fairies." We also talked to Gary Faerie. He was really excited about the new gnomes. He said: "I reminded everyone in the trees of the faerie code. We call it the code of no exceptions." I think it was a good reminder. It says…
Love your neighbor who doesn't…
- *Look like you*
- *Think like you*
- *Love like you*
- *Speak like you*
- *Pray like you.*
- *Vote like you.*
- *Build houses like you.*

Love your neighbor. No exceptions.

Did Wood Biscuit see the sign in my yard? Maybe!

Fri / 2020 June 5 / Journal Entry

I worked on a curriculum for virtual service learning all day. There is still much work to do, but I am getting there. I welcomed the distraction of work.

Wood Biscuit Post

[Picture of John Bender from The Breakfast Club walking across the football field with fist in the air. Wood Biscuit is on the field. The poo sculpture is also included in the scene.]
Last Unofficial Neighborhood Update for a bit: Thanks everyone for

reading posts over the last couple weeks. It was a nice distraction and a fun, creative outlet during this time of social distancing.

At first, I just wanted to change the tone of the conversation in this Facebook group. Then a horse hijacked my posts. Wood Biscuit helped us laugh at our silly problems, reflect on our blessings, give thousands of meals to the needy, and helped us read silly stories that mirrored some of our own shortcomings.

The greatest part of it is that everyone was civil and kind in every post, including the pool activists and dog poop bandits. I must give credit where credit is due. They either took it in stride or hid in the shadows. We found that not many people will challenge a talking horse.

The big question that this has all been leading up to...Does anyone know when the pool is opening?

Sat/ 2020 June 6/ Journal Entry

We had an early morning wake up to go to our License to Carry class at 8:30 a.m. We signed up for it months ago when we bought our guns in March. It finally opened up, and while we both want to get our LTCs, we are unsure about attending a class during a pandemic. The website assured us that the class size was limited. Neither Jose nor I plan to carry our guns on a routine basis, but we do want to follow the law. It is ironic that we are attending this class during all the protests and a global pandemic.

Tues / 2020 June 9 / Journal Entry

George Floyd's funeral broadcast on live television

"Try to see the good in others. When you're tempted to judge someone, make an effort to see their goodness. Your willingness to look for the best in people will subconsciously bring it forth."
Marianne Williamson

I learned three new terms today. "Defund" does not mean "disband," as in, defund the police. There are varying degrees of defunding, but it usually means reallocating some public funds used toward policing to fund public safety, social services, and youth services. "Disease" is a medical term, but "dis-ease" is a psychological term, as applied to COVID-19 and reopening society. Another new term is "ally" which is different from the "supporter" of movements like Black Lives Matter. An ally provides assitance through moral support. A supporter is an individual who contributes time, effort, or money.

The funeral for George Floyd was aired today for four hours. It was a celebration of his life.

There is a growing debate regarding Black Lives Matter versus All Lives Matter. I saw a metaphor about it on Facebook: There is one house on fire on the block. All the houses matter and need to be protected, but the one house that is on fire needs the most attention and resources.

Thurs / 2020 June 11 / Journal Entry

"Sometimes when you're in a dark place you think you've been buried, but you've actually been planted."
Christine Cain

This morning, I woke up perfectly fine, but then I started to cry. I prayed out loud—for me, for the community, the country, even for the president.

I went to the chiropractor. While waiting I heard, "Here Comes the Sun" by the Beatles. It made me feel better. Then, my chiropractor adjusted my spine and neck, which cracked so loud. It was amazing; I felt an endorphin rush in my body. My first sunflower bloomed from the seeds we planted in April. Here comes the sunflower!

Fri / 2020 June 12 / Journal Entry

The inflatable Walmart pool was set up and ready. The yard and patio looked pretty and inviting. It was an excellent day to reflect and relax and get some vitamin D from the sun.

I listened to *Oprah Live*. Oprah said:
Everyone wants to know: Do you see me? Do you hear me? Does my life matter? Am I valued? On Global Wellness Day a good mantra to remember is. "In this moment, I am well." Stop right now. Close your eyes and take four seconds to inhale and four seconds to exhale, and celebrate the breath and the freedom to breathe. Breathe for those who cannot breathe—George Floyd or those who are on ventilators struggling due to COVID-19. Just breathe and repeat, "In this moment, I am well."

Jose and I relaxed in the blow-up Walmart pool since the neighborhood pools are still closed. I asked Alexa to "play Soft Rock." She heard "play Yacht Rock." I didn't realize there was a station called Yacht Rock.

Jose called his mom in Florida and found out she and her partner, Arnulfo, were both tested for COVID-19 and were waiting for the results. Kat and Jordan got pre-approved for a home loan to buy a house. Kyla took one of her board exams to be a chiropractor.

I had a Virtual Virtues meeting with Dr. Bob via Webex. The topic tonight was a discussion about COVID-19 and race relations and the complex feelings of "being apart" and "being a part." I think that sums up exactly what I struggled with last week.

Wood Biscuit Post

Thank you to our Woodbridge Board of Directors for their tireless work. The pools are scheduled to open tomorrow, so let's have a little Bingo fun! If you observe any of these behaviors or conversations, check your box. Can't wait to hear people yell "Bingo" at the pool!

Woodbridge Pool Bingo
The "Bingo card" was nine squares, a three by three. The squares included:
- *complaints about how long it took to open the pools*

- *asking about a partial refund of HOA dues*
- *asking if masks are required in the water*
- *observing a "watcher" a.k.a. "Karen" compliance checker*
- *a Wood Biscuit free space*
- *overhearing "You are not six feet apart"*
- *observing someone with cleaning supplies*
- *random temperature checks*
- *threats to call the police.*

Sat / 2020 June 13 / Journal Entry

Wood Biscuit Post

[Picture of a chubby guy with an inner tube around his waist.] Unofficial Fake Pool Update: The checklist was short. Sunscreen? Check. Floaty? Check. Swimming trunks? Oh no!

This is when local resident Delbert realized that the shelter in place had done some damage. To be exact...23 pounds of damage. "This is all the HOA's fault. They should reimburse me for new swimming trunks. They took so long to open the pools, so instead of swimming I got big bones."

It's incidents like these that are making some residents wonder if they made the right decision to open pools. "I just realized that since we have all been inside, everyone is going to be pale from no sun, gray headed from no hair coloring appointments, and pudgy from overeating. I think I will keep my eyes forward when I drive past the pool," said resident W. Booskett.

These setbacks don't seem to be dampening the spirits of most pool fans. They are sending in their forms and lining up to swim on opening day. I guess it's out with the little ducks and in with the pale butts. #DeepBreath, #ThenButtonIt

Sun / 2020 June 14 / Journal Entry

New York Governor Andrew Cuomo was on TV demonstrating the difference between a face mask and a chin strap. People who do not like wearing face masks over their nose and mouth try to get away with wearing it pulled down under their chin.

Wood Biscuit Post

[Picture of a grandma holding her glasses to get a better view. Wood Biscuit is in the background.]

Unofficial Fake Neighborhood Update: Many tech-challenged residents have found themselves in shock recently when they drove past pools and saw residents splashing around and having fun.

"I hadn't heard a thing about pools opening," said resident Nana Betty. "I checked my mailbox, and I haven't seen the Pony Express come down the street. You figured I would have heard something."

Other paranoid residents were also out of the loop until they received the snail mail notification. Well-known doomsdayer and paranoid resident, Ted K. said, "We were the last to know. I got off all social media and threw away my phone last month. I had to after Bill Gates planned to put microchips in our brains with the COVID-19 vaccine he's working on."

Hopefully everyone will be in the know soon. Then residents can begin to complain about how expensive postage costs were for the association or how they are being discriminated against because they don't use the internet. #BackInMyDay, #DialUp, #AOL

Mon / 2020 June 15 / Journal Entry

I made my weekly trip to Walmart for groceries. It was the first time since the pandemic began that I saw boxes of disposable masks for sale (limit one box per customer). Each box was $14.00.

Tues / 2020 June 16 / Journal Entry

I completed the new mandatory "Back to Work" training about safety protocols. I downloaded a new app, Appian, that is used for employees to do self-checks for COVID-19 and receive a work pass for entrance into campus facilities.

Wood Biscuit Post

[Picture of Wood Biscuit in a car in a garage.]

Unofficial Fake Neighborhood Update: The effects of the COVID-19 pandemic can be seen in many places. People wearing masks in stores, hand sanitizer bottles on counters, and plexiglass partitions dividing us from cashiers. We can't deny that the world is a different place.

One Woodbridge resident used the shelter in place mandate to make big changes in his life. "I've been toying with the idea of cleaning my garage. It's been full of junk for years. I've never actually parked my car inside of it," said local resident Ned. "Then I saw all these morons not wearing masks the last couple of weeks. Then I decided to just tackle it while I stay home and watch the second wave of infections."

This trend of procrastinators finishing long overdue projects seems to be more widespread than we first thought. We also had reports of Nana Betty cleaning out her junk drawer, Willy Bosut reorganizing his clothes closet, Dana Smith picking weeds in her flower bed, and Mack D. having his wife shave his hairy back.

Wood Biscuit made me think about, of all things, my jewelry collection. Occasionally I had pieces of jewelry that were expensive (to me anyway), but more than their cost, they were usually gifts that were presented to me as a token of admiration, love, service, recognition, or thanks. They brought me esteem and value. They meant that I meant something to someone. My value to the world increased, and these items were proof. They needed to be kept safe in case there is any question in my mind or anyone else's mind that I matter, or at least mattered, in this life.

It would be interesting to be a fly on the wall and hear what my kids will say as they pick through my "valuables." More than likely, they will choose a few items that they like for themselves, and either throw away, donate, or sell the rest in a garage sale for $1.00 an item. They will probably pass over the rings I was given by a former admirer, or the bag of charms I collected when I traveled, or the bag of pins that I collected from service and belonging to various organizations. I can bet there will not be a hint of discussion or curiosity about the meaning behind any of it. Why? Because it is not meaningful to them and their understanding of who I am or was.

I truly do not want to burden anyone, especially my family, with all my stuff. I would rather they spend the time together simply remembering me and how I may have added value to their lives when I was here, rather than discussing, debating, deciding, and dealing with my stuff. The mindset to plan ahead for our eventual demise and rid the world of our personal, physical treasures is overwhelming to think about, much less to do. We need to do everyone—our spouse, kids, families, neighbors, community—a favor and clean out and get rid of our crap so they do not have to do it for us.

Wed / 2020 June 17 / Journal Entry

I went to the dentist. New check-in procedures have been implemented at the dentist's office due to COVID-19. I had to call the office from my car to get permission to enter the waiting room. I had to use hand sanitizer, wear a mask in the waiting room, sign new patient information, release paperwork (digitally), and get my temperature taken.

Fri / 2020 June 19 / Journal Entry

"This is a wonderful day. I've never seen this one before."
Maya Angelou

Wood Biscuit Post

[Picture of a silhouette of Sherlock Holmes and Wood Biscuit.]

Unofficial Neighborhood Update: Just so everyone knows…I don't know the location of the treasure and neither does Wood Biscuit. What treasure

might you ask? *The big Woodbridge Treasure Hunt started today. It seems someone has taken quite a bit of time to set up a challenging treasure hunt. What do we know so far? Here are a few things:*
1. *There is a video on YouTube explaining the treasure hunt and what it is about.*
2. *There is an Instagram account that has some posts that will probably give clues in the future.*
3. *There is a Twitter account that seems to be mirroring the clues.*
4. *I suggest you team up with others to crack the clues. I don't think they are going to get any easier as it progresses.*

I started working on the Woodbridge Treasure Hunt to distract me.

Woodbridge Treasure Hunt sign and Facebook post: Welcome. It looks like you followed your curiosity, and you are excited to start the treasure hunt. Let's get a few things out in the open. In the end, there is a prize, but what kind? It has no monetary value. The hunt will be challenging and different. You will use the internet, get some exercise, and find out what the faeries are hiding. It won't be easy, simple, or obvious. If it was easy, it wouldn't be as much fun. There is no physical danger. If you feel like you are in danger you are going the wrong way. If you are trespassing on someone else's property, you are definitely going the wrong way. When you get stuck, reach out to a friend or neighbor and crack the hunt together.

Sat / 2020 June 20 / Journal Entry

Wood Biscuit Post

[Picture of a person going into dark woods with a flashlight. Wood Biscuit is on the trail.]

Unofficial Woodbridge Treasure Hunt Update: So, have you tried looking for the Woodbridge Mystery Treasure? If not, then you should. It is fun. It is rewarding...and it is really, really, really, challenging. Did I mention that it is challenging? Someone has put a ton of time and effort into planning the event and placing clues. Don't assume the game is broken or a clue is missing. The rain and weather won't wash away any clues. They are well made and durable. It's really challenging until it's really obvious where the next faerie clue is. Don't give up. I'm not sure how long the hunt will take, but I suspect multiple days.

We found the first faerie sign. Wood Biscuit was right—the sign was sturdy and durable and made of wood. It looked like the faerie logo and URL site had been professionally engraved into it. It was securely attached to a tree trunk by the pond. The faerie logo was red.

Once I deciphered the first clue, it led us to a pond and park in our neighborhood we had not been to before. We presumed the next clue would be attached to a tree, so we got out and started wandering through the park looking at tree trunks. Sure enough, we found the blue faerie sign hidden in a group of trees. We drove home so I could download the document which had masonic codes, also known as pigpen codes. I googled masonic codes and deciphered the message.

We explored a new section of the neighborhood and wound up back at the park where we found the Blue Faerie. We named this park/pond The Duck Pond because there are ducks everywhere.

The long, wandering walk made me realize the treasure hunt went beyond the Muddy Creek Trail. It was going to be throughout the Woodbridge Community. There are over 8,400 homes in our neighborhood.

Sun/ 2020 June 21 / Journal Entry

Jose and I took a drive to find the green faerie. The green faerie code was easy to solve. Instead of a URL, the sign had geometric shapes on it. When I counted the sides of each shape it produced a phone number. When I called the phone number, a recorded message gave us a new clue.

After an early dinner we used Google Maps to locate our destination to hunt for the yellow faerie. We drove to the west side of Woodbridge and walked the new trail which had some steep hills. We found the yellow faerie and instructions to download layers of a cipher wheel, which is a tool to create encrypted messages.

Mon / 2020 June 22 / Journal Entry

We drove to another park and pond we now call Woodbridge West. I found the bronze faerie, took a picture of the URL, and headed home to work on the clue to find the purple faerie.

Thurs / 2020 June 25 / Journal Entry

"When a train goes through a tunnel and it gets dark, you don't throw away the ticket and jump off. You sit still and trust the engineer."
Corrie Ten Boom

Four months into the pandemic.

COVID-19 cases are on the rise. The mask debate is getting more contentious. Non-mask wearers complain that they can't breathe and that the government is infringing on their rights. The news reported sixteen people from one family got infected at a surprise birthday party, and the elderly grandparents are on life support with no visitors allowed.

I asked my co-worker to proofread my virtual service-learning curriculum documents. In the meantime, I got a lot of work done on my Tier I, II, and III plans for service learning.

I spoke to a friend who is a professor at a private university. She discussed the school's plan to record live classes for students who choose to attend online. This raises the question about "intellectual property" for many professors. Online learning is truly challenging but does not seem to be going away.

I had a virtual Bible study with Kristi. The lesson, as usual, was timely and excellent. Today we discussed sin. We reflected on the sadness and anger that has been prevalent with racial injustice. We discussed how sin equates to failure to live up to what we know is right, true and moral, and it leads to a breakdown of trust. That is why God is so important. He is the source of ultimate hope.

Fri / 2020 June 26 / Journal Entry

"My coming of faith did not start with a leap but rather a series of staggers from what seemed like one safe place to another. Like lily pads, round and green, these places summoned and then held me up while I grew. Each prepared me for the next leaf on which I would land, and in this way, I moved across the pond of doubt and fear."
Anne Lamott

I headed out first thing this morning to find the purple faerie at what we now refer to as Sachse Road Pond. I felt like Nancy Drew. I am glad I wore my Sugar Skull galoshes because I ended up trekking around most of the pond. One side was steep and slippery. I encountered a creek that had resulted from the recent rains. I looked and looked and couldn't find the purple faerie. It didn't feel right. I felt like I was too close to other people's property, and I thought about the first post: "There is no physical danger. If you feel like you are in danger you are going the wrong way. If you are trespassing on someone else's property, you are definitely going the wrong way."

I backtracked and explored the other side of the pond. This tree-covered area is a hidden gem in our neighborhood. I thought it would make a great place to have a picnic. It took about twenty minutes, but I finally spotted the purple faerie. I raced home to start working on the next puzzle.

Dr. Fauci and Dr. Birkt made an appearance during a press conference with Vice President Mike Pence about spikes in cases, hospitalization rates, and death rates. The governor shut bars down at noon and pulled back restaurants to fifty percent capacity or take-out only. The next few weeks are going to be critical to everything—flattening the curve, the economy, and opening schools.

Sat / 2020 June 27 / Journal Entry

I woke up at 3:00 a.m. and could not go back to sleep. I proceeded to work on the puzzle, but to no avail. I Googled and searched for all kinds of ciphers, codes, combinations, alpha numeric puzzles, videos, and images, but I couldn't find anything to help. It was frustrating, and I am not a patient person. I know the puzzle must be easy enough for kids to solve, so why can't I—a person with a bachelor's, master's, and a doctoral degree—figure it out? I worked until 6:30 a.m. and went back to bed.

I reached out to a couple who posted on the Woodbridge Resident page that they are also stuck on the purple faerie. It turns out they both work at Richland, too. Three grown-ups with multiple college degrees can't break a code that, according to the game host, is simple enough for an elementary kid to solve. Well, that doesn't make me feel any better. In fact, right now, I am feeling pretty dumb. I don't get it. At least I have treasure-hunting allies like me.

Wood Biscuit Post

Picture of a treasure chest with Wood Biscuit nearby.

I will start by saying...my wife and I found the treasure today. We are the first people to locate it. The good news is that there is still treasure waiting for you to find at the end.

Sun/ 2020 June 28 / Journal Entry

"When you dance, your purpose is not to get to a certain place on the dancefloor; it's to enjoy each step along the way."
Wayne Dyer

I called Janet. We became friends when I first started teaching in 1986. She has received three deliveries from the Buzz Fairies. This is a group of women on Facebook who support each other during COVID-19. They deliver cookie baskets with adult beverages—sometimes dressed in faerie costumes. I love it! How ironic is it that faeries are so prevalent during the pandemic?

While Janet and I were talking, my Richland allies solved the puzzle.

Thank God! I reflected on what I had learned about myself on this clue. I could not figure out the clue. It kept me up at night. I spent hours Googling and thinking about it. I got frustrated. I started to doubt my abilities. When my colleagues figured it out, I felt dumb. I was overthinking it. So, this is where the lesson lies. This is where, in retrospect, I should have slowed down and trusted myself. I could have figured it out on my own if I had had more patience and trust in myself and the process.

This is the beauty of the treasure hunt. The game host was wise enough to know that the hunt would provide opportunities for the players to seek adventure and experience discoveries that emerged along the way. The treasure is not the prize at the end; it is the lessons we learn along the way. It is about the process, not the product. Once I realized this, I felt like I could relax and appreciate the journey.

In the middle of the treasure hunt, just as the hunters sensed the solution was near, the game host took us back to the faerie village that inspired the treasure hunt in the first place. The clue was in braille--a way for the blind to see. The password to get to the clue was *regressus* which is Latin for "return." I completed the entire puzzle and found the orange faerie. I was on a roll.

Mon / 2020 June 29 / Journal Entry

109 days Safer at Home, 267 days sober

This morning, I woke up and went searching for the black faerie which held the key code to the cipher wheel. She was located under the Creek Crossing bridge. To decipher the last encrypted message, the images of the four layers of the cipher wheel must be aligned to create the cipher code. Then all the other symbols and letters in the encrypted message can be deciphered. There were three pages of the encrypted message, so it took quite a while to decode the final message.

Jose and I headed out. I was so excited I could hardly stand it. When we got to the sign "The Trail Ends Here," we veered off the path into the woods with my iPhone compass in hand. We walked thirty paces northeast. There was a pile of logs on top of a flat, square piece of wooden board. Under the board was a hole with a treasure chest inside. Inside the treasure chest was a message that said, "Please take only one." There was a Ziploc baggie with a letter from the game creator, a silver coin with the faerie logo, and a Woodbridge Treasure Hunt car decal with the faerie logo. The letter said:

Congratulations! You found the Faerie Treasure of Muddy Creek Trail!

If you're reading this, it means you are a formidable treasure hunter and puzzle solver. And I would like for you to have one of these unique coins and braggadocious stickers as a memorable token for your efforts. I don't know who began this new "forest faerie" tradition, but I was pleasantly surprised to see that virtually the entire surrounding community chose to embrace and support it. That was very heart-warming to me, and I felt inspired to create this experience as a tribute to that community-wide effort.

My hope is that this game is seen as a unique and fun way to get people out of their homes, get some fresh air, get some steps in, use their brains, creatively use technology, and work together. After all, I think some fun was in order after several months of collectively navigating one of the most bizarre events in the last century. And I don't know about everyone else, but this exercise made me much better acquainted with the geographical vastness and beauty of the neighborhood we share!

I do have two specific requests to make before you leave. At least consider obliging them if you can. But it's totally up to you.

1. *You found the chest, and I'm just as proud as you are that you did so. But this doesn't mean that the game is over for everyone. Others are still playing and enjoying the experience. So please don't tell anyone the location of the chest.*
2. *If you were able to find and play this game, then, chances are, you're a very lucky person in a somewhat comfortable position in this world (comparatively speaking, anyway). Life is already difficult enough without society suddenly needing to navigate a global pandemic, immediately followed by massive social unrest. And if you are one of the fortunate few to have made it through the last few months with*

only minor setbacks, then perhaps like me, you may feel like you want to try and do what you can to lift up the community which surrounds you. But if you would like to show me any amount of appreciation, you can do so by instead paying it forward to these invaluable Sachse-based charities: La Familia de Esperanza (The Family of Hope) and Five Loaves Pantry.

I thank you again, sincerely, thoroughly, and genuinely, for being part of this, and I hope you enjoyed it! Stay humble, be kind, and keep your eyes open. There's treasure everywhere!

P.S. Once you've claimed your prize and you're alone, please take extra special care to put everything back the way it was before so that everyone gets the same experience. And please notify me via email if additional coins are needed inside the chest. Thank you!

We left the treasure chest as we had found it.

The Woodbridge Treasure Hunt was symbolic. It was a metaphor. It was an exercise that prepared my heart and mind and reminded me of adventure, creativity, problem solving, and discovery. I discovered how small things like faeries, faerie doors, and faerie villages can inspire a community during a global pandemic. I discovered hope. I discovered my neighbors and my neighborhood. I discovered the hunt was as rewarding as the treasure itself. It never was about the buried treasure or the trinket prize inside. It was about the challenges, the problem solving, the feeling of accomplishment. It was about being outside, the fresh air, the weather, and the seasons. It was about nature, trees, ponds, sunsets, ducks, birds, fish, turtles, and owls. It was about connections to nature, to the community, to neighbors, to family, to self.

Tues / 2020 June 30 / Journal Entry

"You were wild once. Don't let them tame you."
Isadora Duncan
Bonus Quote: "Glitter done!"
Unknown
Today's news poll for parents was: Which learning option would you

choose for the fall semester? Online seventy-eight percent, in-person twenty-one percent.

I organized my workspace, which has been a challenge lately. Jose and I have workstations in our home office. My desk space in the office is tight, and I do not have room to spread out materials when I am studying, writing, or editing curriculum. I can work on the dining room table, which allows me to spread out, but I hate typing on my laptop. All my RCHS files are in a box in the guest bedroom, so it is frustrating every time I stop working and get up to get something out of another room.

I organized all our travel trip folders going back to 2012. I love that we have a folder with all our itinerary and travel plans from our trips. We have folders from Jamaica, Washington D.C., Chicago, New Orleans, Memphis, Puerto Rico, Italy, Seattle, San Francisco, Florida, our first cruise to Costa Maya and Cozumel, and more.

Likewise, the Alaskan cruise folder keeps staring at me. Our Alaskan cruise is scheduled for May of 2021, for Jose's fiftieth birthday present. We do not see ourselves flying on a plane and cruising on a floating petri dish anytime soon. So, I canceled our reservation and will get a full refund. It is sad. I feel bad. I really want to do something special for Jose.

Since we haven't been traveling this year, I don't have travel magnets or travel ornaments for this year. The holidays are going to be interesting. So far, we have missed out on our usual holiday happenings and family gatherings: Spring Break, St. Patrick's Day, Easter, Mother's Day, Michelle's birthday, Memorial Day, Father's Day, and graduation. This Fourth of July, which falls on a Saturday this year, is going to be different: no fireworks, no family cookouts, no traveling. It will be okay, just different.

I started thinking about the travel folders, souvenirs, ornaments, and magnets I had collected along the way. I know why I save the things I save, but who else knows? These things that I treasure do not matter to the people who matter to me, so why do they matter to me? Do I need them to remind me? Do I need them when I die? Do I need them to live?

If I died tomorrow, my family may find these items, but would they understand what they signified to me? What if my house burned to the ground tomorrow? Would all that I am be burned up with my little treasure boxes? I learned along the way that stuff is just stuff.

I have come to grips with the concept that my stuff is not worth anything to anybody because it is just stuff. I am reminded of this when I have a garage sale and sell everything for $1.00. Yet, I still have my own treasure troves that I cannot let go. Instead, someone else will be burdened with deciding what to do with my doll collection, my photo albums, and my trinkets.

COVID-19 Statistics in Texas:
June 10th 2,000+ cases in one day
June 17th 3,000+ cases in one day
June 20th 4,000+ cases in one day
June 23rd 5,000+ cases in one day

COVID-19 Statistics:
Confirmed cases worldwide: 7,102, 048
Confirmed deaths worldwide: 404,000
Confirmed cases in the United States: 1,915,712
Confirmed deaths in the United States: 114,000

july

Thurs / 2020 July 2 / Journal Entry

It was reported today that college students are having coronavirus cluster parties. They are paying a cover charge which goes into a pot. Whoever gets COVID-19 first gets the pot of money.

Fri / 2020 July 3 / Journal Entry

113 days of Safer at Home, 270 days sober

"Every time you subtract negative from your life, you make room for more positive."
Andy Van Dyke

I was reminded of the stages of grief: denial, anger, depression, bargaining, and acceptance, and I am reflecting on where I am regarding this pandemic journey. I vacillate between all the stages. I am definitely in the anger stage when I see people debate about masks, see news reports about social injustice, and read insensitive, mean Facebook posts. So, I am going to watch an episode of *Queer Eye* to lighten my mood. Just like today's quote, get rid of the negative to make room for the positive.

Sat / 2020 July 4 / Journal Entry

"May we think of freedom not as the right to do as we please, but as the opportunity to do what is right."
Peter Marshall

We watched Lin-Manuel Miranda's production of *Hamilton* on Disney Plus. I googled the lyrics on my phone so I could follow along. After the musical was over, we painted rocks on the patio and listened to Yacht Rock and then hid the rocks around the neighborhood. Jose made chicken sausage, peppers, and grilled zucchini for dinner. We met the neighbors for a socially distanced driveway get-together, otherwise now known as a "Holly Hills Hangout".

Fireworks displays were canceled to eliminate large crowd gatherings. Unfortunately, people were shooting them off in the neighborhood, so the Woodbridge "Karens" were posting about their children and dogs being terrorized.

Mon / 2020 July 6 / Journal Entry

I saw a Facebook post this morning, "What are the first three words you see?" I saw "alignment," "self-care," and "connection." I spent the day doing just that. My first stop was to the chiropractor for badly needed adjustments (alignment). I did my weekly grocery shopping at Walmart, picked up cupcakes from Smallcakes, got my hair trimmed and my nails done (self-care). I bought a new NIV translation Bible at Barnes and Noble (connection). On a different note, Kat and Jordan made an offer on a house, so they may be homeowners soon.

Tues / 2020 July 7 / Journal Entry

"Fireflies are tiny messengers that whisper in the darkness: Don't lose hope because magic does exist."
Jane Lee Logan

Today I worked on the virtual service-learning curriculum. Sometimes my creativity gets stuck. That is how I felt today. I am so close to finishing the virtual curriculum for the juniors, but I keep hitting a wall with ideas. I tried approaching the task from a different direction today, but it wasn't helpful. It's all part of the creative process. I will try again tomorrow.

Sad news. Immigration officials will not allow students to stay in the country if they have all online classes in college. The students in this situation have the following choices:

1. break immigration law and stay in the country,
2. transfer to an in-person university, which is too late and too expensive, or
3. go back to their home country during uncertain, unsafe, impossible travel times during a pandemic.

Wed / 2020 July 8 / Journal Entry

I thought about the K.I.S.S. strategy (Keep it Simple Stupid). This helped me break through the block I was having on my virtual curriculum project. I discarded the activities that were not working well and cut out work assignments that were designed just to have work. I was able to move forward and be productive. It felt good to knock out work today.

The debate on when and how to open schools in the fall is getting more heated. People are voicing their concerns on both sides of the fence. There are those who are concerned about the spread of the virus with teachers and students. Others are concerned about the social-emotional well-being of students and parents if school continues to be virtual. There are even those who believe that teachers are just whiny and want an extended vacation. Trump is threatening to cut funding if schools do not open.

I was very excited that two of my Facebook friends who are former teachers, Bridget and Barbara, joined Kristi and me for a new Bible study today. Today we studied "The Image of God" from the Bible Project's Church at Home series. To prepare for our study, we read Genesis 26-30. We discussed that if we are all created in God's image, no human is better than another. Kristi stated, "You will never look into the eyes of someone God doesn't love." I want to remember that statement when I am judging someone else. I appreciate these ladies. I know they are images of God. I feel blessed to have them in my life.

One thing I enjoy seeing on these summer evening walks is the fireflies that come out at dusk. I don't see them in the neighborhood like I did when I was a kid, but they are in the woods on Muddy Creek Trail.

Thu / 2020 July 9 / Journal Entry

"Look at where Jesus went to pick people. He didn't go to colleges; he got guys off the fishing docks."
Jeff Foxworthy

We met our Crappie Guided Tour guide at 7:00 a.m. at Lake Lavon. We wore our masks. We were the only boat on the water. We did not see any other people for six hours. It was really nice being in the middle of an empty lake all morning.

Greg, the guide, had a Garmin fish finder which allowed us to see our bait in the water and watch the fish in the water. He gave us fishing lessons and provided everything we needed to catch crappies. He was knowledgeable and patient. We could only keep fish over ten inches long, so we threw back at least ten little guys, but we got to keep twenty-six fish. Greg fileted our fish upon return. We have plenty of fish for several fish fry dinners. It was a great mini-vacay kind of day.

Sun / 2020 July 12 / Journal Entry

Day 122 of safer at home

"Everyone needs time to develop their dreams. An egg in the nest doesn't become a bird overnight."
Lois Ehlert

The news is reporting that foreign students may now stay in all online classes. The colleges and universities fought for their right to stay in the country. The State Fair of Texas has been canceled for October 2020 due to COVID-19. State Fair T-shirts are being sold anyway: "2020 Ain't No Fair," "Texas Fair: Now Serving Nothing Deep Fried on a Stick," "Texas State Fair —Zero Calories."

Mon / 2020 July 13 / Journal Entry

"Let those desert places in our hearts bloom."
Pope Francis

With the weather as hot as it is, we took Dexter and Major on another walk after the sun went down. The streets were still and eerily quiet. There are still no planes in the sky. We do not listen to music when we walk. Much of the time is spent in silence just observing and reflecting. I talked to my friend who is an educator and parent of public-school students about reopening school and her concerns for her own kids, the teachers, and the students. I am so glad I do not have to make decisions about whether my kids will go to school in person or online, or whether or not they can participate in sports, cheerleading, and fine arts activities. I feel blessed that I do not have to worry about my job, homeschooling my children, paying bills, or getting food on the table for my family.

Wed / 2020 July 15 / Journal Entry

After a delicious dinner of homemade Maryland creole crab cakes and sauteed crab fingers, we went to The Duck Pond. The dogs and I laid on a blanket. I brought a sleeve of unsalted crackers and fed the ducks. Surprisingly, the dogs were not concerned with the ducks. The ducks were brave; some got out of the water and came close to us on the grass. Meanwhile, Jose fished. Tonight, he took chicken dog treats for bait. He caught two catfish. The first one was two pounds, and the second one was at least five pounds. He was a big boy. Jose released both back into the pond. It was another nice summer evening at the park. People were riding bikes, walking dogs, and feeding the ducks.

Thurs / 2020 July 16 / Journal Entry

Another early morning walk, and we found more painted rocks. The first one said, "Good Vibes," which I took as a sign of a good day.

Tue / 2020 July 21 / Journal Entry

The mind is like water. When it's turbulent, it's difficult to see. When it's calm, everything becomes clear."
Prasad Mahes

The opening of schools is a moving target. County health officials keep pushing back school opening in person from after Labor Day to late September and even October. Essential workers are struggling to figure out day care for their children since day care centers are closed. High school sports have been postponed.

When I talked to my educator friends today, their heads were spinning about how schools were going to reopen. There are new protocols and rules about masks, face shields, plexiglass dividers, school clinic visits, meal deliveries for students and teachers, and visitors.

There will be no preseason football games for the NFL. Baseball season finally started today. The Rangers played their first game in their brand-new Globe Life Stadium with no fans. To make it more realistic, they piped fan noise in.

Our Bible study group uses resources from The Bible Project which is a non-profit organization that helps people access the Bible. Today our Bible study was about God's generous love. God is the party host, and humans are the party guests. Tim Mackie, one of the co-founders of The Bible Project, pointed out that we should observe the birds. They don't store up food, but they have enough. God provides. He goes on to say: "Man's scarcity problem is not a lack of resources. It is a mindset that God can't be trusted, therefore I should take matters into my own hands. Think toilet paper shortage or gas shortage."

We talked and prayed about what we are most grateful for. I am grateful for this group.

Sad news. Ogres destroyed the faerie village. Someone posted a picture on the Woodbridge Resident Facebook page. It is very disappointing. We took the dogs for a long walk on the trail. I am happy to report that repairs have already started in the faerie village.

Wed / 2020 July 22 / Journal Entry

"Of all the paths you take in life, make sure a few of them are dirt."
John Muir

Jose watched YouTube videos about fishing. YouTube has videos for everything. We went to a different pond tonight that we found on the Woodbridge Treasure Hunt. We call it Woodbridge West. Jose caught three small bass. By the time we left, there were eight guys fishing, and one little boy caught a five pound "monster" bass. He was so excited. It made all the guys smile. We watched the sunset on a blanket because it is July in Texas, and it is only 87 degrees.

Thu / 2020 July 23 / Journal Entry

Jose mentioned this evening that he has given up on the dream of having a truck, boat, or RV. This disappointed me. He is so giving, and he never buys anything for himself. I told him to make an appointment to go look at a truck tomorrow.

Fri / 2020 July 24 / Journal Entry

"The problem is not the problem. The problem is your attitude about the problem."
Jack Sparrow, Pirates of the Caribbean

On our morning walk we spotted the painted rock that said, "Just Do It." It was one of the rocks Jose had painted and hidden over two weeks ago. After he ran a few errands, Jose scooped me up to go look at a truck. Four hours later we left the dealership with a slightly used 2019 Nissan Frontier truck. I named it "Little Greg." Then we decided to take a cue from the faerie village and schedule a remodel of our master bathroom, kitchen, guest bathroom, and laundry room.

Sun / 2020 July 26 / Journal Entry

"But no matter how many fish in the sea, it'd be so empty without me."
Eminem

On our walk today we observed so many new things. Today we found a golf ball, a swim jig lure, painted rocks, new faerie houses, treasure hunters, and dog poop with sprinkles (yes, it's true!). We watched catfish jumping and the ducks doing what ducks do. My new Birkenstock sandals arrived from Amazon, so I wore them on the walk. They may be ugly, but they are so comfortable.

Jose's rod and reel racks arrived from Amazon. We hung them in the garage. They hold four rods and reels and keep them safe and organized on the wall. It makes me happy that it makes him happy.

We loaded up Dexter and Major for their first ride in Little Greg and headed to The Duck Pond for Sunday night fishing. When we arrived, it started to sprinkle, and a rainbow appeared. Then it started to rain harder, so we sat in Little Greg and watched the ducks waddle in groups across the street. We listened to the rain for about twenty minutes. When it stopped, we had the whole pond to ourselves. It was quiet, except for the sounds of ducks quacking and landing in the water.

Jose fished, and the dogs and I watched the clouds turn colors and reflect on the water. I took a picture of Jose fishing (#DoingWhatIDo) with the sunset and clouds reflecting in the water. It was a perfect day.

Mon / 2020 July 27 / Journal Entry

"When life closes a door, God opens a window."
Paul Smith

Our virtual Bible study was about hope. A passage from Romans 8:24 says, "For in this hope we were saved. But hope that is seen is no hope at all. Who hopes for what they already have?" The only thing that does not change during difficult times (like a pandemic) is a good God who promises restoration. Circumstances will come and go, but God is consistent. We need to cultivate the ancient concept of hope.

I have so much hope for humanity. I hope that our lives will be better after the pandemic is over. I hope that our earth will heal, that man will be kinder, and that the health care system, the justice system, the education system, and the political system will be better. I hope that we have generated a population of people who are hopeful. I hope that humankind has reflected and reprioritized the important things in life after this experience. I hope so.

After dinner we walked the trail. It felt spiritual. There were fancy painted rocks that said, "Work for It," "And the Adventure Begins," and "Stay Positive." However, my favorite rock find said, "Hope."

I choose to think that armadillos were the culprits who ravaged the faerie village instead of a person or persons. I choose to think positively. The added bonus for today—we saw not one, not two, not three, but four owls tonight! They were near the faerie village. They most certainly were hunting for ogres.

Thu / 2020 July 30 / Journal Entry

I worked on making sure that all my online documents for virtual service learning are accessible to students with disabilities. Microsoft Word has an accessibility check function that scans and scores each document. It offers suggestions for revisions if needed. This is important for visually impaired students.

Fri / 2020 July 31 / Journal Entry

I sent the kids some "just because" money. Kat and Jordan are scheduled to close on their first home in a week. Kyla is working on her chiropractic internship hours. Christian is working at the Air Force base in Washington state. We are blessed with great kids!

COVID-19 Statistics
Confirmed COVID cases worldwide: 16,000,000
Confirmed deaths worldwide: 644,404
Confirmed COVID cases in the UnitedStates: 4,000,000
Confirmed deaths in the United States: 146,460

august

Sun / 2020 Aug 2 / Journal Entry

"She was powerful not because she wasn't scared but because she went on so strongly despite her fear."
Atticus

My heart is heavy for teachers returning to school tomorrow. Many are fearful. The administrators are fearful, too, but must do what they are told. People are posting nasty things about educators on Facebook. They think teachers are a bunch of whiny babies. There are teachers who must take their own kids to school tomorrow because they can't stay at home with them, even if they would prefer to keep their kids at home and do online school.

I am getting ready for tomorrow, too. I will be assisting with laptop distribution for the RCHS students. It will be a drive-through event. It will be outside. It will be hot and uncomfortable, but not nearly as uncomfortable as my people in public schools. They have no choice. Many are afraid of dying. I feel helpless, but hopeful. I posted a public prayer on Facebook.

God,
I am not very eloquent when I pray, but you know what is on my heart. Lord God, I pray our leaders and decision makers will seek your guidance, wisdom, and strength. I pray for people who work in schools as they struggle with returning to work the next few days. I pray for the parents of students who don't know how to navigate the incredibly difficult situation to keep kids home or to send them to school. I pray for the students who rely on adults to do the right thing. God, I pray for your continued love, grace, hope, forgiveness, protection, and healing. I have faith in you, Lord, that you have a plan that I may not understand. I pray that

you will guide me to show love, support, and leadership to those that need it. Lord, help me manage my own heart and habits to continue to grow with grit and grace. Lord, thank you for all your blessings. Amen

Tues / 2020 Aug 4 / Journal Entry

"You're off to great places, today is your day. Your mountain is waiting, so get on your way."
Dr. Seuss

The news stated that 5,000,000 cases of COVID-19 have been reported in the United States. Today there are 97,000 kids who have tested positive. One person dies every eighty-six seconds.

Some schools started today. A recent poll asked, "Will your child be equipped for virtual learning?" Eighty percent of parents responded yes, while twenty percent responded no.

When COVID hit in the spring of 2020, we paused all service-learning requirements at RCHS. Seniors could graduate, even though there was no ceremony. The juniors were halfway through a semester, and most of them had planned to take advantage of spring break to volunteer and get hours. With the lockdown, juniors entered their senior year behind on the sixty-hour graduation requirement for service hours.

When it was evident that RCHS students would not be returning to school in person in the fall semester, I had to figure out a way for them to meet their service-learning requirements without in-person volunteering. I had to trust myself that I could create an alternative way for students to meet the graduation requirement for service learning.

Most of the non-profit agencies where students used to volunteer were also closed, and people were not encouraged to leave their homes. Some agencies had stayed open to help those in need, but they had strict safety protocols and no opportunities for student volunteers.

The virtual service-learning (VSL) curriculum had to include a way for students to catch up on hours if they were behind, stay on track during another virtual semester, and allow for meeting basic requirements while giving students a chance to go above and beyond and earn extra hours to be eligible for a service award. I created a tiered VSL curriculum so students could create a plan to meet their individual needs. I created simple, easy-to-understand instructions and activities that would allow students to complete their requirements from home. I created meaningful and relevant activities that were not just busy work which would add stress to an already ridiculous and stressful school situation.

I visited online classrooms through Teams throughout the day to discuss virtual service learning (VSL). I was on camera, so I dressed professionally from the waist up. I had workout leggings and house shoes on my bottom half. Before the pandemic, I spent a lot of time and money on accessories. I haven't worn jewelry in months, not even my wedding rings. I started out early in the pandemic dressing and accessorizing each morning to feel normal. I did not go anywhere. If I had a video call, the other side could only see me from the waist up. Over time, the jewelry went by the wayside. It is not important anymore.

Bridget, Barbara, and I had virtual Bible study on "The Water of Life." There have been many times when I felt unrelenting thirst, and I felt like things were getting worse, despite my efforts to make them better. When I turned to God and had faith, He quenched my thirst and made things better. It is comforting. It has been proven to me repeatedly.

Fri / 2020 Aug 7 / Journal Entry

This morning was glorious! The humidity was low, and the temperature was in the seventies. We went for an early walk, but there was quite a bit of traffic on the trail, so we walked to The Duck Pond and had it all to ourselves. My favorite duck, Mo, and the Muscovy duck, The Governor, enjoyed a feast of frozen peas with the rest of their flock.

We drove Little Greg to Home Depot to pick up our new flooring. All we had to do was pull up to a curbside space, text "I am here" to the number on the sign, and they brought our order out and loaded it in the back of the truck. We drove to the design center and selected countertops, tile, backsplash, sinks, and grout for the bathrooms and kitchen.

Mon / 2020 Aug 10 / Journal Entry

When I went to the nail salon today, they had installed plexiglass bubbles for the pedicure chairs. It was impressive.

Tues / 2020 Aug 11 / Journal Entry (C Day)

"The same boiling water that hardens the egg softens the carrot. Everything depends on the individual's reactions to stressful circumstances."
Dr. James Dobson

I had an early appointment for my annual well-woman visit with my gynecologist, Dr. Tang. I considered canceling since I was feeling great, and we were five months into a global pandemic. I contemplated my safety, the safety of the other women, most of whom are usually pregnant, and the staff at the ObGyn office. I was kind of excited because for the first time in years I would be able to share my sobriety, my walking accomplishments, and my general "never felt better for a 56-year-old" health report. Well, not so fast.

I called the office to reschedule my appointment, but they told me I needed to go ahead and come on in. They had safety protocols in place for the patients and staff. So, I showed up for my appointment, took off all my clothes, and slipped into the paper gown that opens in the front. First the breast exam, which I always hate. I do not like to have my breasts touched when my arms are lifted over my head.

Immediately, Dr. Tang felt a lump. She could tell by the look on my face that I was worried.

She tried to downplay my concerns. "Maybe it is scar tissue from your implants. Try not to be worried: it is all part of aging. Have you had a mammogram recently? What about a colonoscopy? Who is your family doctor?" She ordered a diagnostic mammogram instead of the regular screening mammogram. As I was checking out, the receptionist looked at my paperwork and the tone of her voice changed. She was much more serious. I wept in my car. I got home, went to the patio, and cried full boo-hoo sobbing. Jose was sweet and comforted me. I scheduled the diagnostic mammogram for Thursday.

Kristi led our virtual Bible study called "The Character of God." We discussed that God is loving and merciful. In what ways has God shown me mercy? There are too many to count. Our lessons always seem to be timely given the circumstances in the world. I shared a quote I heard from T.D. Jakes this week. He said, "COVID-19 was like God had given us a 'time out.' Our isolation was an opportunity to reflect and think about how to make transformations that matter." Kristi asked for our prayer requests. I shared my day with my friends. Kristi said a lovely prayer, and I cried while we all prayed. I am so grateful for these ladies and for God's mercy.

After dinner, Jose and I reviewed some renovation emails, and I asked him to take me to the pond so I could feed the ducks. We stood on the bank and fed them frozen peas. We walked the dogs around the grass. It was a nice escape.

It was hot and getting dark, so we headed back to Little Greg. Jose said, "Hey Bey, look. It's a painted rock." We have never seen one at The Duck Pond before. I bent down and saw that it said, "TRUST." It was a rock I had painted and hidden on the trail a few weeks ago. Someone had found it and re-hidden it at the park. I needed to find it. I brought it home. I decided to take it with me to the mammogram appointment Thursday. God is good, and His character was on full display.

Wed / 2020 Aug 12 / Journal Entry

The home renovation plans keep my mind busy and distract me from thinking about my upcoming doctors' appointments. The hospital billing office called to inform me my copay for the mammogram would be $600. I called Dad and let him know about my visit with Dr. Tang and my upcoming diagnostic mammogram. I worried for him. My mother died of colon cancer when she was just 52. Now, I informed him I may have breast cancer at the age of 56. While we spoke, a cardinal flew into the backyard. Cardinals are considered by many to be visitors from heaven. I felt my mom's presence when I saw that little red bird.

Thurs / 2020 Aug 13 / Journal Entry

I drove to Methodist Hospital in Richardson with my TRUST rock in my purse. Due to COVID-19 safety protocols, I had to go to the appointment alone. I checked in at a table at the door. They took my temperature, asked me screening questions, and checked my name on a list before I was directed to the Women's Center. I checked in and paid my copay. I changed into an examining gown, held my TRUST rock, and said a prayer. I sat on a bench and waited my turn.

I had a diagnostic mammogram. Based on what showed up on the screen, I was led into a room where they checked my breasts with a sonogram.

The doctor said I needed a biopsy which would be scheduled for tomorrow. The results would be available by Tuesday or Wednesday of next week. He said he felt that regardless of the biopsy results, I would need to have surgery to remove the lump.

Things were happening so fast. My head was spinning.

I had to tell some people, but I was not ready to tell everyone about my situation until I knew more. The hospital billing office called to let me know I owed $2,000, which is in addition to the $600 I already paid. I was still working on my insurance deductible. This made me wonder if we should proceed with the home renovations. We still needed to pay for Kyla's wedding. All I can do is take one day at a time and trust God.

Fri / 2020 Aug 14 / Journal Entry

I was awake by 5:30 a.m. I could not go back to sleep despite all my efforts to NOT think or worry about the biopsy. I cuddled with Jose, and then we went for an early walk since it was supposed to be 105 degrees by the end of the day. The trail was very quiet. The creek was almost dried up. There were brown leaves on the ground. I got text messages from Barbara, Bridget, and Kristi (my Bible Chicks) before my biopsy.

Kristi sent me a link to a YouTube video, "There Was Jesus" by Zach Williams and Dolly Parton. I listened to it and prayed out loud as I drove alone to the hospital again.

"There Was Jesus" by Zach Williams and Dolly Parton
In the waiting, in the searching
In the healing, in the hurting
Like a blessing buried in the pieces
Every minute, every moment.
Where I've been and where I'm going
Even when I didn't know it
Or couldn't see it
There was Jesus.

I sensed things had been expedited for a reason. Amy, the nurse navigator, met me at the hospital. She held my hand and talked me through each step of the procedure. The biopsy was uncomfortable. I had to raise my arms over my head while they did another sonogram. Then they gave me a local anesthesia, inserted the needle several times into my breast to take a sample, and then inserted several pins that would be visible on future scans.

The doctor said he was very concerned. He speculated it was malignant and either breast cancer or lymphoma. I had to endure another mammogram to get pictures of the pins. My head was spinning. I tried to be brave. Now I drove myself home to wait for the results.

I called my contractor's assistant and informed her of my health situation since it could impact the home renovations. Jose came home, and we went to the patio so I could give him a recap. I asked him to call the kids and his mom and let them know what was going on.

Sat / 2020 Aug 15 / Journal Entry

"Sometimes it takes sadness to know happiness, noise to appreciate silence, and absence to value presence."
Unknown

I woke up early and sat on the back porch. I flipped through one of my favorite books, *The 7 Habits of Highly Effective People* by Steven Covey. I have read it many times, and I looked for highlighted text on the faded and dog-eared pages. It was a great reminder of how I need to keep my mindset during this new challenge. I called my sister, Michelle, and asked her to notify Jim, Angela, and my Uncle Michael about my situation. I decided not to tell Mamal. She lost her daughter, my mother, to colon cancer. Why worry her about my situation?

The 7 Habits of Highly Effective People by Steven Covey
1. Be proactive.
2. Begin with the end in mind.
3. Put first things first.
4. Think win-win.
5. Seek first to understand, then to be understood.
6. Synergize.
7. Sharpen the saw.

Mon / 2020 Aug 17 / Journal Entry

According to ABC news, America's approval rating of Trump's handling of the coronavirus is: disapprove sixty-seven percent, approve thirty-three percent.

Joe Biden selected Kamala Harris as his running mate.

Former First Lady, Michelle Obama, delivered a virtual speech to the Democratic National Convention. This is a portion of it:

I am one of a handful of people living today who have seen firsthand the immense weight and awesome power of the presidency. And let me once again tell you this: the job is hard. It requires clear-headed judgment, a mastery of complex and competing issues, a devotion to facts and history, a moral compass, and an ability to listen—and an abiding belief that each of the 330,000,000 lives in this country has meaning and worth. A president's words have the power to move markets. They can start wars or broker peace. They can summon our better angels or awaken our worst instincts. You simply cannot fake your way through this job.

And I know that regardless of our race, age, religion, or politics, when we close out the noise and the fear and truly open our hearts, we know that what's going on in this country is just not right. This is not who we want to be.

So, what do we do now? What's our strategy? Over the past four years, a lot of people have asked me, "When others are going so low, does going high still really work?" My answer: going high is the only thing that works, because ... going high does not mean putting on a smile and saying nice things when confronted by viciousness and cruelty. Going high means taking the harder path. It means scraping and clawing our way to that mountain top. Going high means standing fierce against hatred while remembering that we are one nation under God, and if we want to survive, we've got to find a way to live together and work together across our differences.

And if we want a chance to pursue any of these goals, any of these most basic requirements for a functioning society, we have to vote in numbers that cannot be ignored. Because right now, folks who know they cannot win fair and square at the ballot box are doing everything they can to stop us from voting. They're closing down polling places in minority neighborhoods. They're purging voter rolls. They're sending people out to intimidate voters, and they're lying about the security of our ballots. These tactics are not new.

We've got to show up with the same level of passion and hope for Joe Biden. We've got to vote early, in person if we can. We've got to request our mail-in ballots right now, tonight, and send them back immediately and follow-up to make sure they're received. And then, make sure our friends and families do the same. This is who we still are: compassionate, resilient, decent people whose fortunes are bound up with one another. And it is well past time for our leaders to once again reflect our truth.

So, it is up to us to add our voices and our votes to the course of history, echoing heroes like John Lewis who said, "When you see something that is not right, you must say something. You must do something." That is the truest form of empathy: not just feeling, but doing; not just for ourselves or our kids, but for everyone, for all our kids.

Tues / 2020 Aug 18 / Journal Entry

"What lies behind us, and what lies before us are, but tiny matters compared to what lies within us."
Ralph Waldo Emerson

We downloaded eForm advanced directives and a living will to be proactive.

The image oncologist called to give a report on my biopsy. The news was better than it could have been, so I felt hopeful. Jose suggested we needed a code word during this cancer journey in case we need to signal each other when things get stressful. We agreed on "mistletoe." This is a reference to the movie *Four Christmases*.

I listened to a sermon from Chase Oaks Church on "Embracing Slow." The pastor said: *Jesus never seemed to be in a hurry. He lived and interacted with others at the speed of walking. He had time for people. He was relaxed. However, for most of us, slowing down is one of the hardest things to implement about the Jesus way of life. Jesus has much to teach us about managing our pace and succeeding in the things that matter most.*

I have had a roller coaster relationship with organized religion, but

I have always been a believer. I am really good at praying when I am hurting or in need. I experience spirituality in the everyday moments when I slow down and see God at work and take a moment to acknowledge Him. It is uplifting, celebratory, and peaceful. It helps me make sense of the world and understand my place in it. By reading, praying, studying, and discussing God, it helps me celebrate the gifts and blessings He has given to me. This is a wonderful feeling to feel.

Wed / 2020 Aug 19 / Journal Entry

Jose and I worked a little and had phone conferences with two crucial support systems that will help us through this health crisis. Tracy, the claims specialist, will guide us through the insurance and medical-bill maze. Amy, the nurse navigator, will assist me through the medical procedures.

As I embark on a new, terrifying health journey, I already feel myself veering into doubt, pity, and worry. I feel fragile and vulnerable. I struggle not to slide down the slippery slope of lack of trust. But now more than ever, I must trust more, not less. I have to trust I am strong enough to fight this fight. I must trust that Jose and I will get through this together. I must trust the doctors to heal me. I must trust my friends and family will be there for me. I must trust God. He is the Creator. He has a plan. He is the Rock.

I walked out to the raised garden on my patio and looked at the dandelion rock, the "She believed she could, so she did" rock, and the TRUST rock. I closed my eyes and said a prayer and felt God's presence around me.

Thu / 2020 Aug 20 / Journal Entry

"But as they say about sharks, it's not the ones you see that you must worry about. It's the one you don't see."
David Blaine

We woke up early and went on a morning walk. Jose was in a rare mood, so I got in a mood, but mine lasted most of the day. Our

attempts to manage our worry and stress are manifesting in bad moods. I was flipping through my journal and landed on this quote from a few weeks ago:
"Be a warrior, not a worrier."
Bob Baker

A diagnosis of breast cancer can be devastating for most people. For me, I am deciding consciously every day to treat it like an opportunity. I don't want to face every day and every waking moment with doom and gloom.

First, if this is my last big challenge in life, why waste what precious time I may have being depressed? If this is one of God's teachable moments for me, why not embrace it and marvel at the lessons along the way? Every time God has seen me through dark tunnels, the light on the other side has always been brighter than where I was before.

Breast cancer is scary. I am learning all kinds of information about the various types of cancer and treatments that are available today, as opposed to twenty, thirty, or forty years ago. I am learning that cancer research has developed a "whole patient" approach which treats the whole person, not just the problem, cancer. I am learning that by having an attitude to "seek first to understand," I will be understood.

I feel enlightened. I have had sympathy for cancer patients, their families, and their caregivers, but now I understand. Now I have empathy. I also understand why all the previous COVID experiences led up to this. I understand why I decided to quit drinking last October and why I have been able to stick with it. I understand it is all part of God's plan for little ol' me.

Tomorrow is a new day.

Sat / 2020 Aug 22 / Journal Entry

"Always believe the impossible is possible."
Selena Quintanilla-Perez

I spent some time in the backyard watching the hummingbird. He has been faithful, and he makes appearances multiple times a day to pollinate the purple salvia that is growing in the garden. I have watched him many times. Sometimes he sits still on a branch. I think he watches me, too. He reminds me of the line in The Terminator, "I'll be back." I will call him Arnold. Arnold gives me hope.

I stood by the fence under a tree and waited. Over the course of thirty minutes, the tiny, diligent, faithful bird visited the garden three times. I was able to get closer than ever before and capture photos and videos of my little friend. I got a couple of video clips on my phone and figured out how to clip clips and use slow motion to edit my little hummingbird movie.

At one point, Arnold flew away, but when I turned around, he was right behind me. He was hovering, as hummingbirds do, and looking me right in the eye. It was a split second that seemed long enough to hold a conversation. The bird knew I would not hurt him. The bird was saying, "Hello! I trust you. I see you every day. Can we be friends?"

That little bird showed me the importance of trust. The plants and flowers know he will return tomorrow and do his job to multiply their beauty.

And again, God is revealed to me, and my understanding of trust is fortified. I cannot help but feel God's presence all around me. I will be able to rest more easily and approach each moment more positively because of tiny hummingbirds, faeries, and a merciful God.

Jose and I took the dogs for a trail walk. We found more painted rocks that said, "Believe in Yourself," "See the Good," "Bee Kind," "Prove Them Wrong," and "Sparkly." The lightning bugs were everywhere. We saw a mother and daughter catching the fireflies and putting them in a jar.

It was a great day!

Mon / 2020 Aug 24 / Journal Entry

"Let your dreams be bigger than your fears."
M. Scott Peck

I had a dream I was fighting, and I won. Then I dreamt I was in a huge traffic jam, but I drove around it. Once I got around it, everything was pitch black. Once I turned on my headlights, the car started going backwards on its own.

I have recurring dreams about driving backward out of control all the time. This time, I said out loud in my dream, "Oh the car is in control. Okay." I let go, and my dream turned into a wild, psychedelic trip, but I was calm and relieved.

We headed to our appointment with the surgeon. I bought two bunches of roses on the way to the appointment. One dozen for Amy, the nurse navigator, to show my appreciation for the care she has shown me, and one dozen for the surgeon, Dr. Hughes. I wanted to show my appreciation for the care she will give me. I checked my email in the car. The Bible Project sent an email with prayer requests. I signed up to get periodic emails from them, and they sent me a prayer in return.

Be anxious for nothing, but in everything, by prayer and supplication, with thanksgiving, let your requests be made to God. (Phillipians 4:6)

On the way into the Cancer Center, we passed a painted rock garden. The rocks were painted by patients and placed in the flower bed to spell out KINDNESS. An angel sculpture stood at the front entrance, a calming waterfall in the lobby, origami and other patient art on the second floor, and a meditation room outside of Dr. Hughes' office. We got a very good vibe, despite our anxiety.

As I met with the nurse navigator and surgeon for my first cancer consultation, I instantly felt at ease. What noble professionals they are. Their time and care in all aspects of our meeting created a sense of trust. The messages from the building, the kindness rock garden, origami art, a tranquil water feature, a meditation room, privacy procedures, and COVID protocols helped develop trust.

Small details like bottled water, a three-ring binder, and an outlined discussion were all carefully crafted to add elements and layers of trust. The giant cross on the outside of the hospital, and the angel sculpture leading into the cancer center are powerful symbols that touch the subconscious spirit and elevate trust for the people who will care for you and potentially cure you.

A woman's breasts hold so much power over a woman's self-esteem. When it comes to breast cancer, esteem is a necessary element of decision making that cannot be ignored. It is highly personal for each female. How the breasts look after surgery is just as life changing as battling the disease. If the breasts are respected during all phases of diagnosis and treatment, the effect on the patient's health will be exponentially positive.

Dr. Hughes explained the risks with all the treatment options. To make the best decision for me, I needed all the facts about my diagnosis, surgery options, and treatment options. I needed to know the risk factors for a lumpectomy versus a mastectomy. There were issues with my thirty-five-year-old breast implants—leaking, scarring, removal, deformity, asymmetry, and replacements. There were issues with radiation therapy, endocrine therapy, and chemotherapy. There were risks with treatment during a global pandemic. There were insurance issues, and of course with any surgery, the risk of death.

The meeting with Amy and Dr. Hughes was very thorough. The bottom line—they thought my cancer was treatable and curable. I left with a three-ring binder of information and organizational tools and four more appointments. In just a week I have learned a lot about breast cancer. There have been so many medical advances in the diagnosis and treatment of breast cancer just within my lifetime. It makes me marvel at the risks so many people before me have taken to seek a cure. I am not afraid. I trust that everything will be okay because my future is in God's hands.

We drove to Heritage Ranch to meet Dad and Rosie for lunch at the country club. It was nice to see them in person. We signed my advanced medical orders and living will. Rosie and the waiter were our witnesses. We came home and worked.

Tues / 2020 Aug 25 / Journal Entry

Our virtual Bible study was on the Holy Spirit. The Holy Spirit is mentioned on page one of the Bible. It is an invisible power that sustains life and transforms humans. I see God's life-giving Spirit all around me, especially in the birds, bugs, flowers, and plants in my garden. I am energized thinking about God's invisible presence as I embark on this new cancer journey.

Fri / 2020 Aug 28 / Journal Entry

Today was a long day at Richardson Methodist Hospital. I had an MRI. I had to lie on my stomach with my hands stretched over my head for forty minutes without moving. Then I had blood work, an EKG, and a chest x-ray as required for pre-operation procedures. Jose met me at the Cancer Center for an appointment with my oncologist, Dr. Trumbly. He will take over my care after surgery.

I received an email from Home Depot. Our new toilets have arrived. Our tub has arrived. New bathroom light fixtures and plumbing fixtures have shipped.

Sat / 2020 Aug 29 / Journal Entry

Our office window faces the neighbor's kitchen window. We are exchanging pasta pun signs with the girls next door.

Them: Penne for your thoughts.
Us: This too shall pasta. You are so fusilli. I am laughing so hard I am ravioling on the floor.
Them: Did you hear about the chef that died? He pasta way. We cannoli do so much. He ran out of thyme.

Mon / 2020 Aug 31 / Journal Entry

"Whenever you find yourself doubting how far you can go, just remember how far you have come."
N. R. Walker

Amy, the nurse navigator, called with the results from the MRI. The test showed additional areas of concern in my other breast and under my arms in the lymph nodes. It caught me off guard and sent me into a mini panic attack. I immediately thought about Chadwick Boseman who passed away from colon cancer this weekend. He played Jackie Robinson and Thurgood Marshall. He starred in *The Black Panther* and *Ma Rainey's Black Bottom*, all while battling colon cancer, and nobody knew he was ill. I am scheduled for additional biopsies on Wednesday.

I sent text updates to my inner circle of supporters. I took phone calls from my cousin Jim, my stepsister Nicole, and my dad. I checked on Mamal and picked up the tub and toilet from Home Depot.

Jose is super sweet. I am so lucky he is my husband.

Unemployment numbers are rising. The stimulus money has stopped. Researchers are trying to create a vaccine. Controversy surrounds mail-in ballots for the upcoming election. Virtual schools are getting poor reviews. College football may be canceled. There is a hurricane in the forecast.

COVID-19 Statistics
Confirmed cases worldwide: 25,193,345
Confirmed deaths worldwide: 665,032
Confirmed cases in the Uniated States: 6,000,000
Confirmed deaths in the United States: 183,066

september

Tues / 2020 Sept 1 / Journal Entry

"Be the chess player, not the chess piece."
Ralph Charell

I had a strange dream last night. I was covered by a tidal wave, but I was not wet or drowning. It surrounded me and started carrying me toward an opening. The wave pushed me through to a calm sea. I was never afraid.

A cold front pushed through and brought rain. I finished virtual class visits, paid bills, confirmed appointments, completed paperwork, and checked renovation details. I did the laundry and thoroughly cleaned the kitchen.

Our virtual Bible study topic was God's love. God loves us because He loves us. We have not earned His love. His love has no beginning or end. We should imitate God's love to us by showing it to others. God shows us grace by giving us what we don't deserve. God shows us mercy by not giving us what we do deserve.

Wed / 2020 Sept 2 / Journal Entry

Today was another biopsy. I took half of a Xanax before the appointment because I was anxious. After the biopsy and mammogram, we met with the plastic surgeon. It was a quick appointment. He took measurements and pictures. It looks like I may be eligible for DIEP flap surgery, so the fat tissue from my stomach can be moved to rebuild my breasts after the double mastectomy. In the meantime, I will have Barbie boobs—no nipples.

I decided to order a Fashionista Barbie with gray hair from Walmart.

I found a shirt for her that says, "Bold, Brave, Fearless." She will travel with me to my appointments from now on. Now we are waiting for the biopsy results and a surgery date for the mastectomy. It would be great if I could have all my surgeries before January 1st before my deductibles start over.

Fri / 2020 Sept 4 / Journal Entry

I had an education appointment with a physical therapist to discuss lymphedema, which may occur after mastectomy surgery. Dr. Hughes called with the biopsy results and scheduled surgery in two weeks. My left breast shows invasive lobular carcinoma, while my right breast indicates invasive mammary carcinoma. I was so grateful I did not need chemotherapy before my surgery and lucky to have the biopsy results before the holiday weekend.

We received a quote on the tile and backsplash. I hope we can get started on the renovation soon.

Sat / 2020 Sept 5 / Journal Entry

"Do not squander time. That is the stuff life is made of."
Benjamin Franklin

We headed to The Duck Pond so that Jose could fish. I took frozen peas. As soon as we got out of the truck, the ducks quacked as if they recognized us. They started running or waddling toward us. They must have been hungry, and we must have been the first visitors of the day. When the food was gone, they went back to being ducks-- swimming, bathing, paddling, and chasing each other in the pond.

It was a glorious morning. I sat on a park bench looking at the pond while Jose fished from the shore. I got to enjoy nature and reflect. Instead of wondering, "Why me?" I contemplated, "Why not me?"

I thought about how much time it takes me each day to "get ready"-- to shower and dress. Some days it takes me more time to decide what to wear than to shower and put my clothes on. Even then, many times I am not satisfied with how I look, so I change clothes. Some days, I change clothes multiple times before leaving the house. I put a significant amount of time, energy, thought, and money into the way I look on the outside. Perhaps I need to do the same for what is inside my heart and brain. I thought about God creating me in His image. I am certain "in His image" is not referring to my physical appearance. I believe I need to focus on the spiritual gifts He created in me.

My body was once shiny and new. As I have lived and aged, my body has taken a beating and has begun to show signs of wear and tear. As much as I strive to use my gifts for good, I make mistakes and stumble along the way. I can become easily discouraged and stop trying. I may start crying, denying, and dying. Who wants that? As Andy Dufrain says in *The Shawshank Redemption*, "Get busy living or get busy dying."

Fri / 2020 Sept 11 / Journal Entry

"Meowing time is over. It is time to roar."
Jeremy McGilvrey

My surgery date is set for next Thursday. I spent the day doing RCHS work so I can have a "me" day tomorrow.

This is a prayer I posted today:

Lord, it's me again. Help me to be the image you created me to be. Help me to understand my right hand and left hand are part of the same body, and you provided both for a reason. Help me to recognize that my heart and my mind, which you created, were perfectly placed in my center so I could use them for good. Help me to listen with my two ears more than I speak with my one mouth. Help me be full of love for all the other humans you created in your image and demonstrate that love in my daily interactions in person and on social media. Lord, I am not rich or powerful or famous, but you created me with purpose. Help me to be the best version of me so I can be part of the solution versus part of the problem. This is my prayer today. Thank you, Lord, for all your gifts and blessings. Amen.

Sat / 2020 Sept 12 / Journal Entry

"Little things seem like nothing, but they give peace like those meadow flowers which individually seem odorless, but all together perfume the air."
Georges Bernanos

I found a bald Barbie at Walmart. I bought her to remind me of this time in my life. I put her on the shelf with other important Barbies that remind me of other times in my life. Malibu Barbie was my childhood favorite. Rockette Barbie reminds me of my dancing days. Chef Barbie reminds me of cooking adventures with Jose. Tae Kwon Do Barbie reminds me of getting my black belt at age 50. Firefighter Barbie reminds me of the Garland Citizens Firefighting Academy and the tumultuous times as a principal in Garland. Graduate Barbie reminds me of college times working on my bachelor, master, and doctorate degrees.

Mon / 2020 Sept 14 / Journal Entry

My fifty-seventh birthday
Day 187 of COVID-19
Four days until surgery

"Attitude is a little thing that makes a big difference."
Winston Churchill

Today is my fifty-seventh birthday. I am beginning a new journey. My day started with a birthday wish from Dolly Parton. It was a Birthday Time e-card. She said, "That's right Kim, this one's for you!"

("Nine to Five" music starts.)
Well, it's birthday time! What a day for celebrating!
There'll be songs and gifts and happy congregating,
This is birthday time with your friends and your relations,
It's a time for joy and happy celebrations!

Jose and I met with Dr. Hughes about surgery. We found out the surgery will take about five hours. We learned how to manage the drains that I will have after surgery.

I picked up a prescription of numbing lotion for the dye injections I will get before surgery. I shopped for mastectomy supplies: a surgery pillow, button up shirts and pajamas, and toiletries for the hospital. We cleaned the house. We got everything as ready as we could. Halloween decorations were already on display. I wonder if there will be any trick-or-treaters this year.

Tues / 2020 Sept 15 / Journal Entry

"Stand up like a mountain, have faith like a rock, love like an avalanche."
Bob Goff

I had an appointment for COVID-19 testing this morning. I got a nasal swab and blood test for antibodies. No news is good news, and no news means I could proceed with surgery. I stopped at Walmart to get Saran wrap for the numbing lotion. I downloaded my Sade playlist. Her music feeds my soul.

Our virtual Bible study topic was "The Gospel of the Kingdom". It focused on the unjust trial and execution of Jesus and how death was defeated with love. Again, the lesson was very timely. Question 1: Where do you feel shattered? We discussed our divided country. Question 2: Our Lord is King despite the way the world looks right now. What questions does this bring up for you? For me, I wonder why Christians aren't being Christ-like. Question 3: What truths can you rely on at this time? I trust that God will save us from ourselves. Question 4: Where do you see suffering and pain in the world and in your community right now? We discussed the pandemic, injustice, immigrants, people of color, women, and the planet.

Then we acknowledged that God is here, and He suffers with the oppressed. He suffers injustices. He feels the pain. He takes it on for us because He loves us.

Wed / 2020 Sept 16 / Journal Entry

"How does one become a butterfly? You have to want to learn to fly so much that you are willing to give up being a caterpillar."
Trina Paulus

Today was busy! We met with Dr. Lemmon, the plastic surgeon. I got a post-surgery shirt with pockets that will hold my drains and compression cuffs for my legs to prevent blood clots while I recover. Our countertops, faucets, and backsplash are scheduled for renovation. Laundry is done. We went to The Duck Pond, fished, and walked the dogs. I packed my hospital bag, caught up on "Boob Bills," paperwork, and showered with pre-op surgical soap.

I received a sweet hummingbird charm from Janet and texts, Facebook messages, and calls from friends and family.

The Hummingbird Charm
*When you see a hummingbird, it is very lucky indeed
because it is known as a healer, if you're ever in need.
Despite its small size, it flies great distances and even flies backwards, too.
A reminder to have faith and enjoy all you do.*

Thu / 2020 Sept 17 / Journal Entry

"You know, all that really matters is that the people you love are happy and healthy. Everything else is just sprinkles on the sundae."
Paul Walker

Today was the beginning of a new beginning. Today was Demo Day and the renovations began. It was ironic that my body and my house would be renovated at the same time. It would be expensive. It would not be easy. It would be worth it in the end, and I would have Jose with me every step of the way. I was one lucky girl.

I showered with the pre-op surgical scrub and rubbed numbing lotion on my breasts. Jose had to wrap me in Saran plastic wrap. This was to prepare for the dye injections for the sentinel node procedure and mapping.

I listened to Sade's "By Your Side" this morning. I looked at pictures of painted rocks from the Cancer Center's rock garden. "Be the Queen!" "Miracles Happen," "Love Big!" "Amazing Grace in My Soul," and "Dance, Dance, Dance."

We reported to the hospital at 10:00 am. The surgery was scheduled for 12:30 and took five hours. Jose had a text phone list to update people on my status. I was ready. I was not scared. I trusted God. I knew I was loved and lucky. I knew everything would be okay.

The staff at Methodist Hospital took great care of me. It was a long day for Jose. I didn't notice because I was under anesthesia for five hours. They took me into surgery about noon, and I got to my room around 8:00 pm. Dr. Hughes only took three lymph nodes from one armpit and one lymph node from the other. The hospital gave me a lovely pink blanket. It was made by nurses specifically for breast cancer patients.

Fri / 2020 Sept 18 / Journal Entry

"It is in your hands to create a world for all who live in it."
Nelson Mandela

My care team, the nurses, breast cancer surgeon, oncologist, anesthesiologists, and plastic surgeon all make choices about me and my care. They can choose to do what is easy and give me the minimum care that their job title requires, or they can choose to do the hard work and fight the fight with me.

I, too, can decide. Do I want to bring positive energy to the party or be a negaholic and drag everyone down? Roadblocks, obstacles, and setbacks are going to happen along the way. Our mindset and attitude have to be trained properly to help us find a way through to the other side. Despite being in the hospital, I choose to keep posting my inspirational quotes on the 2020 Vision page and keep writing in my journal.

I was able to get out of bed and pee with the nurse's assistance, and I walked several laps around the surgical floor. I think all the dog walks we took have helped me to get out of bed. I had a good breakfast, but I had some swelling, so I wasn't allowed to eat again until late. They thought I might have an infection, and I might have to go under anesthesia again to clean my wounds. Fortunately, they did not have to do a second surgery, but I stayed an extra night in the hospital.

My face mask, eye mask, and Barbie were my hospital friends. Again, the staff took excellent care of me. They taught Jose how to empty my drains.

I think of God and Jesus. I cannot think of any greater suffering, and it came from a perfect heart of love. I think about the few weeks prior to this when I thought I might die soon from breast cancer. I didn't want to spend any precious time filled with fear, dread, depression, or hate. It feels good to feel good—even when it is hard. Attitude is a choice, and I hope my attitude about attitude is a help to others.

I propped up in bed and watched the news. President Trump gave eighteen interviews with Bob Woodward, Watergate reporter, and allowed them to be recorded. He admitted on tape that he knew the coronavirus was deadly and dangerous for old and young people but downplayed it so people would not panic.

The Notorious RBG, Supreme Court Justice Ruth Bader Ginsburg, passed away from pancreatic cancer.

Sat / 2020 Sept 19 / Journal Entry

"I am a mushroom...on whom the dew of heaven drops now and then." John Ford

I got to go home from the hospital. So many who have suffered from COVID-19 have not gone home. The neighbors chalked my driveway and gave me a goody bag. Jose helped me shower. The Bible Chicks sent me flowers. I felt blessed. The dogs cuddled up to me, and Dexter licked my arm for an hour.

Sun / 2020 Sept 20 / Journal Entry

"We don't know where we are going, but we're going."
Good Spark Garage

I watched a *Sex and the City* marathon and fell in and out of sleep in my recliner. I woke up to the episode when Samantha is diagnosed with breast cancer. I am sore, but I feel better than I thought I would feel considering both of my breasts were removed, and I have four drains coming out of my body like the arms of an octopus. Jose helped me walk down the block and back. I worked remotely for two hours and replied to 132 emails.

Some students are attending school in person. I call them Roomers. Other students are attending school virtually. I call them Zoomers. The teachers must actively engage, teach, and manage all the students at the same time.

Mon / 2020 Sept 21 / Journal Entry

"It's not how you bowl; it's how you roll."
Unknown

I slept well on the couch recliner. I was able to shower, dress, and take a walk down the block and back. Our countertops were measured for installation next week. All the flowers that I received are still pretty. The chalk art on the driveway cheers me up.

Tues / 2020 Sept 22 / Journal Entry

"When it rains, look for rainbows; when it's dark, look for stars."
Unknown

Today, I managed to work a little, then nap, then observe my UT-Dallas student via Zoom, then nap, then lead Bible study on Google Meets, then nap. It is ironic because the topic for our study was "Sabbath Rest." As the Bible Project points out:

"It is about stopping and recognizing that our lives and provisions ultimately come from God. And while He might be leading us through a wilderness at the moment, our ultimate future hope is in God's plan to rescue and renew the world. The Sabbath is an intentional disruption of our daily rhythm to celebrate the simple things, rest, and prepare for more work."

I think about the time we are spending being safe at home. I welcome it. I see it as an opportunity to slow down and celebrate the little things, which for me, have become big things. I enjoy working from home, being with Jose and the dogs, walking, reading the Bible, and gardening. I enjoy observing the birds, flowers, weather, painted rocks, and faeries. I consider being safe at home a privilege. It has increased my awareness and appreciation for what God has provided us.

I didn't take any pain medicine today. The weather is rainy and cooler, but I feel too weak to enjoy it. Hopefully, I will get a good rest tonight and feel better tomorrow.

Wed / 2020 Sept 23 / Journal Entry

"Life is a one-time offer; use it well."
Mark Timm

I am so lucky Jose is taking care of me. My recovery continues, but I was hoping I would feel stronger by now.

Dr. Hughes called with the pathology report. It is ten pages long, so she gave me the *Reader's Digest* version. My left side is now considered IA, but the right side is now IIB. IA means the tumor is small and has not spread to the lymph nodes. It is also referred to as "early stage." IIB generally means the tumor is larger and may have spread to a lymph node. It is also called "locally advanced." There were additional tiny spots found on the right side and in one lymph node. I have two different types of cancer in two different breasts which is unusual. I think she will order genetic testing for this reason. I have three appointments next week.

Fri / 2020 Sept 25 / Journal Entry

I was able to sleep in my bed for the first time since my surgery! I must sleep flat on my back, which is not my preference, but it is a nice break from the couch recliner. I am still moving slowly. I can shower and wash my hair which makes me feel fresh and normal. I need help dressing. Jose must empty my four drains twice a day. It is not my favorite thing. My right side is draining so much more than my left side.

Mon / 2020 Sept 28 / Journal Entry

We met with Dr. Lemmon today. Two of the four drains were removed. Our new countertops were installed today. The renovations (body and home) are making progress.

Tues / 2020 Sept 29 / Journal Entry

"You can't start the next chapter of your life if you keep re-reading the last one."
Michael McMillian

Where has the month gone? I was wide awake most of the night. I fell asleep at 5:00 a.m. and got up at 7:30 a.m. The plumber arrived at 8:00 a.m. I worked six hours from home today. The faucets and countertops look great. I am ready for the rest of the renovations to happen.

COVID-19 Statistics:
Confirmed cases worldwide: 37,716,872
Confirmed deaths worldwide: 1,080,819
Confirmed cases in the United States: 7,988,448
Confirmed deaths in the United States: 214,000

october

Thurs / 2020 October 1 / Journal Entry

Breast Cancer Awareness Month. Think Pink!

"With a new day comes new strength and new thoughts."
Eleanor Roosevelt

We went on a lovely morning walk on the trail. I had a productive day of work in the home office. I told Jose to shut down early and go fishing. He was able to fish for a couple of hours. He is such a good guy and great husband. I just wanted him to have a break from me. He deserves it.

The Holly Hills Gang sent me flowers and a card. My friend, Kristyn, sent a heart box loaded with get well goodies, which was fun. Janet sent me another card. It was a great day!

Fri / 2020 October 2 / Journal Entry

"Be picky with your clothes, friends, and time."
Lilly Pulitzer

We went on another walk this morning. I took a shower and got dressed. I wore a shirt today that said, "I can, and I will." As we approached the doctor's office, an elderly man in a wheelchair waited outside for a ride. He saw my shirt and pointed to his hat which said, "I can, and I will."

We met with Dr. Hughes for a post-op follow-up. Everything looks good, so I will see her in January. We are waiting for the results of the MammaPrint from surgery. I am praying for "no chemo!"

Mon / 2020 October 5 / Journal Entry

My drains came out today! I got my first injections into the temporary implants which will help my skin to stretch for reconstructive surgery. I went to the nail shop and sat inside the plexiglass bubble while they gave me a manicure and pedicure. I bought Jose two fishing shirts, a lightweight jacket, and Tiff's Treats cookies to say thank you for being a great nurse.

Tues / 2020 October 6 / Journal Entry

Happy Soberversary—one year of sobriety!
Day 208 of Covid. Twenty-eight days until the election.

I got to sleep on my side for part of the night. I got to take a real shower for the first time since surgery without the octopus tentacle drains.

Thurs / 2020 October 8 / Journal Entry

Song of the Day: "I'm Bringing Sexy Back" Justin Timberlake

My neighbors posted the perfect song of the day suggestion on their kitchen window that faces our office window. I slept late, showered, and worked. I ordered a breast cancer awareness mask and bracelet and a VOTE mask.

Fri / 2020 October 9 / Journal Entry

I was really wiped out today for some reason. My skin is stretching under my right boob, and it feels like stitches are pulling apart when I move a certain way. It is not fun. It feels like a red-hot poker.

Sat / 2020 October 10 / Journal Entry

I shopped for Christmas t-shirts, sweatpants, and masks for the family on Amazon. I found Christmas 2020 shirts with reindeers wearing masks for the girls and Santa wearing a mask for the boys.

Sun / 2020 October 11 / Journal Entry

"You were assigned the mountain to show others it can be moved."
Shanee Wilson

As Jose and I walk, I get frequent stabbing pains and burning pinches where I guess my skin is stretching. It hurts to the point of bringing me to tears. I commented that a year from now I hope to be back to normal.

I don't know why, but after my shower, the area that had been pinching and pulling started burning to the point that it brought me to tears again. I think I am a little nervous, maybe terrified, about the impending results of my MammaPrint. I feel the devil sneaking in and making me doubt God's grace. God, please hear my prayer and heal me.

Life happened to me, and it was called breast cancer. I underwent bi-lateral mastectomy surgery, and I have been recovering and finding another new normal.

One of my high school classmates messaged me that after she saw my breast cancer post on Facebook, she scheduled a twenty-year overdue mammogram. She must have a diagnostic mammogram next week.

Mon / 2020 October 12 / Journal Entry

Happy Birthday Daddy-O!

"Fight each round, take it on the chin. And never, never, never give in."
Olivia Newton-John

I dreaded getting up today. I was full of doubt and pessimism. I was afraid. I was afraid of the hurt I had been experiencing. I was afraid that another injection would make it worse. I was afraid of my MammaPrint results. In the shower I said a prayer to God to forgive my lack of faithfulness. I prayed for Him to heal me and work His plan and get rid of the devil thoughts that were changing my usual strong, positive self.

We headed to the plastic surgeon, and my skin was on fire. It made me cry in the examination room. The nurse explained that it was normal. The temporary implant is sewn in place on the inside, so what I have been feeling is real. She reassured me that it would go away. The injection of saline did not hurt, and I do not have an infection. This is all good news.

When we got into the truck, Amy, the nurse navigator, called with my MammaPrint results. Both cancers were considered "low risk for recurrence," so chemotherapy is probably not necessary. Again, good news! I will meet with the oncologist Thursday for a full report and treatment plan consultation.

Tues / 2020 October 13 / Journal Entry

"This is a time to make peace with our inner demons, no matter how frightening they may appear. Our wounded selves are always longing to be understood and loved."
Tree Spirit Wisdom

My internal stitches continue to bother me. It isn't a constant pain, but when it hits, it burns with great intensity. On a scale of zero to ten, I can go from zero pain to a ten for no reason.

When I started the Bible study, I certainly had a lot of internal "what if" questions. What if I don't know the answers? What if I have never read the Bible? What if my personal spiritual journey has been too disjointed? What if I am not good enough? What if they discover my sins? What if I lack the skills and confidence to pray out loud?

I think it is interesting that today's quote was about trees, and today's Bible study was about the Tree of Life. Now I truly feel that this Bible study was not by accident. I believe it was part of the plan that God has for me, for us, to discover His love for us and lead us to a personal relationship with Him.

Thurs / 2020 October 15 / Journal Entry

"If you change the way you look at things, the things you look at change."
Wayne Dyer

We met with the oncologist, Dr. Trumbly, today. The report was great. Both cancers appear to be gone and there is a low risk of recurrence. I do not have to endure chemotherapy or radiation. I will begin endocrine therapy which will consist of one pill a day for five to ten years. This will inhibit the production of estrogen. What a relief!

The year 2020 has been a difficult year for everyone. There is much work to do in our country and for our planet. So much around me is on the verge of being restored—our home, my body, our democracy, and my faith. I feel like we are in the fourth quarter of a football game, and I have new energy to get to the finish line.

Since the State Fair of Texas is closed due to COVID-19, Jose ordered tickets online to the Fair drive-through. Our tickets allowed us to drive through the fairgrounds and stop along the way, but stay in our car to pick up french fries, corny dogs, two drinks, kettle corn, and cotton candy. We were allowed to get out of our car and get our pictures taken with Big Tex, who also wore a mask. As we drove through the fairgrounds, we saw the automobiles and the farm animals. We got a midway prize and a T-shirt. There was no line. We parked in a parking lot and ate our fair food.

Fri / 2020 October 16 / Journal Entry

"On weekends, I sit in a lounge chair on my balcony. I love to be outside when the weather is right. I can stay there pretty much all day."
Sue Monk Kidd

Song of the Day: "Can't Stop the Feeling" Justin Timberlake

I love this time of year. We went on a long walk. There was no wind. The air was cool and crisp. I just want to be outside all day. Lots of people were out walking, skating, biking, and fishing. For the past two weeks we have seen Frasier the Crane every time we walk. We saw Frasier catch a fish in the pond by the twelfth hole and faerie village. We spotted a few painted rocks that said, "Smile! God Loves You," and one with the pink breast cancer ribbon that said, "Hope."

We walk in silence most of the time. It has become our ritual, our go-to, our "woosah." One of us may point out the light shining through the trees, a mushroom, a dry creek bed, or changing colors. This is my favorite part of the day. We may hold hands or just pinky fingers. The dogs are visibly happy.

The neighborhood garage sale was this weekend. I would have enjoyed setting up and selling the junk that has piled up since last year, but it is too much work with my recovery. The spring sale was canceled due to COVID-19, and frankly, I did not want to take any chances by being around people. I enjoyed the day on the patio instead. The weather was phenomenal!

We reclined in our zero gravity chairs, listening to the fountain and enjoying the breeze in the shade. Major stretched out on the patio, and Dexter climbed into my lap. When we opened our eyes after a brief snooze, we watched a hawk soaring overhead. I commented that the hawk can soar in the sky without flapping its wings. Then we saw an unusual site. I counted twenty-eight hawks soaring past us in the clear blue sky. I have never seen so many hawks all at once. They weren't circling; they looked like they might be migrating.

Sat / 2020 October 17 / Journal Entry

Happy 95th birthday Mamal! We tried to have an online Google Meet with Mamal, Michael, and Michelle today. Michael sent the link for Michelle and me to join the meeting. Can you imagine seeing your family on a computer screen on your 95th birthday? She received the flowers and candy I sent her for her special day.

Sun / 2020 October 18 / Journal Entry

Song of the Day: "I'm Not Gonna Cry," Mary J. Blige

I started taking my endocrine therapy pills. They make me feel edgy and bitchy. I have had several bouts with my internal stitches. It feels like a hot poker piercing my skin and makes me cry. I need to channel my inner Mary J. Blige.

Mon / 2020 October 19 / Journal Entry

I went to the plastic surgeon today. He filled my temporary implants to the maximum capacity. It could be the end of December for reconstruction surgery. He says it will be a six-to-seven-hour surgery, five days in the hospital and four to six weeks of recovery. I hope I can get the house renovations started soon.

One of the houses in our neighborhood is for sale. I heard the owners do not want to sell it to anyone who is "ethnically challenged." Angry emoji face.

Christian is in town on his way from Washington state to Florida. He got tested for the coronavirus before he came over, and we all wore masks as a precaution.

Fri / 2020 October 23 / Journal Entry

"Live your breast life."
Molly Rae Gaynor

I saw a story on the news about an art installation that developed during the pandemic. There are over 2500 painted rocks at Parr Park. We headed to Grapevine to the Parr Park Painted Rock area with jackets, hats, and gloves because autumn was in the air.

The park was nice but surprisingly empty. The rain and wind had covered the trail in colorful autumn leaves. We found the painted rock installation, and the rocks were grouped by subject matter: Disney, rock-n-roll, Texas, pets, military, college. It is quite remarkable that the rocks remain there.

It was a wonderful outing.

Tues / 2020 October 27 / Journal Entry

"You are an architect of your own destiny. You are the master of your own fate; you are behind the steering wheel of life. There are no limitations to what you can do, have, or be except the limitations you place on yourself by your own thinking."
Brian Tracy

The electrician showed up at 8:00 a.m. He removed sheet rock and installed wiring for our under-cabinet lighting in the kitchen. The demolition for the master bathroom renovation is Monday.

When I got the cancer diagnosis, I did not want to go down a negative tunnel of depression and darkness and "why me's." Why *not* me? Why not put my money where my mouth is, so to speak, and practice what I preach and use my newly found spirituality to navigate the journey.

Maybe, just maybe, something even better is on the other side of this setback. Maybe, just maybe, God has given me an experience that will take my spirituality to the next level. So, I decided to trust Him. This feeling is God's spirit filling my physical body. If we are open and awake to God's presence, we will feel His spirit feeding our spirituality.

When I reflect on "What Would Jesus Do?" I can easily feel small, insignificant, and unworthy. I know I have much work to do on myself before I can judge or preach to someone else. I can start by trying to be an example of kindness, positivity, and spirituality. I shared this Facebook post from Laura Jean Truman:

Keep my anger from becoming meanness.
Keep my sorrow from collapsing into self-pity.
Keep my heart soft enough to keep breaking.
Keep my anger turned toward justice, not cruelty.
Remind me that all of this, every bit of it, is for love.
Keep me fiercely kind.

Wed / 2020 October 28 / Journal Entry

Our new kitchen lights and bathroom lights are installed. I love them. They are LED lights which will last longer, use less electricity, and they are dimmable. I bought moving boxes and rolling racks to prepare for our renovation. I began packing up the master bathroom. The construction dumpster was delivered today.

As we were driving, we saw a duplex covered in political signs and flags. One side was pro Trump ("Trump—Keep America Great!" "Trump—No More Bullshit!" and "All Aboard the Trump Train") and the other side was pro Biden ("Bye Don 2020," "Biden President 2020," picture of Trump's hair—"Nope! Biden 2020"). Over 58,000,000 people have already voted.

Sat / 2020 October 31 / Journal Entry

Happy Halloween! Happy Birthday, Kyla!

This is the first year since I have lived in this house that we have not decorated, dressed up, and handed out candy on the driveway for Halloween. I wanted to dress up like Carol Baskin and Joe Exotic, the Tiger King, but I settled for skull leggings, a Day of the Dead T-shirt, and a Halloween tiara. Tonight is a blue moon, and it is the second full moon of the month.

I spent the day organizing. I organized the kitchen pantry, dresser drawers, bedroom closets, and bathroom storage. We emptied out the master bath and moved into the guest bedroom to prepare for renovations. I was exhausted. There were no trick-or-treaters due to COVID-19. Sad emoji.

COVID-19 Statistics:
Confirmed cases worldwide: 40,000,000
Confirmed deaths worldwide: 1,122,111
Confirmed cases in the United States: 8,444,414
Confirmed deaths in the United States: 225,159

november

Sun / 2020 November 1 / Journal Entry

Daylight Savings Time, fall back one hour

"If you never try, you'll never know."
Germany Kent

Our home renovation is a precursor to the one I will be facing on my own body in a few weeks. The lessons I learn will be preparation for the tests I will face. I spent the day preparing for dust, destruction, and disruption. Tomorrow is demo day. It is a risk. It is expensive. How will it all turn out? Will there be more problems or unforeseen repairs? Do the contractors know what they are doing? Will we be safe from each other and COVID? Can we afford this? Is this a wise investment?

I spent two days getting physically prepared for the workers. I finished packing and moving the bedrooms and bathrooms. I removed items from counters, walls, cabinets, and closets. I moved things Jose and I would need for the next four weeks while we slept in the guest bedroom and used the guest bathroom. I, of course, got side-tracked with other mini projects as I packed and moved things. I organized the drawers, shelves, and closets. I organized the medicine cabinet and pantry. I did laundry before packing the bed linens so they would be ready to use when I unpacked them in a few weeks. It was more than physical preparation. It was mental preparation.

We decided back in August to go ahead and proceed with this renovation. We met with the contractor and picked out tile, flooring, and countertops, and then…. we waited.

Waiting is not something I like to do. Once I decide, I like to get moving and get it done. Unfortunately, COVID-19 has created new obstacles for ordering and delivering lots of things, including my tile. So as October passed, I started to get stressed out. When would the renovations start? When would they end? How would this play out with the holidays? How would this play out with my breast reconstruction surgery?

I have been stressing about this renovation. First, I would rather move into a new place than go through the process of updating our house. I have avoided projects like this for years. The main reasons —the mess, the mayhem, and the money. I need to have the right attitude and not get hung up on every detail and bump in the road. This too shall pass. The dust and mess will eventually emerge into a new, bright, fresh, clean space. The pains, the drains, and scars will eventually heal and reveal a new body with new life and new chances.

When you are OCD like me, it is difficult to give over control to the situation or to other people. In other words, it is difficult to trust. This is another opportunity to examine myself. I think I will give myself an "F" for trust last week. Is it OCD? I have never been officially diagnosed with obsessive compulsive disorder. In fact, it may be a convenient excuse for becoming a raving lunatic who wants things done a certain way by a certain time.

My patience will be challenged as I deal with frustration, excitement, and the wide array of emotions I will experience during the home and body renovation process. I need to be aware of the way I treat the doctors and the contractors. I need to respect their skills, training, and experience to measure twice and cut once. I need to leave them alone, stay in my lane, make their job easier, and treat them the way I want to be treated—as a professional.

With each new day comes new learning. Once I begin to think that there is nothing new to learn, I begin to lose. I want to reflect each day about the progress on the work and my progress on the journey. I want to learn, grow, and improve. God has presented these opportunities, and I do not want to squander them.

God gave his Son to renovate us and to give us a second chance. I have been given the gift of a home renovation, a body renovation, and a spiritual renovation. I feel energized to continue to do the work, walk the path, fight the fight, and explore all that God has given me. I pray these experiences help me find peace, hope, grace, and love. I feel blessed, happy, and fulfilled. I feel safe. I feel saved.

Wood Biscuit Post

Picture of Woodbridge ballot with Wood Biscuit in the corner:

Just a reminder to everyone who complained about the handling of the swimming pools during the COVID epidemic. There are two seats on the board of directors open. I'm sure all of the experts that posted about how the neighborhood should be run have already sent in their applications. If not…I can provide you with a postage stamp or instructions on how to contact the management company if you lost your letter to run for the board.

Mon / 2020 November 2 / Journal Entry

Demo Day

"Sometimes good things fall apart so better things can fall together."
Marilyn Monroe

Song of the Day: "Wrecking Ball" Miley Cyrus

Today is demo day. Is it a coincidence the neighbors chose this song of the day to post on their kitchen windows: "Wrecking Ball?" We had to get up early to prepare for the contractor's arrival. The first guy came and covered everything in plastic. He marked an "X" on everything that was to be demolished. It reminded me of a doctor preparing for surgery—reviewing the orders, prepping the patient, marking the limb for surgery, or in this case, amputation.

I am sitting on my patio enjoying seventy-two-degree weather on the second day of November. I can hear Niko, the demo guy, hammering and chiseling the bathtub, shower, and tile floor. I must admit, he knows what he is doing. He is quick, quiet, efficient, and clean.

Tues / 2020 November 3 / Journal Entry

Election Day

"This has been hard on all of us. Treat others the way you would want to be treated. We all will need it."
Unknown

Dr. Lemmon's office called to schedule my reconstruction surgery. It will be on Saturday, December 12th. I can spend the holidays recovering and watching hours of Lifetime and Hallmark movies. I was caught off guard by the call. I got a nervous feeling in my stomach because it is a little over a month away.

Tues / 2020 November 3 / Facebook Post

"I met those of our society who had votes in the ensuing election and advised them:
- *To vote without fee or reward for the person they judged most worthy.*
- *To speak no evil of the person they voted against.*
- *To take care their spirits were not sharpened against those that voted on the other side."*

John Wesley, October 6, 1774

I had virtual Bible study today. Bridget led us on the topic of "Witness." A witness is someone who sees something important or amazing and shares their experience with others. One of the questions posed to us was, "How can you bear witness to what you have seen, heard, and learned about Jesus?" For me, I try to model it by walking the walk, behaving on social media, and developing a stronger personal relationship with God before I profess to know Him. Our Bible study prayers revolved around renovation and restoration.

Wed / 2020 November 4 / Journal Entry

"I walk around like everything is fine, but deep down, inside my shoe, my sock is slipping off my foot."
Aubrey Marcus

We went to bed not knowing who the president would be. Trump declared victory at 2:00 a.m. The media is being very cautious about calling winners of any states. There were more voters than ever before. There weres more mail-in votes than ever before due to COVID-19.

Different states have different rules about poll times, mail-in voting, and when they start counting the votes. Many news sources state it could be several days before we know who will be president. Of course, it comes down to the electoral college and who carries the states that have the electorate votes. Trump is filing lawsuits to stop the count. It takes 270 delegates to win.

Juan worked on our patio posts which revealed an ant infestation. This led to a call to an exterminator. Niko worked on the drywall in the kitchen. Paolo moved the drain and pipes for the tub and shower.

I ordered Advent-ure Challenge Calendars for us and the kids. It has twelve challenges you must scratch off. It will be our 2020 COVID Christmas holiday advent-ure since we will not be able to gather together and celebrate as a family this year.

Thu / 2020 November 5 / Journal Entry

Wood Biscuit Post

Picture of sign "Wood Biscuit Wins!

Unofficial Neighborhood Update: Local imaginary horse claims win in neighborhood election.

Although the candidates haven't been announced and no votes have been cast, Wood Biscuit has claimed victory in the 2020 Woodbridge board member elections. "I just filled out my form and then voted for myself. Then I decided to stop all voting. So, I'm pretty sure that means that I won," said Wood Biscuit in a phone interview.

Many residents are upset and asking questions. The most common question is, "How can a winner be determined if other residents haven't had the chance to vote yet?" It seems irregular and hasn't followed the protocol of earlier elections. Current HOA board members and the current management company are checking the validity of the horse's claim of victory. Thus far, they are still not commenting on the situation.

When Wood Biscuit was pressed for more details about his claim of victory, he responded, "If you want to hear me unfiltered, then you will need to go over to WoodBook. It's my new social media site that isn't biased against horses. It's kind of like Parler or Weme, but there are fewer conspiracy theories, sore losers, and paranoid residents."

Only time will tell if the victory claims of the horse are real. The only clear winner this time is the WoodBook app. It is up to five downloads this week and is ranked 6,132,764th in the AppStore.

Sat / 2020 November 7 / Journal Entry

"Live each day as if it were your last."
Marcus Aurelius

The leaves were changing into bright autumn colors, so I suggested we take Dexter and Major to The Duck Pond and enjoy the day. Jose caught three fish. I fed the ducks frozen peas and watched them play in the water.

I met a group of elementary-aged girls who called themselves the "Claws and Paws Guild." They come to the pond and pick up trash periodically. I saw Frazier the Crane and took videos of him flying back and forth across the pond. I lay on the park bench and admired the shades of yellow, red, orange, and green in the leaves of the tree above me.

I listened to the ducks and felt blessed.

Joe Biden will be our president, and Kamala Harris will be our first female vice-president. My heart is hopeful for the new things we may have on the horizon: new leadership, new hope, new policies, new life.

I have learned a lot about the election process, and at my age, fifty-seven, I have to admit, I have taken for granted my right to vote. I have not participated in elections until recent years. I am very excited that so many more people took part in the process this year despite the pandemic.

I already feel encouraged that we have had the highest number of voters to ever turn out for an election, with almost sixty-seven percent of eligible voters casting votes. Despite COVID-19 safety concerns, that is approximately 155 million people. I feel invigorated that people have found their voice, especially those who have been suppressed and voiceless for so long.

My Facebook friends are crying, either because they are happy Biden won or sad because Trump lost. Several of my Trump supporter friends have gone radio silent. Others are posting that they are leaving Facebook and joining Parler where they won't be censored.

Sat / 2020 November 7 / My Facebook Post

Lord, it's me again. November is the month of gratitude, so thank you for the opportunity to thank you. Today I am grateful for so many things, but mostly for a feeling of hope I feel this morning. This year, 2020, has been like no other.

Now in the last quarter, I feel gratitude. Thank you for the opportunity to live in this nation. Thank you for democracy and the right to vote. Thank you to our veterans who fought and active military who serve to protect our rights. Thank you for the ability to choose so many things in my life including my attitude, my words, and my actions. Thank you for the ability to celebrate holidays.

This year will be different, but thank you for the opportunity to be creative and enjoy new ways to be thankful and celebrate. Today Lord, I thank you for the opportunity to spend time with you in nature and wonder over all you created. Thank you for your blessings and for your son, Jesus Christ, who was sent to save each of us including little ol' me. Your perfect love for us, despite our failing you, demonstrates your almighty faithfulness, and for that, I am humble and grateful. Amen.

Sun / 2020 November 8 / Journal Entry

Jose's godfather, Sammy Avila, passed away last week. We found out today he died of COVID-19.

Wed / 2020 November 11 / Journal Entry

"God changes caterpillars into butterflies, sand into pearls, and coal into diamonds using time and pressure. He's working on you, too."
Rick Warren

We took the dogs for a walk on the trail this morning. Leaves were changing, falling and crunching under our feet. It was gray and misty. The trail and bridges were covered in fresh, fallen leaves. As we walked, more leaves fell. The colors and sounds were soothing to my soul. I took a few videos and put together a video of falling leaves when I got home.

I spoke to God while walking and thanked Him for all that He has created and provided for us. I worked on the patio today and captured a video of a monarch butterfly who has been hanging around the patio the past few days. The monarchs migrate from Canada to Mexico every year. It is amazing.

There are a few political signs and flags still up. Trump has yet to concede the election. Trump refuses to meet with Biden to discuss the transfer of power. Maybe a socially distanced Thanksgiving is part of God's plan to keep relatives from discussing politics this year. Just a thought.

There are several holiday "dork" trips I really want to do this year, but my better judgment is telling me no. We have been so good for the past eight months, and the coronavirus cases are spiking again. Even though they are advertised with social distancing protocols, Jose and I shouldn't risk it. Activities like Meet and Greet Dr. Seuss's The

Grinch, Luminova at Globe Life Park, and I Love Christmas Movies at the Gaylord Texan are right up my alley in "Dorkville." They will have to wait until the pandemic is over. I am going to forego these guilty pleasures so I may have many more Christmases with Jose and the family in the future.

Thu / 2020 November 12 / Journal Entry

The "Advent-ure" challenge calendars arrived. It could be a lot of fun! My friend Janet is creating personalized letters from Santa on Santa stationary straight from the North Pole. I ordered one for each family member as part of the Advent-ure challenges.

Tue / 2020 November 17 / Journal Entry

We won't be gathering with our family this Thanksgiving. We have come too far to screw it up now. Zoomsgiving is better than I.C.U. Christmas.

Barbara led our Bible study on "Sacrifice and Atonement." One of the discussion questions asked, "What is one sacrificial act of humility you can do to build unity in your church or family?" I thought about sacrificing our Thanksgiving holiday tradition to stay safe for ourselves, our family, and our community.

Thu / 2020 November 19 / Journal Entry

"By perseverance the snail reached the ark."
Charles Spurgeon

I had to get a bone density scan and blood work before I met with the oncologist, Dr. Trumbly. He gave me a survivor's packet of information. He said my blood work was "boring," my bone density scan was "mostly normal," and he told me to take calcium and vitamin D supplements.

I straightened the painted rock garden at the cancer center on my way out. It was a lovely day. I am blessed.

Sat / 2020 November 21 / My Facebook Post

God, it's me again. This weekend begins our holiday season. The 2020 holidays will be different from previous years, but different doesn't mean bad. I am faithful that you have new blessings, traditions, and memories in store for us. This year has provided time and opportunity to slow down, reflect, pray, and show gratitude for so many things that are easily overlooked in our busy lives.

I pray today that you will help people to make the best decisions for themselves, their families, their friends, neighbors, and community to keep us all safe and healthy. I pray you will lay special blessings on all who must work during this upcoming holiday. Keep them safe and give them energy. Let them feel essential and appreciated.

Please wrap your loving arms around our first responders, doctors, nurses and other health care workers. Give them renewed hope and encouragement to continue to do the magnificent work they do each day.

Lord, help each of us, especially me, to focus on you and the blessings you provide every day. Take care of my loved ones, and let them know how much I love them and miss them. Let them know I am waiting for the next time we can gather to hug, laugh, eat, and celebrate. Until then, I trust you and thank you. In your Son's name I pray. Amen.

Sun / 2020 November 22 / Journal Entry

It has cooled off and feels like fall. We walked the dogs and started cooking recipes I found when I googled "Thanksgiving for Two." We prepared three sets of dinners for two: one for Kat and Jordan, one for Kyla and Taylor, and one for us.

The to-go boxes included:
- Dinner rolls
- Slow Cooker Grape Jelly Meatballs
- Roasted Garlic and Herb Turkey Breasts
- Stuffin' Muffins

- Dad's Gravy
- Spinach and Artichoke Zucchini Bites
- Sweet Potato Bites
- Green Bean Casserole Bundles
- Homemade Cranberry Sauce
- Deviled Eggs
- Buttermilk Pie

I made another box that included their Christmas 2020 pajamas, T-shirts and masks, a jigsaw puzzle, autumn hand soap, air freshener, and a pumpkin spice candle. I added Thanksgiving paper plates, napkins, and utensils.

The girls came by at 5:00 p.m. and called from their cars in the driveway to pick up their Lozada Thanksgiving To-Go boxes. Jose and I enjoyed our own early Thanksgiving dinner. Then we put our feet up and watched the Dallas Cowboys beat the Minnesota Vikings 31-28.

Mon / 2020 November 23 / Journal Entry

I bought a 500-piece Rudolph the Red-Nosed Reindeer puzzle and started putting it together for one of the Advent-ure challenges. I ate Thanksgiving leftovers for lunch and helped Jose get the yard decorations out. I washed my car and got the waving Santa and reindeer antlers and nose on my car. I will count that as another one of the Advent-ure challenges.

The holidays are approaching, and schools are closing due to rising cases. Businesses are closing due to the economy and rising cases. Millions of people are traveling for the holidays despite the CDC warnings. 101 people are diagnosed with COVID-19 each minute. There is a possibility of two vaccines on the horizon.

Dolly Parton contributed $1,000,000 towards research for the COVID-19 vaccine.

Tue / 2020 November 24 / Journal Entry

I deep cleaned the living room while Niko and Paolo framed the tub and shower. I dusted walls, cleaned windows, and polished furniture and knickknacks. Juan continued electrical work and installed hardware, while I set up the formal Christmas tree. It took me until bedtime to decorate it.

I led the virtual Bible study with the Bible Chicks on the topic of "Temple." The idea of a unified body of Christ in the Garden of Eden seems like a fantasy when we look at the divisiveness and brokenness in our world today. In the end, we must practice The Golden Rule: to treat others the way we want to be treated.

Wed / 2020 November 25 / Journal Entry

"Almost everything will work again if you unplug it for a few minutes, including you."
Anne Lamott

I had a hard time sleeping because I was so sore from cleaning and decorating. I started early again today and worked on the den and kitchen. The workers came for a half day and finished up the painting and the electrical work. The kitchen renovations are done, one day before Thanksgiving!

The house, my body, the presidency, the nation, the holidays, and the year 2020 have all undergone major challenges. It's November, and the seasons are changing. The leaves are falling. It has all been rough, but I have remained hopeful. We are in the fourth quarter of 2020, and I see so much opportunity and possibility.

Thu / 2020 November 26 / Journal Entry

We watched the Macy's Thanksgiving Parade which was pre-recorded due to COVID-19.

I thought about the two times I went to New York and saw the parade in person. This year's parade had cars instead of balloon handlers, no crowd, and pre-recorded performances. The parade always marks a happy Thanksgiving holiday and the official beginning of the Christmas season for me.

The news reported that there are currently 90,000 people hospitalized due to COVID-19. One person per minute dies from the coronavirus in the United States. Some hospitals report they are out of patient beds.

Fri / 2020 November 27 / Journal Entry

"We cannot direct the wind, but we can adjust the sails."
Dolly Parton

I finished decorating our hodgepodge family tree in the den. Despite the pandemic, I was able to add new ornaments to commemorate this year including a Dr. Pepper Museum ornament, Texas Ranger Museum ornament, RBG ornament, a grill, fishing and taekwondo ornament, toilet paper ornament, and a 2020 ornament.

We put on our Christmas sweatpants and T-shirts. Jose's shirt has a Santa with a mask, and my shirt has a reindeer with a mask. We made breakfast for dinner—pancakes, bacon, and breakfast potato scramble—and watched *How the Grinch Stole Christmas*. This counted as one of the Advent-ure challenges.

Sat / 2020 November 28 / Journal Entry

"How cool is it that the same God that created mountains and oceans and galaxies looked at you and thought the world needed one of you, too."
Unknown

I went to McDonald's to pick up lunch. I tuned in to the Christmas radio station and listened to Christmas carols while I drove. I had the Santa arm waving on the back windshield wiper at stop signs and stop lights. I went through the drive-through and bought lunch for the car behind me. It was another Advent-ure challenge.

Mon / 2020 November 30 / Journal Entry

I had a pre-op appointment with Dr. Lemmon. The nurse gave me a paper gown and paper underwear and took mugshots of my torso. She told me to face front, turn diagonal, turn to the side, repeat on the other side.

With the rise in COVID-19 cases since Thanksgiving, hospitals are reporting rising cases, and there is a distinct possibility that my surgery could be delayed if there are no beds available at the hospital. If my surgery gets pushed past January 1st, I will have to meet a new deductible of $3,000 out of pocket. I can't help but feel pissed off about this. It hasn't happened yet. I do trust God has a plan, so I intend to focus on that and pray on it.

Several days ago, I made a post on Facebook for friends to send me Health Care Heroes cards to distribute at the hospital. I received several cards in the mail.

COVID-19 Statistics:
100,000 new cases a day for five days in a row
1,000 deaths a day for five days in a row
Confirmed cases in the United States: 10,022,557
Confirmed deaths in the United States: 237,979

december

Tue / 2020 December 1 / Journal Entry

Day 422 of sobriety, Day 264 of COVID
"He who has not Christmas in his heart will never find it under the tree."
Roy L. Smith

The past nine months (264 days) have been anything but normal with the pandemic, breast cancer, working from home, virtual service learning, etc. It has been an opportunity to study God, build my faith, reflect, write, pray, grow, and count my blessings.

I reposted a Facebook post:

Hallmark Pandemic Movie Plot

A high-powered atheist finds herself stranded in her hometown during a pandemic lock down after she came home to take care of her mother with dementia via music and naked art therapy. Against her better judgment, she falls in love with the son of the son of a sailor man. Together they learn the true meaning of Christmas.

Wed / 2020 December 2 / Journal Entry

"The magic is inside you. There ain't no crystal ball."
Dolly Parton

Kat called to tell us she and Jordan are "expecting." I am going to be a grandma! Dad is going to be a great-grandpa! Mamal will be a great-great-grandma. 2021 will be a big year. Kyla will graduate from chiropractic school. Kat and Jordan will become parents. Kyla and Taylor will get married. Jose will celebrate his fiftieth birthday.

I thought to myself, "What if I miss it all? What if this is my last Christmas?"

Thu / 2020 December 3 / Journal Entry

"When you arise in the morning, think of what a precious privilege it is to be alive, to breathe, to think, to enjoy, to love."
Marcus Aurelius

The installers came and finished the floor in the master bathroom and closet. The shower glass and bathroom mirror were installed. The end of the home renovation is in sight. I worked all day. This is going to be a busy week wrapping up projects and getting ready for surgery and Christmas.

I bought clothes for the two angels I adopted from La Familia de Esperanza. I chose a sixteen-year-old girl and a seventeen-year-old boy. They each got shoes, socks, gloves, hat, pants, shirts, and a jacket. I bought snacks for Jose's basket for Health Care Heroes. I bought ornaments and bags to go with the Big Mood stickers and cards for my nurses. I bought candy-cane snacks for our postal workers. I bought canned goods to take to the drive-in movie tonight.

We returned to the site of the Leaning Tower of Dallas which is now an open field. There is a pop-up drive-in movie theater showing Christmas movies on a big inflatable screen with the downtown Dallas skyline in the background.

We took Little Greg and packed blankets and pillows in the truck. We arrived early and watched old-timey drive-in commercials before the movie started. I had some battery-operated Christmas lights that we draped around the visors and rear-view mirror. We ordered popcorn, hot chocolate, and a grab bag of Christmas candy on the drive-in app. They texted us when it was ready to be picked up at the concession stand. We tuned in to a radio station to hear the sound. We snuggled in Little Greg and watched *Elf* on the giant, inflatable screen and ate drive-in movie snacks. It was a great date night.

Sat / 2020 December 5 / Journal Entry

"Some of our best lessons are shared with people we will never meet in this lifetime. But imagine seeing them in heaven one day and hearing them say 'Remember when you...'"
Unknown Author

My reflection: Great Blessings for 2020

- Cousin trip to Waco
- Kat and Jordan's marriage
- Baking
- Gardening
- Walking
- Painting
- Faerie village
- Painted rocks
- Woodbridge Treasure Hunt
- Working from home
- Masks
- Virtual meetings
- Bible Study
- Holly Hills Hangouts
- Fishing
- Feeding the ducks
- Creative celebrations
- Drive-by to-go boxes
- Adopt-a-Senior
- Nature
- Kyla and Taylor's engagement
- Kat and Jordan's baby
- Home renovations
- Body renovations
- Streaming services
- Essential workers

During the month of December, I receive a daily email from Biola University Center for Christianity, Culture, and Arts Advent Project. I listened, read, and reflected on today's email.

Today's Advent Prayer:

God, our Father, we know that rulers will rise and make claims to power and authority, some for good and some for ill. Help us remember that the true King arrived in humility and continues to rule in sacrificial love.

Tonight, we had the First Annual Holly Hills Socially Distant Christmas Carol Sing-A-Long. A family from the neighborhood came out to lead us. The Jones family, Gragert family, Ipe family, and Mussetter family came out. Most everyone wore festive sweaters and holiday hats and scarves. We gathered in my front yard and sang Christmas carols. We even had a "Fa-la-la-la-la" battle. It was the first time I have caroled since junior high school.

I invited the Jones family over to experience Carl, the hot chocolate snowman bomb. They enjoyed it, and I got to show off our home improvements.

Sun / 2020 December 6 / Journal Entry

After dinner Jose and I went to Starbucks. My car was decked out with battery operated Christmas lights, reindeer antlers and nose, and the waving Santa on the back window. We bought coffee and frappuccino and paid for the car behind us. Merry Christmas from Mr. and Mrs. Claus. We came home and watched *Christmas Vacation* after Jose listened to all the Hallmark *Christmas Vacation* ornaments on the hodgepodge tree.

We watched my favorite Christmas movie, *White Christmas*. Nicole called to check on me. We laughed because Jose was doing his own rendition of "Sisters-Sisters" from *White Christmas*, while we chatted on the phone. We also watched *It's a Wonderful Life*. There is a scene where George reads a telegram about Mr. Gower's son. It says he died of influenza. It was dated 1919, the second year of the Spanish flu pandemic that killed 675,000 people in the United States and fifty million worldwide.

Mon / 2020 December 7 / Journal Entry

According to a post circulating on Facebook, these are the deadliest days in United States history:

- Galveston Hurricane 1900   8,000
- Battle of Antietam 1862   3,600
- September 11, 2001   2,977
- December 3, 2020   2,861
- December 2, 2020   2,762
- December 1, 2020   2,461
- December 4, 2020   2,439
- Pearl Harbor 1941   2,403

Tue / 2020 December 8 / Journal Entry

It was another early morning. The laundry room floor was installed. The toilets and baseboards were installed. I am ready to put our closet, master bathroom, and bedroom back together.

Wed / 2020 December 9 / Journal Entry

We dusted and swept our bedroom. We moved back into our closet. Our house is almost back to normal. There is more to do tomorrow and Friday, but we will be in good shape for my surgery on Saturday.

Thu / 2020 December 10 / Journal Entry

It's a big day!

The master bath renovation is complete. The bathroom has been put back together. The garage is almost back to normal and clean so we can park the vehicles inside the garage for the first time in weeks. We spent the night in our own bedroom last night.

Sat / 2020 December 12 / Journal Entry

"No matter how you feel, get up, dress up, and show up."
Regina Brett

We arrived at Baylor Plano Hospital at 8:30 a.m. Besides me, there was only one other surgery scheduled. I remember rolling down the hall into the operating room, but that is all. The surgery took eight hours. During DIEP flap surgery, an incision is made along your bikini line, and a portion of skin, fat, and blood vessels is taken from the lower half of your belly, moved up to your chest, and formed into a breast shape. The tiny blood vessels in the flap, which will feed the tissue of your new breast, are matched to blood vessels in your chest and carefully reattached under a microscope.

Once I was in my room I just slept and had a liquid diet. The hardest thing was getting up to walk. It is an important part of recovery to get moving after surgery.

Advent-ure Challenge: The Twelve Days of Christmas—Day #1
Post a picture of a Christmas craft (all pictures and challenges were completed prior to surgery and recovery). I did the Rudolph the Reindeer jigsaw puzzle. Jose decorated the front yard and live oak tree with Christmas lights.

Sun / 2020 December 13 / Journal Entry

Hospital day #2. I slept mostly. I was able to start eating solid food.

Advent-ure Challenge: The Twelve Days of Christmas—Day #2
Post a picture in your ugly sweater. I wore my light up Dallas Cowboys sweater. Jose wore his red and green glitter tracksuit sweater and his Santa pandemic beard.

Mon / 2020 December 14 / Journal Entry

"Candy canes remind us to stick to it, even when life throws us a curve."
Kristen Stokes

My pain is not unbearable. The nurses keep me fairly sedated. I ate and walked around the surgery floor with assistance. All the nurses comment on my Barbie, my unicorn pillow, my cat sleep mask, and my glitter nails. I gave a thank-you treat bag to each nurse who has been taking care of me.

Advent-ure Challenge: The Twelve Days of Christmas—Day #3
Post a picture in your Christmas pajamas eating breakfast for dinner. Mission accomplished on Friday, Nov. 27th.

Tue / 2020 December 15 / Journal Entry

More of the same at the hospital. They removed some monitoring wires and the catheter. My pain is a little higher today. I was ambitious and thought I might be able to meet the Bible Chicks on Zoom, but I bailed until next week. Sad emoji.

Advent-ure Challenge: The Twelve Days of Christmas—Day #4
Post a picture drinking hot chocolate and watching a movie. Mission accomplished at the drive-in movie when we watched *Elf*.

Wed / 2020 December 16 / Journal Entry

I got a good sleep last night, so I felt better waking up today. I am sitting in a chair waiting for breakfast. I am very blessed to have the nurses I have had taking care of me.

Advent-ure Challenge: The Twelve Days of Christmas—Day #5
Post a picture buying coffee for a stranger. Mission accomplished at the drive-through at Starbucks.

Thu / 2020 December 17 / Journal Entry

Today was my first day at home. I am feeling grouchy. Jose is a good nurse, but I am having a difficult time getting comfortable. I am very groggy and fussy. Stupid robocalls keep interrupting my naps.

Bah humbug!

Advent-ure Challenge: The Twelve Days of Christmas—Day #6
Post a picture of your car decked out in holiday decor. Mission accomplished! Battery-operated lights on the inside, antlers and nose and waving Santa arm on the outside.

Fri / 2020 December 18 / Journal Entry

"I stare at the mirror to remember who I am and who I am not."
Suzanne Collins

I feel more alert today. Jose helped me take a shower, change my wound dressings, and feel normal. It is time to get back in the swing of my daily routines. My body looks like a Frankenstein project.

Advent-ure Challenge: The Twelve Days of Christmas—Day #7
Post a picture of stocking stuffers. Mission accomplished when I purchased four stuffed animals at PetSmart (two from me and two from Jose) and donated them to the Wylie Children's Medical Clinic.

Sat / 2020 December 19 / Journal Entry

I slept pretty well in the recliner, but I moved to the bed where I got several more hours of zzz's. I feel stronger and less sore today. I am very happy the home renovations are finally finished. We still need to put the guest bathroom back together, but there is no hurry since nobody is coming over during the holidays.

Advent-ure Challenge: The Twelve Days of Christmas—Day #8
Send a letter or card to a loved one. Mission accomplished. I sent "Letters from Santa" that Janet made for me. Jose sent personal holiday cards.

Sun / 2020 December 20 / Journal Entry

I am feeling better. Good sleep is the best healer. I took a long shower.

Advent-ure Challenge: The Twelve Days of Christmas—Day #9
Post pictures or videos singing Christmas carols. Mission accom-

plished. I posted a video of the Holly Hills Christmas Carol Sing-A-Long.

Mon / 2020 December 21 / Journal Entry

"Sleigh all day!"
Dolly Parton

I had another good night's sleep. I was able to mostly shower and dress myself. We went to Dr. Lemmon for a follow-up appointment, and the last three drains were removed! Now, I have to wear a compression girdle for at least four weeks as I continue to heal. The nurse asked me to rate my pain on a scale of zero to ten. I told her "one." She said I was tough because that is an unusual answer considering the surgery I had.

I took a nap when I got home, did a little office work, put the guest bathroom back together, and walked down the block and back. Jose held my hand, which I really like.

Advent-ure Challenge: The Twelve Days of Christmas—Day #10
Post a picture decorating cookies. Mission accomplished. Jose made ninja cookies, and I made a cookie Christmas tree.

Tue / 2020 December 22 / Journal Entry

"An ounce of goodness every day can soothe the heart in many ways. An ounce of goodness 'just because;' don't wait until Christmas to be Santa Claus."
Charmaine J. Ford

It is somewhat strange yet oddly comforting that I have not purchased one Christmas gift, wrapped one present, or planned holiday gatherings this year. I am content to be at home with Jose and the dogs and forgo the hustle and bustle that normally takes place over the holidays. I can focus on resting and recovering but also on reflecting on the true meaning of Christmas.

Jose is planning our Christmas day Zoom bingo with the kids. I sent them each $200 as an early stocking stuffer so they could enjoy the holiday a little more. Kyla is broke, Kat has morning sickness, and Christian is completing employee evaluations. In other words, they are "adulting."

Advent-ure Challenge: The Twelve Days of Christmas—Day #11
Post a picture delivering a gift basket. Mission accomplished. Jose delivered a gift basket with Health Care Hero holiday cards and snacks to the nurse's station when I was in the hospital. I had gift bags prepared for my nurses who cared for me.

Wed / 2020 December 23 / Journal Entry

Christmas Eve's Eve

Today I slept late. I took a nap. I wore my compression girdle. I didn't feel bad. I didn't feel great. It was a "meh" day.

Advent-ure Challenge: The Twelve Days of Christmas Day #12
Post a picture of your version of a Charlie Brown Christmas tree. Mission accomplished. We have two Charlie Brown trees. One for Jose. One for me.

Thu / 2020 December 24 / Journal Entry

"There are three stages of man: he believes in Santa Claus; he does not believe in Santa Claus; he is Santa Claus."
Bob Phillips

Jose and I spent the day in our Christmas pajamas and in our recliners. We flipped channels and watched portions of *White Christmas, It's a Wonderful Life, Holly Dolly Christmas, Thank God for Kids, The Christmas Story,* and *Four Christmases*. It was unusual to not be cooking, wrapping, running to Walmart, entertaining, doing dishes, opening presents, and go, go, going all day. It was a blessing to be at home with the dogs and our decorations. It was nice to be able to sit back, reflect, relax, and heal.

Fri / 2020 December 25 / Journal Entry

Christmas Day

We slept in. Jose set up a Zoom bingo meeting with the kids. Technology allowed us to be together even though we were in Sachse, Kyla and Taylor were in Euless, Kat and Jordan were in Little Elm, and Christian was in Destin, Florida. Kyla and Taylor had on homemade Christmas sweatshirts, and Christian had on a festive cardigan. Jose was sporting his Santa hat and Santa beard. They played Zoom bingo for gift cards.

Jose and I made beef tenderloin with chive butter, roasted Brussels sprouts with almond slices, and mashed sweet potatoes for dinner. Then we binge-watched six episodes of *The Mandalorian*. Merry Christmas!

Mon / 2020 December 28 / Journal Entry

"Today's forecast—mostly magical with a chance of miracles."
Jim Rohn

Kat is due August 6th. Kyla's wedding is set for August 7th. Jose turns fifty on August 16th. August will be busy! We received pictures of the sonogram. Our grandchild looks like a gummy bear. Heart emoji.

I had to get up early to go to an appointment with Dr. Lemmon's nurse. She checked my healing progress and gave me an extra compression girdle. Then I passed out for a two-hour nap. I felt drugged.

Tues / 2020 December 29 / Journal Entry

I got a text that Rosie's sister, Liz, had died during the night due to COVID-19.

The cases continue to rise. Over 300,000 people have died from COVID-19 in the United States.

Wed / 2020 December 30 / Journal Entry

"For my part I know nothing with any certainty, but the sight of the stars makes me dream."
Vincent Van Gogh

It was rainy and cold and a good day to sleep in, so I did. There was no activity on my work email, so I shut it down, submitted my timesheet, and closed out my 2020 planner. Life does go on, but 2020 was unusual. I feel like so many people are hopeful that everything will magically be back to normal when the calendar changes to 2021, but I believe the biggest challenges are still ahead of us.

At 10:30 p.m. our phone rang. Mamal was crying and confused. Michael had gone back to his home in Terlingua, Texas, the day before. He had spent the last three weeks, including Christmas, with her. When she called us, she was worried that he had not come home to her house. She said he had been gone all day, he hadn't come home, and it was late. She was worried and confused.

We decided to get in the car and pick her up. We drove to Arlington, packed her bags, and drove home. We got her to bed around 1:30 a.m. I "slept" on the couch because Jose had a canker sore, and his mouthpiece made him snore like a freight train. I fell into bed around 5:30 a.m.

Thurs / 2020 December 31 / Journal Entry

I got Mamal up and dove headfirst into a conversation about her future, which was completely futile. She is stubborn and does not remember anything. It was a fitting way to spend the last day of this unusual year. My positivity and sunny disposition were worn thin.

Times Square is closed for the ball drop. Jose and I toasted at midnight with Welch's Sparkling Grape Juice. A COVID-19 vaccine is ready. Operation Warp Speed has begun. The vaccine requires two doses administered four weeks apart.

Over 885,000 U.S. citizens have filed for unemployment. The government will issue $600 stimulus and survival checks.

There are 4,000 deaths per day in the United States.

Most of the Facebook posts are about how awful 2020 was. The last day of the year made me sad. I don't like to be sad. The last few days of 2020 did not unfold like I had imagined. I am the positive, optimistic one, but not on this New Year's Eve nor on New Year's Day in the wee hours of the morning.

COVID-19 Statistics:
Confirmed cases worldwide: 82,282,392
Confirmed deaths worldwide: 1,800,000
Confirmed cases in the United States: 19,655,574
Confirmed deaths in the United States: 341,000
Confirmed cases in Texas: 1,738,920
Confirmed deaths in Texas: 27,539
Confirmed cases in Dallas: 189,252
Confirmed deaths in Dallas: 1,955

2021

january

Fri / 2021 January 1 / Journal Entry

"We all get the exact same 365 days. The only difference is what we do with them."
Hillary De Piano

Rock of the Day: Flower—"Grow through what you go through."

I was up all night. The past two days finally caught up with me, and I went to bed around 6:30 a.m. By 10:00 a.m I was sweaty, grumpy, and sad. I thought about Jose and how he never complains. I thought about what he tolerates—mainly me. He sat next to me on the bed while I cried. I got up, took a shower, and prayed. I thanked God for all our blessings and asked for strength and guidance for the new year.

I thought about the quotes I posted today and took my own advice. I put on "my big girl panties" and spent the next six hours de-decorating. It was a welcome distraction.

I felt better mentally to be doing something. It is what I normally do each year, and I was able to do it physically, even though I am still recovering from surgery. Jose took down the front yard decorations. Mamal doesn't know about my cancer or surgeries. She stayed bundled up under blankets by the fire.

Sat / 2021 January 2 / Journal Entry

"The new year stands before us like a chapter in a book, waiting to be written."
Melody Beattie

Jose paid attention to my "system" of putting away decorations. We left the trees and lights up for one more night.

Sun / 2021 January 3 / Journal Entry

"Don't impress others with what you have; impress them with who you are."
Unknown

Bonus Quote: "You can get excited about the future. The past won't mind."
Hillary De Piano

We watched a documentary on minimalism late last night. I have been giving this concept a lot of thought. I woke up early this morning and gave it a lot more thought. I thought about what stuff is functional and what stuff is crap. I have been intentionally unsubscribing from emails that fill up my inbox and tempt me to buy more stuff, which equates to more crap. I am going to minimize how many posts I "like" and "love," and I am going to "hide" ads that come across my timeline on Facebook. I am going to delete apps off my phone that I don't use. I am going to put today's quotes into action.

I keep re-reading these quotes. So much of the "stuff" I/we keep is stuff from the past. I have dishes, furniture, knickknacks, collectibles, and jewelry that are remnants of the past. I sincerely believe my ancestors would be okay with me letting go of this stuff.

Mon / 2021 January 4 / Journal Entry

It is time to get back into a routine. I got up, got dressed, and showed up. I went to the doctor and got a check-up. My wounds are healing. I have two more weeks of wearing the compression girdle full time, then I will wear it part time for a few more weeks. I am going to start taking my estrogen blocker, anastrozole, and my supplements, calcium, and vitamin D again.

Tue / 2021 January 5 / Journal Entry

"Every morning's dew is the fresh breath of a new beginning."

Jessica Edouard
Bonus Quote: "A grateful heart is a magnet to miracles."
Jane Fuller

Rock of the Day: Toucan—"Toucan Do It!"

I made breakfast for Mamal: French toast bites, sausage, and fruit. I gave her a quiz. She didn't know who I was or my name. I wonder where she thinks she is. Mamal eats whatever we make for her. I tried another quiz. She still doesn't know who I am or my name.

Jose and I did New Year accounting. We wrapped up 2020 expenses and earnings. We set up new 2021 ledgers and got files moved for storage and shredding.

I met virtually with the Bible Chicks finally! We caught up on the holiday, the COVID-19 vaccine, and school starting for the spring semester. We discussed our new Bibles and our plan for 2021 Bible study. We discussed our focus words for 2020 and our new focus words for 2021 which guided our prayer for the new year (devote, change, grow, complete).

Dear Lord,
We pray that we will DEVOTE our time and hearts to this Bible study so that we can CHANGE and GROW in order to COMPLETE a study of your work to further our relationship with you. Amen.

Wed / 2021 January 6 / Journal Entry

"Everything that is tearing us down today will become a memory, and the memory will be shared as an anecdote or a story or a poem or a play or a warning. It will be shared with another human being who will then understand that he's not alone in his sadness. This is why we show up for others and tell our tales and listen to others. The great congregation meets daily, and you are someone's angel today." Tennessee Williams

I woke up and got Mamal up so that I could help her get a shower before I started my day. Thank goodness we have a new walk-in shower with a bench. I made breakfast. I did a little work while Jose made lunch. I had a Zoom call with Janet. We both had quite a bit to share about the holidays. Then we became productive and started discussing our new focus words for 2021. Her word is "dream," and mine is "complete."

Then Jose came in and said, "Shit is hitting the fan on the news." Trump had a rally, still claiming the election was stolen from him. Our 45th president, Donald Trump, spoke to a crowd that marched to the capitol building. They stormed the Capitol. Elected officials were under attack and went into lockdown.

For the rest of the afternoon, evening, and night, we watched our democracy under attack by citizens of our country.

I am mad, and I am sad. Our nation's reputation, democracy, and security are vulnerable. Many people are calling for the impeachment of #45.

Fri / 2021 January 8 / Journal Entry

Day 460 of sobriety

Shopping at Walmart in the evening is good. It is not busy, so I can socially distance myself in the aisles. Almost everyone is wearing their masks. The weather forecast is for snow or a wintery mix. I am glad I am shopping tonight. Tomorrow the store will be busy as everyone prepares for "snowmageddon."

Sun / 2021 January 10 / Journal Entry

"I pray this winter will be gentle and kind -- a season of rest from the wheel of the mind."
John Geddes

I got Mamal some oatmeal and hot coffee. She dressed and fed herself. I did not fuss over her. I was laser focused on my Bible study. It began to snow large snowflakes. It was quiet and peaceful. I worked on the discussion questions and did some soul searching.

Mon / 2021 January 11 / Journal Entry

When Mamal was drinking her morning coffee she asked, "How did I get here?" "Why am I here?"

That turned into a frustrating and futile conversation. I am trying to let everything roll off my back, but it is so sad that she does not know my name or who I am. She does not believe me when I tell her we were worried about her and brought her here so that we could take care of her. I try to be honest and tell her she cannot take care of herself, but she argues, and I feel like the bad guy.

I am sad. I am tired of the coronavirus. I am upset that I have had cancer in the middle of a pandemic. I am disgusted with politicians and the division in our country. I am disappointed in society. I am worried about my family members and my dogs. I am worried, and I am mustering up all I can to be faithful and strong and positive. It is exhausting.

So, I had a mini meltdown, ate one of my favorite comfort food meals, spaghetti, and settled in for mindless TV time watching *The Bachelor*.

Tue / 2021 January 12 / Journal Entry

"The undertaking of a new action brings new strength."
Richard L. Evans

Finally...a good night's sleep. I felt refreshed after sleeping and taking a shower. My current struggle is that I feel caught between a rock and a hard place with Mamal. I need to let go of feeling responsible to fix everything, be in charge of everything, and do everything. I do not want to feel animosity toward her or her decisions. I do not want anyone to judge me for what I feel, do, or say.

I need to pray and trust God. He loves me. He loves her. He has a plan. God can fix this; I cannot.

I had an appointment with Dr. Hughes. Today was one month since my reconstructive surgery. I gave her a dozen pink cupcakes. She asked me about my pain level. I told her I had not taken any pain meds since my second day at home.

She was surprised I could sit up and stand straight and raise my arms above my head. She said many of her patients are still at a forty-five-degree angle and still on pain meds two months after surgery. I cannot imagine trying to live a normal life with a long-drawn-out recovery. I feel very blessed. I drove home with the radio blasting Pink and Eminem. I have not jammed out to the radio like that for months.

Today's Bible study topic was "Why God Gave Choice." We have choices every day to trust God or go our own way. God is God. God created man. Man is not God. Man is not capable of being God. God wants a relationship with man, but man has to stay in his lane. The trouble begins when man wants to be God and when other men treat a man, or worship a man, as if he was God, with no regard for God.

Again, we finished the study with our focus word prayer:

Dear Lord,
We pray that we will DEVOTE our time and hearts to this Bible study so that we can CHANGE and GROW in order to COMPLETE a study of your work to further our relationship with you. Amen.

Mon / 2021 January 18 / Journal Entry

Martin Luther King Holiday, "Freedom!"

I think Mamal was up at the crack of dawn today. She was so excited that she was going home, and Michael was coming to town.

Jose and I had a nice dinner, just the two of us. We watched mindless TV, *The Bachelor*. With Mamal gone, the heater is off. We can breathe again. A Kroger commercial keeps playing over and over again. It plays a version of Flo Rida's "Low." Every time it would come on when Mamal was here, she would tap her feet and clap her hands. I miss her already.

Trump was impeached for the second time. COVID-19 cases are still rising. The vaccine is slowly getting administered. Facebook memes suggest that Chick-fil-A or Amazon should get involved and administer the vaccine to get it out faster and more efficiently.

Wed / 2021 January 20 / Journal Entry

Inauguration Day

It is Inauguration Day. As a woman, I felt it appropriate to celebrate the inauguration of the new president and new madame vice president with my pearls.

I am ready for the next chapter for our country. Lady Gaga sang the National Anthem which brought tears to my eyes. Jennifer Lopez sang "This Land is My Land" and "God Bless America," and I cried. History was made when the first female vice president, Kamala Harris, was sworn in by Justice Sonia Sotomayor, and I cried. Joe Biden was sworn in by Chief Justice Roberts, and I cried. I cried tears of joy and hope.

Joe Biden's speech was full of hope, unity, and respect. He asked for a silent prayer for the 400,000 lives lost to COVID-19. Garth Brooks sang "Amazing Grace." Amanda Gorman, the National Youth Poet Laureate, recited "The Hill We Climb." Democracy prevailed, and we had a peaceful transfer of power. I received my copy of *Vogue* magazine with Madame Vice President Harris on the cover with her pearls and Converse tennis shoes.

After dinner, we watched *Celebrate America* with music from Bruce Springsteen, Bon Jovi, Justin Timberlake, The Foo Fighters, John Legend, Tim McGraw, Tyler Hubbard, Demi Lovato and Katy Perry. It was a celebration of essential workers, teachers, and health care heroes. The evening ended with a silhouette of the President and First

Lady, Joe and Jill Biden, hugging each other as they watched the night sky light up with fireworks.

"The Hill We Climb" (excerpt)
Amanda Gorman

For there is always light,
if only we're brave enough to see it.
If only we're brave enough to be it.

Tue / 2021 January 26 / Journal Entry

I attended the virtual Bible study. We discussed how God has met us through physical, mental, emotional, and spiritual suffering. We shared where we currently need God to rescue us in our lives.

One of my goals this year is to read the Bible. I finished Genesis, which I have done many times before. I got busy reading Exodus. I think it is a boring section to just read on its own. The Bible Project video resources helped me understand for the first time the significance and symbolism of the story.

Fri / 2021 January 29 / Journal Entry

"I want to organize my life, not my clutter."
Unknown

I am interested in creating a capsule wardrobe and purging most of the clothes from my closet. I figured out how to organize my photo albums on my phone. I cannot stop thinking about minimalism. I posted about minimalizing your Facebook feed by hiding, snoozing, or unfriending people and ads.

I am concerned that the pandemic deaths continue to rise. Some people continue to be adamant about their right to go without masks. Some of my Facebook friends shame those of us who wear masks and call us "sheep." More and more of my Facebook friends have posted that they know someone who has had COVID-19 and died.

I watched *The Social Dilemma* and a series about QAnon called *The Story of Q*. It was eye opening to see how the big tech companies and the internet conspiracy theorists influence world events.

The news reported that we have hit another coronavirus milestone. There have been 100 million confirmed cases of COVID-19 worldwide. The United States has reached twenty-five million confirmed cases of COVID-19. President Biden is warning that we will probably hit half a million deaths soon. The vaccine roll out is still unpredictable.

february

Tue / 2021 February 2 / My Facebook Post

Lord, it's me again. My prayer is short and sincere. Forgive me Lord. I try to live by the Golden Rule and treat others as I would like to be treated. Please guide me to do better. My words, whether spoken or written, matter. My beliefs and opinions are true to me, but I never wish to be disrespectful or hurt someone who holds a different view from me. Lord, I know better. Help me do better. Amen

This is the point of my prayer: I do not need to wait on or rely on someone else to do something about injustice. I do not need to depend on a miracle to wipe out sorrow and suffering. Why? Because I am God's miracle. He provided me with everything I need to be part of the solution, to add value, to be the change, to make a difference, to get into good trouble, to spread the good news, and to do what Jesus would do.

Wed / 2021 February 3 / Journal Entry

Dad called to let me know that both he and Rosie were notified they have appointments to get their COVID-19 vaccine shots this week. Jose and I are still waiting patiently for our notification.

Thu / 2021 February 4 / Journal Entry

I spent the day in a virtual leadership conference with Raise Your Hand Texas. Normally, we would be in a lovely conference center with everything, including the hotel rooms, provided by RYHT. It is an indulgent and inspiring experience, but I am not going to lie, I am a fan of virtual conferencing from home. I do not miss driving four to five hours to San Antonio, Houston, or Austin.

Fri / 2021 February 5 / Journal Entry

Kat is thinking about having a baby shower. We are not sure how it would work during a pandemic, the vaccine rollout, and keeping her and the baby safe. Kyla traveled to Florida for a chiropractor's conference. It makes me nervous. Dad and Rosie got their first COVID-19 vaccine shots today. Thank goodness!

Sun / 2021 February 7 / Journal Entry

The Super Bowl is on. There was a moment of silence for the 440,000 lives lost due to COVID-19 in the United States. Sad emoji. Health care workers made up a large portion of the socially distanced audience. Normally, we would have invited the kids over for Super Bowl Sunday, but this year it was just the two of us.

Wed / 2021 February 10 / Journal Entry

The weather is getting very cold. We made a trip to Walmart and Central Market to beat the snowmageddon-panicked shoppers and the last-minute Valentine's crowd this weekend.

Thu / 2021 February 11 / Journal Entry

Today was a "snow day" due to icy conditions and freezing temperatures. There were massive accidents on the roadways. There was a hundred-car pileup in Fort Worth. At least five people were killed. I spent the day watching Trump's impeachment trial.

Sat / 2021 February 13 / Journal Entry

All 254 counties in Texas are under some sort of winter weather alert. The entire state of Oklahoma and Arkansas are under alerts, too.

Sun / 2021 February 14 / Journal Entry

Wintery weather arrived. Several inches of snow blew in overnight.

There are power outages everywhere. The morning temperature was zero. The weather report is predicting another round of freezing snow and rain.

Mon / 2021 February 15 / Journal Entry

President's Day

We have been fortunate to have had electricity and heat all day. Mamal has not. I tried calling her at 8:00 a.m. Her landline was busy, so I had to assume she had lost power. I texted her neighbor, Tina. Power had been out since 1:30 a.m. I called the Arlington Police Department non-emergency number. They drove by and checked on her.

Kat lost power off and on throughout the day in Little Elm. So did Dad in Fairview. I sent text messages to my mentees and the kids about dripping faucets so their pipes do not freeze. Schools and businesses are closed, partially due to the holiday and some due to the weather. Many schools announced last Friday that they would have virtual classes if the weather closed the campuses. There are so many power outages, even virtual classes have become a challenge.

Tues / 2021 February 16 / Journal Entry

This morning the temperature was zero degrees. The sun was out, but the wind chill was below zero. The weather report predicted another round of freezing snow and rain, so we decided to take advantage of the window of time and drove to Arlington to get Mamal. Her phone was not working at her house, and she had been without power for thirty-two hours! We packed the truck with bottles of water and extra blankets. We drove slowly. The highway had one good lane all the way to Arlington.

When we arrived, she was sitting in her chair bundled in blankets. She did not hear us come into her house. The thermostat said 43 degrees. She had not eaten. We packed her bag and drove her to our house.

Wed / 2021 February 17 / Journal Entry

Happy Birthday, Kat!

"Climate is what we expect. Weather is what we get."
Mark Twain

It's official. Snowmageddon 2021 is now called SNOWVID-21. We received even more snow last night, but we were lucky the ice storm passed by us. Work and school were canceled. We were fortunate to have electricity, food, and water. Mamal was with us, safe and sound, and we enjoyed a warm breakfast and a toasty lunch.

In the afternoon, we had hundreds of robins visit the backyard. They covered the yaupon holly trees. It was an unusual site, and several neighbors texted me about it. Once they flew away, I saw that they were eating the berries off of the trees. There are hardly any leaves left. Obviously, the robins were looking for food. I decided to take advantage of the snow and build snow people in our zero gravity chairs. I gave them hats, scarves, sunglasses, and blankets. I posted a picture of them with the caption "SNOWVID-2021 —the snuggle is real." I saw a great snow hack on Facebook to remove snow from dog fur...use a kitchen whisk. Brilliant!

Thu / 2021 February 18 / Journal Entry

139 hours of temperatures below freezing

My morning routine since SNOWVID begins with letting the dogs out, which with freezing temperatures, requires a lot of encouragement for them to go outside and do their business. Then I whisk the snow off their legs and dry their feet. I light the fire, turn on the TV, and open the blinds. I shower and dress before anyone else wakes up. Today I made crescent rolls, maple brown sugar oatmeal, sausage links, and grapefruit for breakfast.

After we got Mamal settled in the chair by the fire, Jose and I went for a walk on the trail. It was quiet and pretty. We saw a family sliding on cardboard down a snow-covered hill. The ponds and creek were frozen. The squirrels were digging for buried nuts. We saw several cardinals. Their red wings stood out against the snowy woods. We saw three Texas vultures feasting on a frozen armadillo. We saw a few frozen birds and a frozen mouse. We have experienced record-breaking freezing temperatures. We saw a few snow people that had been built in the yards in the neighborhood.

We made lunch and ventured out to Walmart. The milk, eggs, meat, chips, produce, and frozen food were gone. Shelves were bare. There was no bottled water. Many people have had pipes freeze and burst in their homes and businesses. The City of Arlington had a main water line break, so there is no water to most homes in Arlington. People who do have water have been told to boil it if they have electricity. I cannot imagine what would have happened had we not brought Mamal to our house.

The TV shows daily Electric Reliability Council of Texas (ERCOT) briefings, but they are full of energy-tech jargon. Today, Republican Senator from Texas, Ted Cruz, was spotted on an airplane on his way to Cancun. Social media roasted him for leaving his fellow Texans in the midst of a global pandemic and statewide disaster nightmare while he went on vacation.

We made calls to check in with the family. The sun came out, and the snow started to melt. Tonight, we will have temperatures in the 20's, so everything that melted will refreeze, which will create cobblestone ice and black ice and cause problems tomorrow.

NASA's rover, Perseverance, made history and landed on Mars today.

Fri / 2021 February 19 / Journal Entry

Happy Birthday Rosie!

The sun is out, but the temperatures are still below freezing across much of the state. The snow is starting to melt. Now that people are getting electricity back on, after days without it, water pipes are thawing, bursting, and flooding. Mamal keeps telling us to take her home. Even though she is in front of the TV, she does not understand the weather, power, or water issues. We stayed in the house today, but we had three square meals. School has been shut down all week, so next week will be back to business.

Sat / 2021 February 20 / Journal Entry

Mamal is not having a good day. She has been fussing and cussing, which is unusual for her. She said she wet herself during the night, but I did not find any evidence. I think she dreams or hallucinates. I tried to get her to let me help her take a shower, but she refused. I know she does not like to get undressed because she gets so cold. She moves slowly, so it is difficult for her to get her clothes back on. She is modest and stubborn and does not want me or anyone else to help her. She would rather not fool with it.

She claims she has taken a "whore bath" and washed the hot spots, but again, I have not seen any evidence of it. I finally convinced her to sponge off after I set up the bathroom and set out clean clothes for her. It was a battle. Her neighbor texted me to report the power was on, the water was restored, and they are no longer required to boil water. No telling what we will find when we go back to her house. We left all the faucets dripping, so I hope her pipes did not burst.

Jose and I took a long walk around the neighborhood. The streets were mostly thawed. We walked on the golf course and discovered a unique snow sculpture of a giant penis and testicles. Major lifted his leg and left a yellow spot in the exact area where the pee hole would be. It was vulgar, but it was funny. We needed a good belly laugh. The ponds are still frozen, but the dogs were happy, and I enjoyed the fresh air and sunshine.

Sun / 2021 February 21 / Journal Entry

Day 503 of sobriety
Day 346 of COVID-19

"As with the butterfly, adversity is necessary to build character."
Joseph Wirthlin

The temperature shot up to seventy-two degrees today! It was lovely. I made a big breakfast, then we took Mamal home. Her house was colder on the inside than it was outside. The faucets were still dripping, so thankfully, she had running water and no broken pipes. We cranked up her heat and got her settled. Michael will be in town tomorrow. He called and admitted it is getting harder and harder for him to come every two weeks to stay with her.

We stopped at Central Market and shopped for fresh produce, milk, and eggs. It was busy, but all the shelves were fully stocked. We took the dogs on a two-mile walk. There was hardly any evidence of SNOWVID 2021 left behind. It is hard to believe that five days ago the temperature was below zero, and today it is in the seventies. That is Texas weather for you.

Kat called to tell us she is having a baby boy, and his name is Jensen Carson.

Fri / 2021 February 26 / Journal Entry

While we were at Walmart, I got a notification that I am eligible for my first vaccine shot next week.

march

Mon / 2021 March 1 / Journal Entry

Day 354 of COVID-19

I drove to work for the first time in almost a year. It has been 354 days since I worked with students in person. That is the longest stretch since I started teaching in 1986.

In order to enter a building on campus, I had to go through COVID safety protocols. I had to sign in to the Appian app, answer COVID-19 questions, and receive a ticket to enter a building. All building doors are locked and limited to one entrance with a person at the entrance who scans your ticket before you are admitted inside. Water fountains are taped off or covered. Bathrooms are restricted to two people at a time. Face masks are required. COVID-19 protocol posters are everywhere. There are very few people on campus.

I started my study hall gig today on an empty campus. Nine students spread out in a lecture hall that seats 100 people. It was a quiet and boring four hours. The students worked on their scheduled classes on their laptops while I supervised them. The study hall provides them with a quiet place to work and uninterrupted internet.

It was an unusual day to be in a classroom with students. They were seated six feet apart and were wearing masks. I reflected on my employment at Dallas College and Richland Collegiate High School. The opportunity to be a part of these institutions during my retirement, my breast cancer, and the pandemic has been a blessing. I am forever grateful that I was able to continue my employment as the Service Learning Coordinator, and I feel blessed that I was able to do my work from home.

Tues / 2021 March 2 / Journal Entry

*Listen O Israel! The Lord is our God, the Lord alone.
(Deuteronomy 6:4)*

I was able to finish reading Deuteronomy today. It is the farthest I have ever gotten in reading the Bible. The weekly Bible study with The Bible Chicks is an opportunity to learn and understand God's promises. When we share our weekly hour of devotion, the lessons seem so personal and simple to process. But as I walk through each week's challenges, it is easy to forget those messages of hope.

God is faithful. He knows there will be bumps along the way. I understand God has a plan for me and Jose. God has never failed me before, so why would it be any different now?

A younger me would not have thought this way. I like to think I have grown wiser with age, and that wisdom gives me the strength and confidence I need to maintain this positive attitude. A sense of calm and peace takes over when I accept that God has a plan for me. It is His plan, not my plan.

His blessings may not come while I am alive but may be what is in store after I die. To do this, to practice this trust and faith in God, I must understand what God has spoken to us in the Bible. I must set aside time to study His word and His message to me -- not look for words that fit my message to myself.

Love the Lord, your God, with all your heart and all your soul and all your strength. And, love your neighbor as yourself. (Luke 10:27)

Wed / 2021 March 3 / Journal Entry

"As you grow older, you will discover that you have two hands, one for helping yourself—the other for helping others."
Maya Angelou

Jose went to Fair Park for his first vaccine. He said there were over 500 cars in line for the first shot. There were ten lines of cars.

He had a QR code that was scanned, and within fifteen minutes he drove through and had the shot in his arm. He had to wait fifteen minutes afterward before he was released to make sure he did not have any adverse reaction to the vaccine. There was another entrance for people receiving the second dose. Michelle got her appointment today. My appointment is set for tomorrow.

Thu / 2021 March 4 / Journal Entry

I was nervous and excited to get my first vaccine shot today. I had to drive to downtown Dallas to one of the many Baylor hospital buildings. At first, I was worried because there was a long line of cars snaking through the parking lot just to get to the building. I received the Pfizer vaccine, then sat for fifteen minutes to make sure I did not have adverse reactions. I was overwhelmed with emotion when I got my shot. It was such a relief and almost a year to the day when we shut down.

I picked up lunch and drove to Richland. The police were directing a long line of cars in the Richland parking lot. It looked like a vaccine hub, but it was the North Texas Food Bank distributing food. I had time to enjoy lunch by the lake. The weather was seventy degrees and beautiful. Two geese came up to me and stared at me while I ate. Then we were joined by a squirrel. I could have reached out and touched all three of them. I think they were happy to see a person!

Our dove couple has returned, and Jose spotted the barn swallows last night.

We took the dogs for a walk on the trail. It was very quiet except for the squirrels. We actually heard two different squirrels vocalize. We spotted several painted rocks. Are they a sign of spring? The woods are starting to get green.

Fri / 2021 March 5 / Journal Entry

My arm, shoulder and neck are sore from the vaccine, but it is a small price to pay to avoid getting the deadly disease.

Sun / 2021 March 7 / Journal Entry

"Every woman's success should be an inspiration to another. We're strongest when we cheer each other on."
Serena Williams

Last summer, I felt very confident and capable of creating a virtual service learning (VSL) curriculum on my own from my house during a pandemic. Working from home, taking daily walks, enjoying patio time, hunting faerie villages, and photographing painted rocks all helped contribute to the creative juices. I used the hours to research, write, edit, plan, and revise a VSL fall curriculum. I felt very good about the product I presented, and I felt even better as students contacted me to ask questions and complete assignments.

In November, I had been recovering from a double mastectomy. I was weeks away from reconstructive surgery and the holidays. Pandemic cases were on the rise, especially after Thanksgiving, so the spring semester VSL curriculum needed to be developed and finalized. I felt happy and grateful that I had planned ahead, and I had material to develop a new and improved spring version of the fall curriculum.

Fortunately, my self-esteem was high, so it fueled my creativity, or perhaps it was vice versa, and my creativity was high, so it fueled my esteem. I felt good and got the job done. Or...I got the job done and felt good. After making tweaks on the fall curriculum, I posted the spring curriculum, and we are currently halfway through the semester.

It is six days from the one-year anniversary of the shutdown. I will always remember the date because it fell on Friday the thirteenth.

Tue / 2021 March 9 / Journal Entry

"The Bible is meant to be bread for daily use, not cake for special occasions."
Suzanne Woods Fisher

I had a great virtual Bible study with the Bible Chicks. We prayed and learned more about the topic, "Understanding Ancient Law." There are over 600 ancient laws that were given to ancient Israel. This is not a behavior code for us. These instructions are how to relate to God and then to the community.

By studying God's word, I have been reminded repeatedly that I am not in charge. God is. Wow! What a gift! I can let go of my own sense of specialness and let God be in control. Well, I can't "let" God do anything. I accept that God is in control. And by the way, who else would I choose to be in charge?

I made a commitment to make time to study every week and show up to a Bible study to discuss, share, and pray. I take time to prepare notes and answer reflection questions. I come with an open mind and heart to learn. I have learned to spend more time with God. I have learned to appreciate time with friends. I have come to realize, on more than one occasion, the lessons were meant for me at this time.

Thu / 2021 March 11 / Journal Entry

One of the things I noticed during the past year was Mamal's lack of understanding about the global pandemic. In many ways, it was a blessing. Her world, her schedule, and her behavior did not change much due to the pandemic. She has no transportation to go anywhere, so staying at home is normal. She has no friends, so isolation is her habit. She rarely watches television or the news, so the news has little effect on her. Her lack of understanding does not negatively impact her. Perhaps that has helped me to understand her wish—to stay in her home—even better.

We have similar traits, habits, and behaviors, she and I. I can understand who I am by understanding who she is. I am her blood. I will be much like her.

Fri / 2021 March 12 / Journal Entry

Happy Anniversary!

Attitude is a choice, and I choose to be positive. My positive attitude has made a difference in the success or failure of Virtual Service Learning (VSL). By being proactive, instead of reactive, I can plan and troubleshoot so students, parents, and administrators are not burdened with unnecessary service-learning stress. My attitude is can-do. I can figure out a way to make it work. My attitude is full of gratitude. I am grateful that I have had the opportunity to use my talents, skills, and experience to run this program while working from home.

I truly hope that students will have a better understanding of service learning than they did prior to the pandemic through the VSL curriculum. I was very intentional when I selected activities for them to do from the safety of their home. I wanted them to come away with an attitude of helping others in a variety of ways that would ultimately help them develop good citizenship and kindness.

So, despite the shutdown of school campuses, the sixty-hour service-learning graduation requirement has continued. My job as the coordinator has not really changed. I still look for opportunities for students to serve. I still track student hours. I still order awards. Over the past year, the location of my workspace and the daily tasks have transformed. The agencies where the students used to volunteer may have transformed. The safety protocols have changed for sure.

I am proud of my work, contribution, and experience. I believe the curriculum is designed to make students better, more thoughtful people who will contribute to society in a positive way.

The beauty of the VSL curriculum is that it provides opportunities and choices. It allows for creativity. It relies on students to decide how much time and effort they want to invest and what kind of reward or outcome they want to seek. They have the power to choose their plan. They also have the ability to alter their plan if they need to or choose to do so. Isn't this the point? Students are learning and experiencing their own empowerment.

Well, I would love to pat myself on the back and take all the credit for this amazing VSL program. The reality is, I had very little to do with it. I was just the vessel. God made it all happen.

Sat / 2021 March 13 / Journal Entry

Coronaversary

It was one year ago today that the World Health Organization announced the global pandemic, thus the name, Coronaversary. President Biden held a memorial service for all the lives lost from the pandemic. Over 500,159 lives have been lost in the United States. That is almost as many lives lost in World War I, World War II, the Korean, and Vietnam Wars combined (534,370). It equates to approximately one life per minute lost last year. Flags are flying half-staff to honor victims of the pandemic.

Tonight, we watched President Biden give his first speech to the nation:

A collective suffering. A collective sacrifice. A year filled with the loss of life—and the loss of living for all of us. We've seen frontline and essential workers risking their lives, sometimes losing them, to save and help others. Researchers and scientists racing for a vaccine. You lost your job. You closed your business. Facing eviction, homelessness, hunger, a loss of control, and, maybe worst of all, a loss of hope. Watching a generation of children who may be set back up to a year or more—because they've not been in school—because of their loss of learning.

Weddings, birthdays, graduations—all the things that needed to happen but didn't. The first date. The family reunions. The Sunday night rituals.

But this virus has kept us apart.

Grandparents haven't seen their children or grandchildren. Parents haven't seen their kids. Kids haven't seen their friends. The things we used to do that always filled us with joy have become the things we couldn't do and broke our hearts.

Too often, we've turned against one another.

A mask—the easiest thing to do to save lives—sometimes it divides us. States pitted against one another instead of working with each other. Vicious hate crimes against Asian Americans, who have been attacked, harassed, blamed, and scapegoated. At this very moment, so many of them—our fellow Americans—they're on the frontlines of this pandemic, trying to save lives, and still, still, they are forced to live in fear for their lives just walking down streets in America. It's wrong, it's un-American, and it must stop.

The only way to get our lives back, to get our economy back on track, is to beat the virus. But this is one of the most complex operations we've ever undertaken as a nation in a long time. We've been working with the vaccine manufacturers—Pfizer, Moderna, Johnson & Johnson—to manufacture and purchase hundreds of millions of doses of these three safe, effective vaccines. These companies, competitors, have come together for the good of the nation, and they should be applauded for it.

And we're mobilizing thousands of vaccinators to put the vaccine in one's arm. Calling on active-duty military, FEMA, retired doctors and nurses, administrators, and others to administer the shots. And we've been creating more places to get the shots. We've made it possible for you to get a vaccine at nearly one — any one of nearly 10,000 pharmacies across the country, just like you get your flu shot.

We're also working with governors and mayors, in red states and blue states, to set up and support nearly 600 federally supported vaccination centers that administer hundreds of thousands of shots per day. You can drive up to a stadium or a large parking lot, get your shot, never leave your car, and drive home in less than an hour. We've been deploying and we will deploy more mobile vehicles and pop-up clinics to meet you where you live so those who are least able to get the vaccine are able to get it. We continue to work on making at-home testing available.

With the passage of the American Rescue Plan—and I thank again the House and Senate for passing it—and my announcement last month of a plan to vaccinate teachers and school staff, including bus drivers, we can accelerate the massive, nationwide effort to reopen our schools safely and meet my goal, that I stated at the same time about 100 million shots, of opening the majority of K-8 schools in my first 100 days in office. This is going to be the number one priority of my new Secretary of Education, Miguel Cardona.

But to get there, we can't let our guard down. The scientists have made clear that things may get worse again as new variants of the virus spread. Because even if we devote every resource we have, beating this virus and getting back to normal depends on national unity.

I signed into law the American Rescue Plan, an historic piece of legislation that delivers immediate relief to millions of people. It includes $1,400 in direct rescue checks—payments. We are bound together by the loss and the pain of the days that have gone by. But we're also bound together by the hope and the possibilities of the days in front of us.

Tue / 2021 March 16 / Journal Entry

Barbara and I discussed this week's Bible study topic, "Making Sense of Divine Violence." It focused on the book of Joshua and encouraged the reader to look deeper into the greater context of the battles and destruction. Context helps the reader understand the true message and guards against taking things literally or isolating verses. The reflection questions asked us to think about violence in our lives. We discussed police shootings, attacks on Asian Americans, and the border crisis.

Barbara and I desperately want to be allies to people in marginalized groups, but sometimes we do not know how to do it. Thank goodness Jesus led by example. We said a prayer to help us demonstrate love and allyship.

Sat / 2021 March 20 / Journal Entry

Social media is a powerful platform. The power of the words and pictures I choose to post must be intentional. God has provided me with many resources. It is my goal that I will be able to provide wisdom, guidance, inspiration, and fuel to empower others to be better, know better, and do better.

Sat / 2021 March 20 / My Facebook Post

Hello Lord! It's me again. Thank you for this glorious spring equinox. The day and night are of equal length, and I am grateful for all the signs of new life around us. Thank you for vaccines. Thank you for masks. Thank you for hope. Thank you for upcoming, exciting life events: a graduation, a weekend getaway, a wedding, a grandbaby, a milestone birthday, and HOPEFULLY, with your good grace, holiday celebrations.

Lord, I pray that your healing hand will continue to curtail this pandemic. Guide us all to make wise, kind decisions that will keep us healthy and safe so we can praise you and your countless blessings. This is a lovely day and night that you have made. Amen.

Sun / 2021 March 21 / Journal Entry

Christian's birthday!

We watched *We Are Texas* on Matthew McConaughey's YouTube channel. It is a fundraiser for the devastation caused by Uri, the SNOWVID winter storm. The event raised nearly eight million dollars and featured artists and performers from the Lone Star State.

Mon / 2021 March 22 / Journal Entry

I had an early doctor's appointment with Dr. Lemmon. It had been rescheduled due to SNOWVID. They took "after" pictures of my breasts and belly since my reconstruction surgery in December.

Dr. Lemmon said he needed to go in and drain some fluid and do surgical revision on my scars. He will also do some work to make my breasts more symmetrical because two different surgeons worked on each side of my body during the breast reconstruction. It will be a day surgery, and it is covered by my insurance since it is cancer related.

Tue / 2021 March 23 / Journal Entry

The reflection question for Bible study was particularly powerful this week, "How often do you consider God's feelings when you make choices?"

Honestly, I do not think I have ever considered God's feelings. I have not thought about it that way. I do think about the consequences of my choices on me, but not how they affect God. The last line in Judges 21:25 says, "Every man did that which he saw was right in his own eyes."

This reminds me of our world right now with the pandemic, masks, social media, vaccines, and privilege.

Thu / 2021 March 25 / Journal Entry

Jose and I got the second dose of the vaccine. This time there were no lines. We parked right up front, walked in, got our shots, and headed out after a fifteen-minute wait to make sure there were no adverse reactions. By the afternoon, my neck and shoulders were stiff and sore. I started getting grumpy. I took Advil and relaxed on the couch.

Sun / 2021 March 28 / Journal Entry

Jose got a text message about cheap crawfish for sale for $2.75 per pound. He decided to host an impromptu crawfish boil. He called the girls and did all the cooking. The weather was nice, so we sat outside.

It was the first time we got to spend time with Kat, Jordan, Taylor, and Kyla in over a year. We talked about our grandbaby to be, who I call Gummy Bear. We chatted about upcoming wedding plans. Jose enjoyed cooking and hosting. The kids enjoyed the food. The dogs enjoyed the weather. It was a great day!

The pandemic has given me many blessings and opportunities to get in touch with and develop my spirituality. I have created routines that help me take notice of God's creations and gifts. I have marveled at so many things during the pandemic, and I have counted my blessings.

I feel spiritual. I feel connected to the Holy Spirit, and I am not afraid.

Mon / 2021 March 29 / Journal Entry

The Derek Chauvin trial began today. It is being televised due to COVID-19. I watched the opening arguments and the nine-minute video of Officer Chauvin pressing his knee on George Floyd's neck. It was disturbing. Chauvin did not "let up" or "get up" for nine minutes.

Tue / 2021 March 30 / Journal Entry

I worked at Richland and ran into an old friend. He was so excited to see me and must have hugged me forty times. I have not been hugged by someone other than Jose in over a year.

The CDC has released new guidelines that two weeks after being fully vaccinated, it is safe to gather indoors in small groups without masks with other vaccinated people or with unvaccinated family members who are not considered high risk. I met virtually with the Bible Chicks and our discussion centered around the story of Ruth and "loyal love." We talked about God's "impartial mercy" towards all humanity and that we should have the same for one another. And finally, we were encouraged by "relentless hope." No matter how difficult life can be, God is always there.

april

Mon / 2021 April 5 / Journal Entry

I was at Richardson West Junior High School by 8:00 a.m. to observe one of the UTeach student teachers. It was the first time I observed a teacher in person since the pandemic began.

Tue / 2021 April 6 / Journal Entry

Our Bible study topic was "When You Feel Powerless" and the book of I Samuel. I do not need to worry about my power because God is all powerful. I was reminded that when I feel powerless, I can turn it over to God and be encouraged that He is working on it. Much of the discussion revolved around I Samuel 2: 1-10 also known as Hannah's prayer:

"Then Hannah prayed and said: 'My heart rejoices in the Lord; in the Lord my horn is lifted high. My mouth boasts over my enemies, for I delight in your deliverance. There is no one holy like the Lord; there is no one besides you; there is no Rock like our God. Do not keep talking so proudly or let your mouth speak with such arrogance, for the Lord is a God who knows, and by him deeds are weighed. The bows of the warriors are broken, but those who stumble are armed with strength. Those who were full hired themselves out for food, but those who were hungry are hungry no more. She who was barren has borne seven children, but she who has had many sons pines away. The Lord brings death and makes alive; he brings down to the grave and raises up. The Lord sends poverty and wealth; he humbles, and he exalts. He raises the poor from the dust and lifts the needy from the ash heap; he seats them with princes and has them inherit a throne of honor. For the foundations of the earth are the Lord's; on them he has set the world. He will guard the feet of his faithful servants, but the wicked will be silenced in the place of darkness. It is not by strength that one prevails; those who oppose the Lord will be broken.

The Most High will thunder from heaven; the Lord will judge the ends of the earth. He will give strength to his king and exalt the horn of his anointed."

Wed / 2021 April 7 / My Facebook Post

Lord, it's me again. Sometimes I feel anxious. I lie awake, and my heart races. My brain starts spinning, and I grow more anxious as I try to figure out the source of my worry. It can be debilitating. But there are other times when I am at great peace. I look around, and I am in awe. I am grateful. Lord, help me remember you are always with me. You are with me when I feel like all is lost, and you are with me when I feel like all is right. Lord, you know my heart. Hear my prayers, and hear my praises. Amen

Mon / 2021 April 12 / Journal Entry

This is the second Easter that many families will not gather at church or for in-person holiday celebrations.

Sat / 2021 April 17 / Journal Entry

Jose and I finally took a weekend road trip. We decided to go to Waco so he could visit the sites I toured on my cousin's trip a year ago. We were finally able to board the dogs.

We chose to visit sites that required masks, limited visitors, or were outside. Normally the hotel would serve a complimentary breakfast, but due to COVID-19, it is grab and go. We grabbed muffins, coffee, and water and watched the news.

The news reports three million people have died from the coronavirus. Over two million vaccine shots in arms have been administered. The CDC announced that fully vaccinated people can go without masks whether inside or outside. As people begin to go back to work and school, many pets are experiencing anxiety when they are left alone at home.

President Joe Biden mailed letters regarding the American Rescue Plan and direct payments of $1,400 per person for pandemic relief.

Tue / 2021 April 20 / Journal Entry

The Derek Chauvin verdict came in today. He was found guilty on all three counts: second-degree unintentional murder, third-degree murder, and second-degree manslaughter.

Fri / 2021 April 23 / Journal Entry

I cleaned out our closets, kitchen cabinets, bathroom cabinets, garage, and attic. It is time to get this minimalist goal under way!

Sat / 2021 April 24 / Journal Entry

The early bird gets the worm. I opened the garage door at 8:00 a.m. By 10:30 a.m. we were shutting down. I made $410 selling everything for $1.00.

We took what little was left of our merchandise to a donation site. Project Garage Sale is checked off the list. The Minimalism Project has just begun.

may

Tue / 2021 May 4 / Journal Entry

May the 4th Be with You!
Looking Fourth-ward

Look at the birds of the air. They do not sow or reap or stow away in barns, and yet your heavenly Father feeds them. Are you not much more valuable than they?
(Matt. 6:23)

Manny, the chameleon, made an appearance on the brick wall. Fred and Ethel, the barn swallows, are back with baby birds. I joyfully watched the four baby barn swallows wait as Fred and Ethel took turns catching insects and feeding each baby, one at a time.

Arnold the hummingbird is back. He pollinates the purple salvia plants with purpose. He touches every flower, collects the sweet nectar, and carries it to its destination to grow. He returns, over and over, because his work is not yet done.

Tue / 2021 May 4 / My Facebook Post

Lord, it's me again. It's been over a year since I have been in the safety of my cocoon. But now, like many others, I am emerging. I am breaking out and spreading my wings. Some days I will stay close and stay guarded. Other days I will be adventurous and travel many miles. Sometimes I will fly solo. More and more, I will gather with others.

I recognize the blessings and gifts you have bestowed upon me. You have provided these opportunities, these resources, this life. My prayer, Lord, is that you will continue to keep us all safe in this new season and chapter of our lives. I pray that we take time each day to honor you and gaze at your garden, smell the flowers, feel the breeze, listen to the bird's song, and taste the sweet nectar of life. Amen

I met with the Bible Chicks virtually to discuss "What God Does About Suffering." When a person or community or nation is suffering, look for glimmers of hope. Look for the helpers who provide justice, mercy, and love. We are called to be gardeners for the benefit of others and ourselves. We are to model ourselves after Jesus, who served and loved his enemies and his friends. We are to practice patience, kindness, love, and self-control. Through daily tasks, we can move God's world forward.

Fri / 2021 May 7 / Journal Entry

I watched the UTD graduation ceremony on Zoom. I continue to keep this journal because we are still in the COVID-19 crisis. Some countries like India and Japan are experiencing surges of cases due to new variants. While many adults in the United States have been vaccinated, others refuse to get the shots. We do not know how long the vaccine will be effective. On the outside, things look like they are getting back to normal. I hope we do not experience a setback.

Sat / 2021 May 8 / Journal Entry

"To the world you are a mother, but to your family you are the world." J. L. Tate

Kat's baby shower was today. About thirty family members from both sides of the family came. Everyone wore masks because Kat is not vaccinated since she is pregnant.

Tue / 2021 May 11 / Journal Entry

Today's Bible study was "The Message of the Prophets." I had never studied the prophets, and when I heard the word "prophet," I thought of fortune tellers. Prophets are not fortune tellers. They were people who had encounters with God and spoke on His behalf. The prophets warned us and provided us with hope. God knows that man is hardheaded and needs constant reminders to choose God rather than follow our own sinful ways. It is a long passage, but I think it is important.

Hear the word of the Lord, you rulers of Sodom; listen to the instruction of our God, you people of Gomorrah! 'The multitude of your sacrifices—what are they to me?' says the Lord. I have more than enough burnt offerings, of rams and the fat of fattened animals; I have no pleasure in the blood of bulls and lambs and goats. When you come to appear before me, who has asked this of you, this trampling of my courts? Stop bringing meaningless offerings! Your incense is detestable to me. New Moons, Sabbaths and convocations—I cannot bear your worthless assemblies. Your New Moon feasts and your appointed festivals I hate with all my being. They have become a burden to me; I am weary of bearing them. When you spread out your hands in prayer, I hide my eyes from you; even when you offer many prayers, I am not listening. Your hands are full of blood! Wash and make yourselves clean. Take your evil deeds out of my sight; stop doing wrong. Learn to do right; seek justice. Defend the oppressed. Take up the cause of the fatherless; plead the case of the widow. 'Come now, let us settle the matter,' says the Lord. 'Though your sins are like scarlet, they shall be as white as snow; though they are red as crimson, they shall be like wool. If you are willing and obedient, you will eat the good things of the land; but if you resist and rebel, you will be devoured by the sword.' For the mouth of the Lord has spoken.
(Isaiah 1:10-20)

Tue / 2021 May 18 / Journal Entry

"You have always been enough."
Jessica Edouard

During today's virtual Bible study, Kristi stated, "When we are stressed, it is because we listen to the lies that anxiety tells us." Today's lesson was "What Good News Looks Like." Good news looks and sounds like victory, restoration, abundance, blessings, generosity, hope, and healing. The reflection question encouraged me to imagine what the world will look like when God brings renewal. I envision peace, harmony, joy, and a planet that looks like a garden.

So what can I do about my anxiety? I will be aware of the lies that anxiety tries to tell me, and I will pray and stay the course.

Thu / 2021 May 20 / Journal Entry

Jose and I headed to the Ranger game at the new Globe Life Stadium. When we purchased the tickets, there was still a mask mandate in place. Today there were 23,000 people in attendance, most without masks, including us. I felt like I had jumped into the deep end of the ocean. It was surreal.

Sun / 2021 May 23 / Journal Entry

I hosted brunch for my Holly Hills neighbor ladies. Jose calls us the Eastside Pink Ladies. Our menu consisted of Quiche Lorraine, a rainbow charcuterie board with fruits and vegetables, a cheeseboard with nuts, almonds, and crackers, orange and cranberry scones, chocolate truffles, lemon bars, and assorted macarons. It was the first thing that we had all done together, other than Holly Hills Hangouts, during the pandemic. It was nice to entertain in the house.

Tue / 2021 May 25 / Journal Entry

"Some people walk in the rain; others just get wet."
Bob Marley

I felt pretty fussy, but Bible study set me straight and lifted my spirits. Our timely topic was "What God Wants from Us." It is simple. He wants an intimate relationship with us. God loves us like a loving spouse, not a demanding boss.

We were asked to describe what it would look like if we demonstrated our love to God like we demonstrate love to our spouse. Our behavior would demonstrate: trusting Him, spending time with Him, thanking Him, cherishing Him, honoring Him, being faithful to Him, and asking for forgiveness from Him. Our closing prayer to God was simple—help us love You back.

Wed / 2021 May 26 / Journal Entry

I prayed while I drove to work. I spent time with God. I asked for a new attitude. I want to learn and grow from the lessons I learned during the pandemic.

I had a positive conversation with the interim principal about my status at RCHS. She reassured me that I am valuable, and the school is secure. Another friend told me she appreciated my positive posts on Facebook each day. I have to say, I felt like God listened to my prayers and answered them today. It was a great day!

Thu / 2021 May 27 / Journal Entry

"When someone says you can't do it, do it twice and take pictures."
Tami Xiang

I moved all my RCHS boxes and files back to school today. My workspace in Kiowa is ready to go forward. The home office is back to its original design.

Fri / 2021 May 28 / Journal Entry

Beginning of Memorial Day Weekend

The news reports that fifty-nine percent of people twelve years old or older, 166,000,000, have received the vaccine. Masks are no longer required in stores or schools.

Holiday weekend travel has 37,000,000 people on the move. The Transportation Safety Administration (TSA) screened two million people yesterday. Airplanes are eighty to ninety percent full. Gas prices are over $3.00 per gallon nationwide. Movie theaters and summer camps are opening to full capacity. Researchers are searching for the origin of the coronavirus. They have speculated that it was transmitted to humans from bats and that it could have been manufactured and leaked from a lab in China.

It's Memorial Day, and the parades, parks, beaches, and family barbecues are underway. 135,000 fans are at the Indianapolis 500. The Vietnam variant has emerged, and Vietnam has restricted travel.

COVID-19 Statistics:
Confirmed cases worldwide: 169,071,044
Confirmed deaths worldwide: 3,513,320
Confirmed cases in the United States: 33,378,322
Confirmed deaths in the United States: 598,910

june

Tue / 2021 June 1 / Journal Entry

"Don't be afraid of opposition. Remember a kite rises against, not with, the wind."
Hamilton Wright Marble

Today's Bible study topic was "God's Mercy on Our Enemy." One of man's biggest flaws is thinking that our enemies should be, or already are, God's enemies. We must trust God's judgment to love and forgive. We must love our neighbors as we love ourselves, even if they are our enemy. Wow! This is a challenging concept.

Wed / 2021 June 2 / Journal Entry

Summer of Freedom and National Month of Action

As I drove, I prayed to God thanking Him for all the blessings and opportunities He has provided, especially as we get out of the throes of the coronavirus. I asked Him to help me continue to make time to read, study, and pray as my schedule fills up with normal life activities again.

It is sad but true. I just realized that since quarantine, reading, studying, and praying are new activities, not "normal" ones, for me. That got my attention.

We had a belated Memorial Day Holly Hills Hangout with the neighbors. We all chipped in and brought food and fixings for a hamburger and hotdog cook out. There was no rain, and the weather was perfect. It made for a fun evening.

Sat / 2021 June 5 / Journal Entry

"Do the dew."
Simon Lowden

I woke up early. When I raised the blinds of the bedroom window, I could see the dew on all the patio plants. It must have rained early in the morning, but the sun was shining, and it made everything glisten and sparkle like garden diamonds. It was spectacular. I grabbed my phone and experimented with picture taking around the yard for about thirty minutes before the sun got too high. I spent another hour trying different editing tools on my phone.

Tue / 2021 June 8 / My Facebook Post

God, it's me again. Each day I try to stay on the right path. It seems so simple, but there are slippery slopes all around it. Walk with me from point "A" to point "W." Guide me through the challenges along the way. Forgive me when I stumble.
From asking to acknowledging
From breaking down to building up
From cursing to commending
From dreading to dreaming
From envy to empathy
From fuming to forgiving
From grouchy to giddy
From helpless to helpful
From I can't to I will
From joyless to joyful
From being a killjoy to a kind soul
From loathing to loving
From mean to merciful
From neglect to notice
From opposition to proposition
From pessimistic to optimistic
From questionable to admirable
From resentful to respectful
From spiritless to spiritual

From thoughtless to thankful
From unhappy to overjoyed
From victim to victor
From worrier to warrior
Thank you, Lord. Amen

Thu / 2021 June 10 / Journal Entry

The January 6th Insurrection investigation committee televised testimony from four of the officers.

Officer Gonell testified, "The physical violence was horrific and devastating. We held the line to defend the democratic process. We don't want medals; we want justice and accountability."

Officer Fanone, who was beaten with a flagpole while he was on the ground, testified, "I was electrocuted again, again, and again. I suffered a traumatic brain injury and a heart attack. I screamed, 'I have kids.' The indifference shown to my colleagues is disgraceful."

Officer Hodges recounted his experience of being crushed in a door.

Officer Dunn requested a moment of silence for Officer Brian Sicknick who died as a result of the injuries he suffered from the domestic terrorists who attacked the Capitol. Dunn said, "It was the saddest day for all of us."

Thu / 2021 June 24 / Journal Entry

Rock of the Day: Frog
"Take the Leap. Every journey begins with the first hop." Unknown

Mamal is moving to Oxford Glen Assisted Living and Memory Care. She is moving to the Holly House. I live on Holly Hills Lane. There are O.G. (Oxford Glen) blocks in the lobby. Jose calls her "O.G." (Original Gangster). There are painted rocks at the entrance. The receptionist's name is Cheryl (her daughter/my mother's name). It just feels right.

I often wonder if the connections I make in my head are creative conjectures of coincidence or if I am noticing God's presence and work all around me. I like the latter explanation.

Fri / 2021 June 25 / Journal Entry

I woke Mamal up and cooked a quick breakfast for her. I got her dressed and fixed her hair even though she wanted to stay in her robe. I showered, dressed, and packed her bags. Michael showed up, which surprised her. He got her in the car, and we followed him to Oxford Glen.

He told her in the car, "I'm taking you to your new home."

The director greeted her, and we got her into a house with other residents who greeted her and started talking to her. Michael and I set up her room and finished paperwork. I hung a sign on the door that said "Miss Gladys," and I put a picture of her holding a sign that said, "The party has arrived," in the display case by her door.

We took her to her room, but when she saw her name on the door, she started saying, "No, no, no, no." We took her in, showed her around, and used redirection techniques to deal with her objections.

I finally sat down and told her, "You don't want to be a burden to your family."

She said, "No."

I said, "We love you very much. This is not easy for us, but it is best." We took her back to the other residents and left. It was hard. It was weird. It was a relief.

Sat / 2021 June 26 / Journal Entry

We took the dogs and Michael for a morning walk on the trail. I saw a cardinal as soon as we set out. I took it as a visitor from heaven. We met Michelle for lunch, and Michael gave her a recap of moving

O.G. to O.G. He went back to O.G. to visit O.G. From now on, when I speak of Mamal I will refer to her as Miss Gladys or O.G. (Original Gangsta). I think it may be a coping mechanism to help me separate my feelings for my grandmother and deal with an elderly person with dementia.

Wed / 2021 June 30 / Journal Entry

I had an appointment with Dr. Lemmon for my upcoming surgery. It is a day surgery at a surgical center, so I anticipate a speedy recovery. Taylor's bachelor party is a deep-sea fishing trip on the coast. It is the day after my surgery, and I want Jose to go. I should be fine.

After dinner, Jose and I went to The Duck Pond. I fed the ducks frozen peas and watched the sunset while Jose fished. He caught his personal best, a 14.3-pound catfish. He attracted a crowd of kids, moms, and other fishers at the pond. I am so glad I was there to get pictures and a video before he released it back into the pond. We found a painted rock that said, "I Love Wood Biscuit."

july

Tue / 2021 July 6 / Journal Entry

The barn swallows had a convention on our porch today. All day they gathered—there must have been ten of them! Whenever I let the dogs out, the birds flew *Top Gun* flight patterns around the back yard.

Our virtual Bible study was another timely lesson about the three-hands approach to life. The first approach is to fold your hands, which means you have checked out and stopped trying. The second approach is to have tight, clenched fists to control life's outcomes, and it brings stress and anxiety. The last approach is to have an open hand held up to the sky and outstretched to God that is receiving the blessings God has for us. I thought it was a powerful lesson. The discussion questions asked us to think about the specific things we are currently trying to control. Then it challenged us to consider what it would look like and feel like to have an open-handed approach to these things and trust God.

Thu / 2021 July 8 / Journal Entry

Check in at the surgery center was 6:00 a.m., and the surgery was at 7:00 a.m. I got home around 11:30 a.m. I felt a lot of pain and nausea. I was surprised because I thought the surgery would be easy compared to the other two which required hospital stays. I slept most of the day.

Fri / 2021 July 9 / Journal Entry

"I bend so I don't break."
Jean de La Fontaine

Jose left to go to Port O'Connor for Taylor's bachelor party. They are going deep-sea fishing. I am worried sick. The coast is flooded. It's a long drive. It's the ocean.

Kyla flew out to Florida for a bachelorette party. I am worried sick. It's Florida. There are 20,000 new COVID-19 cases per day for the third day in a row. It is the Delta variant which is rampant in unvaccinated areas like Florida and Texas.

Jordan is in Kansas visiting his best friend, and Kat is home alone waiting for Jensen's arrival. My pain is unbearable, so I am taking pain pills. I have no appetite. I feel much worse than I expected.

The Virtual Virtues group had a Zoom meeting. Dr. Bob posed a question, "How do you cope when you are really down?" Some of the ways suggested by the group included: cathartic crying, attitude of gratitude, humor, serving others, learning something new, being extra empathetic, pulling away, being vulnerable, being creative, accomplishing something, praying, asking for help, and approaching the problem with the left or right brain. I thought this was a timely, lovely discussion with a community of people I admire deeply.

Sat / 2021 July 10 / Journal Entry

"Some see a weed; others see a wish."
Roma Downey

I decided not to take any more pain pills. I need to get out of my brain fog. I slept most of the day. The dogs have not left my side. Major comes to me so I can hold his collar. He backs up so he can pull me up so I can stand up. I feel awful. I have tried to eat, but I have no appetite. I am worried. I am fussy. I am alone. I am fighting to feel better. I have too many things I want and need to do.

Sun / 2021 July 11 / Journal Entry

Jose is on his way home. I am not going to lie; I am ready for him to be home. I tried to eat half of a peanut butter sandwich, and it was a challenge. I am weak and grouchy. I feel like shit. I have cried a lot.

Mon / 2021 July 12 / Journal Entry

"H.O.P.E. = Hold On. Pain Ends."
Triston Harper

Today was awful. I felt awful. I was not in pain, but every breath was painful. I cried all day. Jose felt helpless.

I could not put my finger on the source of my sorrow, but it was deep, and it was real. I prayed. I cried. I sucked it up. I cried. I went outside. I cried. I got off the couch. I cried. I had no appetite.

Finally, I called the surgery center. I spoke to Stephan, a nurse with a British accent and wonderful bedside manner. I am not sure how Stephan "identifies" but "they" treated me with care and respect. They asked me questions, reassured me, and asked me if I wanted to harm myself. I must have sounded pathetic. Stephan contacted Dr. Lemmon. His nurse called and asked me the same questions.

Why is it easier to talk to strangers when I feel like shit?

They called in a different prescription for nausea. It seemed to help. I ate a good dinner. I wrote a check for $8500 and mailed it to the caterer for Kyla's wedding. I felt like throwing up as I wrote it.

Tue / 2021 July 13 / Journal Entry

"We don't see things as they are; we see them as we are."
Anais Nin

I feel better today. I can be fairly strong and positive most days. I can handle a lot of irons in the fire. I thrive on managing stress. But once in a while, it all comes to a head. I get knocked to my knees, and the only way through is to turn it over to God. I had to be reminded to unclench my fists and open my hands to God's blessings. I am blessed with so much.

I studied "Wisdom from Sensual Love Poetry" and the Song of Solomon from the Bible Project's Reflection series. I was reminded of the gift I was given with Jose's love for me. I was reminded that we have our own little Garden of Eden on the corner of Holly Hills Lane and Creek Crossing. I was reminded that God wants a relationship with me.

Wed / 2021 July 14 / Journal Entry

"I took a walk in the woods and came out taller than the trees."
Henry David Thoreau

I felt 100 times better today. I did a few things around the house which made me feel useful and actually relaxed me. I worked in the office on wedding stuff for a few hours. My brain is no longer foggy. I watched the birds in the backyard. I helped Jose make dinner, and we took the dogs for a 3.5 mile walk on the trail and to The Duck Pond. We sat on the bench, watched the ducks and the clouds, and I felt normal, except for the drain attached to my body. I didn't nap today. It was an excellent day.

Thu / 2021 July 15 / Journal Entry

"Like seashells, we are beautiful and unique, each with a story to tell."
Unknown

I had an early appointment at Dr. Lemmon's office. It's funny—his office is being renovated. I am still under renovation. The drain stayed in, and I got a prescription for an antibiotic. The nurse said the drain hole was "angry." I got blood work at Quest for my oncologist, Dr. Trumbly.

Sun / 2021 July 18 / Journal Entry

The rainbow that I have put in the sky will be my sign to you and to every living creature on earth. It will remind you that I will keep this promise forever.
(Genesis 9:13)

I decided to tackle the Bible study. It was called "Learning How to Grieve from Lamentations," and it was just what I needed to transform my mindset.

The book is full of poems of suffering and grief. We are called to express our anger and suffering and loss to God and to understand we do not have God's view of the situation. He wants us to wait within the suffering. He wants us to be in it. We cannot avoid it. We need to go through it. God will not necessarily fix the situation. God grieves when we do, and He cares deeply. We are called to remember God's character.

"I remember my affliction and my wandering, the bitterness and the gall. I well remember them, and my soul is downcast within me. Yet this I call to mind and therefore I have hope: Because of the Lord's great love we are not consumed, for his compassions never fail. They are new every morning; great is your faithfulness. I say to myself, 'The Lord is my portion; therefore, I will wait for him.' The Lord is good to those whose hope is in him, to the one who seeks him; it is good to wait quietly for the salvation of the Lord. It is good for a man to bear the yoke while he is young. Let him sit alone in silence, for the Lord has laid it on him. Let him bury his face in the dust—there may yet be hope. Let him offer his cheek to one who would strike him and let him be filled with disgrace. For no one is cast off by the Lord forever. Though he brings grief, he will show compassion, so great is his unfailing love. For he does not willingly bring affliction or grief to anyone." (Lamentations 3:19-33)

Sat / 2021 July 24 / Journal Entry

"Start each day with a positive thought and a grateful heart."
Roy T. Bennett

The wedding is two weeks from today. I had a dream that we went into lockdown again. The first thing I saw on my phone this morning was a news story that Austin, Travis County, has moved to Level 4-COVID-19. The county guidance is urging everyone to wear masks, indoors and outdoors, whether vaccinated or not. I sent the article to Kyla since she is in Austin with her bridal party celebrating her bachelorette party. I sent a text to Taylor and his mom. She responded that she is worried too. I checked the status of their honeymoon destination, Aruba. Aruba is at Level 3. I had a mini meltdown about it all. I cried a little; I prayed a lot.

Sat / 2021 July 24 / My Facebook Post

Lord, it's me again. I am saying a breath prayer. I breathe in your name and breathe out my petition to you.

Breath—Lord, the coronavirus postponed, canceled, restricted, challenged, and transformed so many aspects of our lives. It also helped many of us appreciate all the blessings we take for granted.

Breath—Lord, I am selfish. I have plans.

Breath—Lord, I want our family and friends to travel and gather for my daughter's wedding. I want to be able to hold my soon-to-arrive grandbaby. I want to continue to visit my ninety-five-year-old grandmother in memory care. I want to rebook the Alaskan cruise I purchased for my husband's birthday. I want to see students' faces. I want to celebrate birthdays, Thanksgiving, and Christmas with loved ones.

Breath—Lord, help us help ourselves. Help us help others. Help us, the American people, rise up as a nation and show the world that we can unite to fight this virus. Help us lead the way.

Breath—Lord, help us eradicate the virus that has stolen the breath of so many lives.

Breath—Lord, I have plans. I hope they fit into yours. Amen

I met the Bible Chicks at Painting with a Twist. We were the only ones there. It was the first time we had all been together in person. We chose a therapeutic and fun cactus painting. We painted four potted succulents with the words, "Grow in Grace."

A high school friend hosted an alumni get together at a local bar later that evening. It was the first time I had seen those people since the pandemic started, and the first time I had been to a bar since I quit drinking. The bar was packed.

There must have been over 200 people there. I was the only person who was not drinking. I was the only person with a mask.

People stared, but I did not care. If someone asked me about it, I told them I was vaccinated, but I had just recovered from surgery. I had a wedding and a grandbaby on the way, and I was being cautious because I did not want to screw it up. Nobody was rude to my face. I did what was right for me.

There have been four million confirmed deaths due to COVID-19 worldwide. COVID-19 "long haulers" are people who have suffered from coronavirus and continue to have long-lasting effects including:
- Fatigue and mental fogginess
- Difficulties with sleep
- Intermittent chest pains and shortness of breath
- Digestive problems
- Changes in menstrual cycles
- Intermittent fevers
- Hair loss

These are the latest updates on COVID-19:
- 186,597,197 or 65% of people in the United States have been vaccinated.
- 83% of new cases are due to the Delta variant.
- There are 35,000 new cases per day, or over 1,000 per hour.
- Children under 12 cannot get the vaccine.
- 23,000 pediatric cases were reported this week.
- 80 USA Olympians have tested positive despite being in a "bubble."
- Schools are opening.
- Masks debates for schools are increasing.
- The Center for Disease Control recommends masks indoors for everyone.
- Texas Governor Abbott has banned mask mandates.
- While the coronavirus could infect two to three people, the Delta variant appears to infect six to nine people.

COVID-19 statistics:
Confirmed cases worldwide: 191,593,295
Confirmed deaths worldwide: 4,127,963

Confirmed cases in the United States: 33,875,385
Confirmed deaths in the United States: 604,546

Fri / 2021 July 30 / Journal Entry

"There's always light if we are brave enough to see it. There's always light if we are brave enough to be it."
Amanda Gorman

Today was Duck Camp for the new RCHS students. It was nice to see students again.

august

Wed / 2021 Aug 4 / Journal Entry

Three days until the wedding!

"Mother is a verb. It's something you do, not just who you are."
Dorothy Canfield Fisher

I was awake at 5:00 a.m. I had a crazy dream. I was in the passenger seat of a car with no driver. It was speeding out of control and driving in reverse. I was trying to stretch my leg to hit the brake while herding baby kittens and rabbits from jumping out of the back windows and doors.

I forgot to take my estrogen blocker medicine last night. I felt funky all day. I prayed. I cried.

One member of the wedding party is considering not attending the rehearsal because it could be a super-spreader. Our son, Christian, called to say he was on his way to get a COVID-19 test. A co-worker tested positive. A relative called to say that she will not be attending. Her daughter tested positive for COVID-19, and three other relatives must be tested because they had been around the daughter.

COVID has been hard. We have not gathered or celebrated as a family in over a year. We talked on the phone and had a Zoom bingo game at Christmas. We had drive-bys for meal pick-ups for the kids. We had a crawfish boil, sat outside, and still have not hugged members of our family.

I am very frustrated that people like me, who stayed home, wore masks, followed the science, sacrificed travel, holidays, and gatherings, AND got vaccinated, are the ones who continue to follow the rules and suffer. It is about doing what is right for all of us, not being stubborn and selfish. I am stressed about the wedding. Rant over.

Sat / 2021 Aug 7 / Journal Entry

Wedding Day!

"Happy marriages begin when we marry the ones we love, and they blossom when we love the ones we marry."
Tom Mullens

The bridal party arrived on time. The groom's party arrived on time. The DJ arrived. His photo booth assistant canceled due to his wife testing positive for the coronavirus. The cakes were delivered on time. The photographer arrived on time, and we took as many pictures as we could without the bride and groom seeing each other.

I was in high gear as a wedding coordinator. I had my clipboard and timeline and kept everyone organized and on time.

Guests arrived. The wedding started on time. The wedding party gathered in the grand ballroom for a toast and more pictures while the guests enjoyed cocktail hour and appetizers in the atrium. We opened the door for the guests to find their tables. The wedding party was introduced. The bride and groom danced their first dance. The officiant said a prayer, and Jose and I made the rounds to the tables and invited them to go to the buffet for dinner. I took off my blingy sandals and put on blingy Birkenstocks so I would be more comfortable. The DJ played classic wedding dinner music.

The guests started dancing to traditional wedding music. The cakes were cut and served. The garter and bouquet were thrown. The DJ cranked up the party music, and everyone had a blast. We sent the bride and groom off with bubbles and bells. I changed clothes and started breaking down all the decorations and cleaning up. All went well. We got out of the venue with time to spare. Jose and I went back to the hotel. My feet were throbbing, and I fell fast asleep.

Mon / 2021 Aug 9 / Journal Entry

Lolli and Pop Day!

Our little Gummy Bear, Jensen Carson, arrived at 1:59 p.m. He weighed seven pounds one ounce, and he is perfect! We were able to Facetime with Jordan, Kat, and Jensen. My heart is so happy. I am a new Lolli, and Jose is a new Pop. God is great!

Tues / 2021 Aug 10 / Journal Entry

*"It dances today, my heart, like a peacock it dances. It dances.
It sports a mosaic of passions like a peacock's tail,
It soars to the sky with delight, it quests,
Oh wildly, it dances today, my heart, like a peacock it dances."*
Rabindranath Tagore

Tues / 2021 Aug 10 / My Facebook Post

Lord, it's me again. Thank you for the many blessings you provided to me and my family this weekend. The list is long and in no particular order. Thank you for safe travels, healthy relatives, safety protocols, reliable vendors, a newly renovated venue, delicious food, lovely weather, friends and family, festive music, a new son-in-law, a wonderful wedding, a new grandbaby, lots of laughter, magical memories, and prayers answered. Amen

Thu / 2021 Aug 12 / Journal Entry

"You are capable of more than you know. Choose a goal that seems right for you and strive to be the best, however hard the path. Aim high! Behave honorably. Prepare to be alone at times, and to endure failure. Persist! The world needs all you can give."
E.O. Wilson

I posted this morning about doing my part, even though I am only one person. Decisions based on what is best for children and not what is convenient for adults, will always be the right decisions.

I headed to my RCHS office to work on awards. Every person I saw wore a mask. I went to Kiowa at lunch time. Less than half of the students and much of the staff were not wearing masks. By the end of the day, we received a district-wide email from Dr. May mandating masks on campus, switching to a virtual conference day, offering incentives for vaccinated employees, and thanking us for all we do.

Good afternoon,

As we prepare to open our doors to students and the community more broadly for the Fall term, the uncertainty created by the pandemic continues to be a reality for all of us. Unfortunately, the virus has created a new weapon with the Delta variant. We must now remain vigilant and keep fighting the virus with the tools we know can work, such as masking, vaccinations, social distancing, and handwashing.

Dallas County Health and Human Services has issued a mask mandate today for all public institutions of higher education, including Dallas College. Effective immediately, it requires employees, students, and visitors to wear masks at all Dallas College campuses and events.

Finally, with Conference Day scheduled for next week and more than 1,000 employees set to attend in person, we have decided to transition to an all-virtual event.

I remain grateful for all you do to make Dallas College a safe place as we continue to serve our students. We will stay agile and continue to monitor the situation as it is shifting rapidly. If you have any questions or concerns, please contact the Critical Response Office or me.

Joe May

Fri / 2021 Aug 13 / Journal Entry

"Love and hate are two horns on the same goat."
Tate Taylor

I went to RCHS. Some of the adults were not wearing masks despite the directive from Dr. May. I think they were "pretending" they had not seen the email. I felt so frustrated and viewed it as a bad example for the students.

Mon / 2021 Aug 16 / Journal Entry

Jose's fiftieth birthday!

"I am only one. But still, I am one. I cannot do everything, but still, I can do something; and because I cannot do everything, I will not refuse to do the something that I can do."
Helen Keller

I ordered yard signs for Jose's fiftieth birthday. It was the least I could do since we did not have a party or go on the Alaskan cruise.

The CDC is predicting that hospitalizations will increase by three times the current rate. The news reports 9,100 deaths this week and an average of 2,000 new cases per day. The mask battles are increasing. Airlines are canceling flights. Nurses and doctors are breaking from the relentless battle.

I worked all day at Richland.

Dr. May sent two emails within three hours regarding masks:

1:10 pm
Good afternoon,
Just a few days ago, I informed you of our plan to require face masks for all employees, students and visitors throughout Dallas College. This decision was in response to a mask mandate issued by Dallas County Health and Human Services (DCHHS) for all public higher education institutions in the county. Late yesterday evening, like you, I learned of the new order issued by the Texas Supreme Court, which temporarily blocks the mask requirement issued by Dallas County.

Even though the Texas Supreme Court has said that we can no longer make mask wearing a requirement, I strongly encourage all employees, students, and visitors to continue wearing masks at all Dallas College locations and events.

My job is not to engage in a political discussion about what has become a polarizing issue; it's about helping to ensure the health, safety and wellbeing of our students and employees. For the past sixteen months, masks, social distancing, handwashing, and now the vaccines have proven themselves as effective tools that keep us safe. Now is not the time to lay down our weapons in this arduous fight. I am calling upon you to accept this personal responsibility to protect yourself, your colleagues, and our students. In this fight, we need to depend on each other.

Thank you for your continued vigilance as we seek to provide educational opportunities to our students in a safe and healthy environment.
Joe May

3:52 p.m
Good afternoon,
I noted earlier today that the external mandate around masks is fluid and subject to change. This afternoon, minutes after my earlier email, Dallas County Judge Clay Jenkins issued an amended order reinstating the countywide mask mandate. Effective immediately, employees, students, and visitors must wear masks at all Dallas College locations and events.

While I support this decision as it aims to protect us all against COVID-19, I fully understand the chaos and confusion this political back and forth creates within our Dallas College community. As I've said before, your health and safety remain our top priority. Therefore, regardless of whether or not there is an external mandate, I implore you to continue following proven preventive measures. These measures include wearing masks, being vaccinated, social distancing, and handwashing. These actions have been proven safe and effective without regard to what our state and local officials decide.

As we prepare to welcome more students back to our campuses, we all need to model the behavior that best ensures our collective safety. We will keep you updated as this situation evolves.
Thank you,
Joe May

This is maddening! How are we going to end this global crisis when information about the pandemic changes so quickly?

Tues / 2021 Aug 17 / Journal Entry

Barbara and I were the only ones able to meet for virtual Bible study today. We discussed "Who Does God Choose to Work Through?" It was a study on Esther and Mordechai. Esther, like Jesus, sacrificially valued other's lives over her own. What a timely lesson, particularly as the debate and battle continues over masks.

Wed / 2021 Aug 18 / Journal Entry

The local news station reports coronavirus cases in schools are rising. Garland ISD has 440 cases, Dallas ISD has 121 cases, Frisco ISD has 103 cases, and Arlington ISD has 101 cases.

Thu / 2021 Aug 19 / Journal Entry

"If you want to make everyone happy, don't be a leader, sell ice cream."
Steve Jobs

I had my annual well-woman visit with Dr. Tang. It was a little over a year ago (8/11/20) that she found a lump in my breast and saved my life. I gave her a dozen pink roses and a big thank you hug.

Sat / 2021 Aug 21 / Journal Entry

"When we are asleep in this world, we are awake in another."
Salvador Dali

I have been sleeping so well. It is a true luxury to have a good night's sleep. I have very vivid dreams. I enjoy waking up and remembering my dream adventures, especially when they are not nightmares. My dreams since retirement and sheltering at home have been quite pleasant. I love my sheets and my bed. I love my eye mask and ceiling fan. I love to sleep.

Sat / 2021 Aug 21 / My Facebook Post

The past few weeks have been full of celebrations: a wedding, a new grandson, a milestone birthday, and family gatherings. It was also my one-year cancerversary.

Early detection allowed me to enjoy and appreciate life's magical moments.

Lord, thank you for helping me enjoy my "breast" life.

Mon / 2021 Aug 23 / Journal Entry

I had an appointment with Dr. Lemmon this morning. His nurse checked my scars. I seem to be healing well. I will go back in October.

This was the first day of the fall semester at Richland Collegiate High School. Many classes were canceled due to a teacher shortage. Unfortunately, last year many educators across the country left the profession for a variety of reasons. Dallas College reports that sixty-six percent of students chose in person learning versus thirty-four percent who chose online classes.

Tue / 2021 Aug 24 / Journal Entry

There are fifteen districts in DFW with mask mandates, including the largest districts: Dallas, Garland, Richardson, Plano, and Mesquite ISDs. The Plano ISD school board voted to allow parents to opt out of the mask mandate by filling out a form and stating medical, religious, or philosophical reasons. High school football games are being canceled due to COVID-19. Dallas College will give employees $500 and students $200 for proof of vaccination.

Our virtual Bible study lesson was "There's Hope in the Nightmare." We studied Daniel chapter seven and his visions. One of the takeaways from this lesson was a reminder that the Bible should not be interpreted literally or out of context. Daniel dreamed of four gruesome beasts that came and rebelled against God. There is a lot of imagery, and even Daniel is confused by his dream. With further reading, the arrogant kingdoms are destroyed by the Highest One. The end of the book of Daniel is a message of patience, faithfulness, and hope.

Thu / 2021 Aug 26 / My Facebook Post

"There's an important difference between giving up and letting go."
Jessica Hatchigan

This morning as I scrolled through posts on social media, I saw a post on a friend's timeline that stopped me in my tracks. I read it and re-read it. I felt shock, then anger, then sadness. I thought about it and pondered how I was going to react to it, if at all.

Lord, I was clearly bothered by the situation. So much so, I turned it over to you Lord. I prayed for wisdom and guidance. I prayed for tools to navigate my feelings and my response. I prayed for understanding. I prayed for the bigger issues this situation represents in our world. I prayed for you to heal all our hearts. I prayed and waited.

Lord, I continued to think about it throughout the day. There was so much terrible news today, my prayer and my "problem" seemed insignificant compared to everything else that is happening in the world. And then Lord, it happened. My friend messaged me about a totally different issue. It led to a phone call. It opened the door for a respectful conversation about my morning. My friend listened and responded in a caring, concerned manner. My friend was the friend I have always known, and not the perception of the post I had created in my mind.

Thank you, Lord for hearing my prayer. Thank you for guiding me to stop and think before I posted my reaction this morning. Thank you for creating an opportunity for us to come together and talk and listen to each other. Thank you, Lord for giving us the tools to navigate this "bump" in our friendship, and work through a social media misunderstanding. Lord, you are always faithful. I realize how busy you were today, and I appreciate the time you took for little ol' me. Amen

Tue / 2021 Aug 31 / Journal Entry

"You can do things. Do you know this? Do you believe it? You should. It's true. You can do great things."
Richelle E. Goodrich

Our virtual Bible study topic today was "Treasured by God." It covered the book of Malachi, the last book in the Old Testament. It discussed the "scarcity" mindset of the Israelites and what they feared was what they ended up creating—a downward spiral of fear and scarcity. The book of Malachi delivers a message of hope. We join generations of people who have experienced division. We are not alone.

september

Sun / 2021 Sept 5 / Journal Entry

Coronavirus deaths have surpassed the 1918 Spanish flu pandemic deaths in America (675,000). We reached a new pandemic milestone. According to the news, 700,000 Americans have died from COVID-19.

The news reports that there are over 1,100 deaths per day due to COVID-19. Over forty million people in the United States have tested positive for COVID-19. One in four cases are children. Even though the school year just started, forty-five Texas school districts with 40,000+ students have had to shut down due to COVID-19.

College football stadiums are packed, and there are few, if any, masks in sight. Thirty-eight million people are traveling for the holiday weekend. TSA is doubling fines for airline passengers who refuse to wear masks. People still refuse to wear masks and get vaccinated. President Biden is requiring all federal workers to get vaccinated. Seventy-five percent of adults have received at least one shot of the vaccine. These are strange times.

Tue / 2021 Sept 7 / Journal Entry

"There are two ways to live your life. One is as though nothing is a miracle. The other is as though everything is a miracle."
Albert Einstein

The new Mu variant is already in sixteen states. There is no definite date for the release of the third booster shot. There have been over 1,400 school closures in thirty-five states since school started. More schools start today.

I had an early Zoom meeting with Region 10 called "The 4-1-1 on the 9-1-1 on Testing." There are new testing vendors, new testing platforms, new deadlines, and new training for state mandated testing.

A new Tik Tok challenge called the "Devious Lick Challenge" encourages students to show off video recordings of themselves stealing and destroying items in schools. It started with taking wet floor signs, hand soap, and hand sanitizer dispensers, but quickly evolved into vandalism and theft of laptops, projectors, fire extinguishers, and more. School officials and administrators have spent the past week investigating this nonsense. I saw evidence of this at Richardson High School on Thursday.

Meanwhile, the RCHS students are posting positive Post-it notes in our bathrooms at Dallas College. This is one of the service-learning activities for Random Acts of Kindness week (smiling emoji):

- It'll get better.
- Have an amazing day!
- I am grateful for you.
- You are pretty.
- You are power!
- On a scale of 1-10, you're an 11!
- You are not alone.
- Lookin' cute.
- You are strong!
- 10/10
- I like your style.
- Make yourself a priority.
- Perfection!
- Quierete como eres.
- You got this!
- You are beautiful!

Sun / 2021 Sept 12 / Journal Entry

I woke up early to enjoy patio time and to work on Bible study. The backyard was busy with hummingbirds, gnats, dragonflies, and monarch butterflies. The fountain was bubbling, the sun was bright, and the air was cool. The backyard is my reflection, meditation, and peaceful place. Mr. Mockingbird serenaded me for four hours in my Garden of Eden on the corner of Holly Hills and Creek Crossing.

Sun / 2021 Sept 12 / My Facebook Post

Lord, it's me again. I want to thank you for all the inspirations for new beginnings that you have shown me in the past few days. Cooler weather, birthdays, caterpillars, and butterflies are small symbols of rebirth. Memories and messages of unity after 9/11 encourage small acts of kindness and hope. Beginning the New Testament, reading Matthew, and studying the baptism of Jesus offer promises of new creation and life. And the simple power of prayer, Lord, continues to amaze me.

It seems the more time I spend with you, the more you reveal to me. It's funny how that works. Thank you for this day and the time to notice your blessings and handiwork. Amen

Wed / 2021 Sept 15 / Journal Entry

Cases continue to rise, and people continue to die. I think about Christian, Kyla, Taylor, Jordan, Kat, and Jensen. I worry and pray for my children and grandchild to stay safe from the coronavirus. Life seems to be back to normal, but for many families, it is anything but normal.

Fri / 2021 Sept 17 / Journal Entry

I had a Zoom meeting with Virtual Virtues. I am so grateful for the "helper space" each month. We discussed experiencing weird vibes, being frozen, being present, finding silver linings, channeling color, discovering hidden treasures, and welcoming warm fuzzies. We also talked about the birth of new babies, the tragedy and death of 9/11, and collective grief and national unity.

I truly value this power hour each month.

Sun / 2021 Sept 19 / Journal Entry

Last year was the first year we didn't decorate for Halloween because of the pandemic. We decided to close that chapter and to forgo our Halloween traditions. We offered the decorations to the girls. They took what they wanted. The rest will go in the garage sale in a few weeks. Time to minimize the attic.

Sat / 2021 Sept 25 / Journal Entry

"If you don't like where you are, move. You are not a tree."
Jim Rohn

My fortieth high school reunion party further solidified my feelings of being blessed at this juncture in my life. After talking to multiple people, I feel like I am the luckiest of all. I am semi-retired, healthy, and happily married with a great family. I have a new and blooming relationship with God. I have good friends. So many of my classmates are broken, battered, unemployed, struggling, lost, cynical, and angry. It is sad.

Life from the pandemic seems to be over. My fortieth high school reunion was held on a big patio, the weather was gorgeous, and nobody, including me, wore masks. I did have my sparkly sequined mask in my pocket as a precaution. There is something strange about being around people you know and having a sense that you won't get sick from them…I hope.

COVID-19 Statistics:
Confirmed cases worldwide: 233,299,536
Confirmed deaths worldwide: 4,733,159
Confirmed cases in the United States: 43,950,004
Confirmed deaths in the United States: 709,218

october

Tue / 2021 Oct 6 / Journal Entry

Jose and I went to Stone Park for the National Night Out in the Woodbridge neighborhood. The creator of the Woodbridge Treasure Hunt, Brad Holley, recognized me from my Facebook profile picture and introduced himself to me. He said he wants to do another treasure hunt soon. I told him I had included him in my COVID chronicle project.

Wed / 2021 Oct 13 / Journal Entry

"Even if you are on the right track, you'll get run over if you just sit there."
Will Rogers

I had an appointment with Dr. Lemmon. They took photos of my "after" surgery results. My scars are healing well, so he set up a referral to the medical tattoo artist. He also gave me silicone tape to wear for fourteen weeks on one of the scars. It should reduce the Frankenstein effect of the scar.

Fri / 2021 Oct 15 / Journal Entry

"To improve your zest for life, fill it with vitamin C's—courage, cheerfulness, confidence, and creativity."
Unknown

...and caterpillars! (me)

There was a big monarch butterfly that stayed in the yard fluttering around the milkweed all afternoon. The next day I found three monarch caterpillars on the milkweed. I googled articles and videos on raising caterpillars. I promptly began setting up my butterfly nursery.

I cut a portion of milkweed, put it in a bud vase, and covered the top of the vase with a paper plate to prevent accidental drowning. I laid paper towels on the floor of the nursery to catch caterpillar frass (poop). I put two upside down red solo cups on each side of the nursery and poked a hole in each to hold a long milkweed stem for hanging and crawling. I took the three caterpillars and carefully placed them in the nursery. I named them after Disney princesses Moana, Mulan, and Merida. I checked on them constantly throughout the day, and I felt happy.

Sat / 2021 Oct 16 / Journal Entry

I found a fourth caterpillar and added him to the nursery. I named him Mufasa.

Since the caterpillars had eaten so much, there was a lot of frass. I spent a lot of time throughout the day observing the caterpillars. They seem to be larger today. They got very active right before sunset, so I took several videos of them eating. Sometimes they get very still as they shed their skin, then they turn around and eat it to help them grow.

Wed / 2021 Oct 21 / Journal Entry

When I woke up this morning Merida, Mulan, and Mufasa were clustered together in the leaves. Moana was hanging upside down from the top of the nursery in a "J" shape. It is chrysalis time! I really wanted to stay home and watch the caterpillars all day.

By the time I got home in the afternoon, Moana had fully formed a chrysalis and was in the pupa stage. The other three caterpillars were on the top of the nursery.

Thu / 2021 Oct 22 / Journal Entry

When I left for work Merida, Mulan, and Mufasa were still on top of the nursery. When I got home, they had all formed their chrysalides.

The weather is perfect. I went out to the back yard and saw a huge monarch butterfly on the milkweed. It made me glad.

Tue / 2021 Oct 26 / Journal Entry

This week's Bible study focused on the illogical story of Jesus: His humble birth, His unfair trial, His sacrificial death, and His resurrection. To understand Jesus requires a transformation of logical thinking. It requires trust.

Wed / 2021 Oct 27 / Journal Entry

Merck announced a pill that reduces hospitalizations and deaths from COVID-19 by fifty percent. They emphasized the pill is not a replacement for the vaccine. They tested it on 775 people—four pills every twelve hours for five days. The FDA approved mix and match Pfizer, Moderna, and Johnson & Johnson vaccines for the booster shot. Vaccines and booster shots are free.

The FDA recommends vaccines for children five-to-eleven years old. People who are vaccinated are five times safer than people who have had COVID-19. Antibody protection after vaccination is much more predictable than antibody protection after infection.

According to local news station WFAA, when the pandemic started, hospital stays and treatment were free. Now that vaccines are readily available, people are responsible for their bills. The average cost for in-network outpatient service related to COVID-19 is $1,164. The average in-network cost to be hospitalized with COVID-19 is $24,000. The average network cost for a patient who needs a ventilator is $99,198. The average costs for the same out-of-network treatments range from $3,157 to $378,052.

The news reported that over 140,000 children in the United States had their primary caregiver die of COVID-19.

november

Mon / 2021 Nov 1 / Journal Entry

One of my Facebook friends and a J.J. Pearce High School classmate died from the coronavirus. I saw him at the bar about a month ago. He told me how much he enjoyed my Facebook posts and positive energy. He told me he respected my decision to wear a mask. He was a good guy. He was not vaccinated. I am sorry for his family's loss.

Tue / 2021 Nov 2 / Journal Entry

Moana emerged from her chrysalis today. She turned into a magnificent monarch butterfly!

Since it is November, The Bible Chicks decided to say gratitude prayers today. We prayed for the health and healing of our loved ones. We prayed for the blessings of our families and the opportunity to be grandmas. We prayed for the opportunity to travel. We prayed for the miracles of butterflies and the opportunity to be a mobile presence for God and witness to others.

Wed / 2021 Nov 3 / Journal Entry

"Butterflies are God's confetti thrown upon the earth in celebration of His love."
K. D'Angelo

I decided to let Moana fly free. It was a perfect day. Jose took pictures as I carefully took her out of the nursery and let her go. She flew up to the crepe myrtles on the side of the house. I watched her for twenty to thirty minutes while she made her plan to head to Mexico. I was happy and sad. I had tears on my face.

I made lunch, and we ate on the patio. A monarch circled our yard several times while we ate lunch. I like to think it was Moana. Meanwhile Merida and Mulan's chrysalides are changing colors from green to black.

Thu / 2021 Nov 4 / Journal Entry

It's raining. I headed to Richland and told Jose to check the nursery every hour. By eleven o'clock Mulan and Merida arrived. The weather will be wet and colder the next few days, so I will keep them in the nursery until Saturday when it gets warmer. I ran out of milkweed, so I googled "how to feed monarchs." I bought some watermelon on the way home.

I led the butterflies to the watermelon in their nursery so they could fuel up before I release them tomorrow. #MonarchMom

I made an online appointment to get our COVID-19 booster shots and flu shots.

I headed to Socrates Cafe in person. We gathered at the Arapaho Methodist Church. Everyone wore masks. We discussed how we managed stress with diet, exercise, sleep, and creativity. We also discussed how to talk to people who have adopted conspiracy theory mindsets and are anti-vaxxers.

Sat / 2021 Nov 6 / Journal Entry

It was a beautiful sunny morning. The monarchs were active, so I released them one by one. Their next stop is Mexico. It was a heartwarming experience, and I can't wait to raise caterpillars again next year.

Sun / 2021 Nov 7 / My Facebook Post

Daylight Savings Time

I posted this prayer:

Lord, it's me again. There is no reason for a caterpillar to believe that it will become a butterfly. Metamorphosis is hard. Change is challenging. Transformation takes trust. Lord, thank you for all the reminders in nature and the seasons that change can be good. Through faith we can look forward to it instead of fighting it or fearing it.

Lord, thank you for providing the ultimate gift of transformation and salvation. It is a gift I cannot earn but only receive. Thank you for your Son. Amen.

Fri / 2021 Nov 12 / Journal Entry

The airport was not busy, but it was already set up for rows and rows of stanchions for TSA screening for the holiday travelers next week. Our flight was on time. Everyone was compliant and wore their masks. Plastic partitions divided the zigzagged security lines. It feels good to travel again.

I read *Oprah's Favorite Things 2021 Holiday Edition* on the flight to visit Christian where he is stationed in Fort Walton Beach, Florida. It was about gratitude. I also read an article in *The New York Times* that asked the question, "How does this end? Is it time to move back to normalcy?"

Mon / 2021 Nov 15 / Journal Entry

770 days of sobriety
612 days of COVID-19

I sat on the beach in Florida and wondered if this is where my pandemic story ends. Jose and I have had three vaccinations. We have been very disciplined throughout the pandemic. We have worn our masks...but not here. We have walked, shopped, and toured without a piece of fabric on our face. Life seems virtually back to normal.

When we get home, we will celebrate the Lozada Thanksgiving with the girls and their spouses. I will decorate for Christmas. I will hang my travel ornaments. I will edit the name of my Facebook group from 2020 Vision to Ama21ng Po22ibilities. I will give out new focus words and reflect on my focus word, "complete." I will make a list of things I have completed this year. But for now, I am going to put my feet in the white sand, lie back on my beach mat, close my eyes, and listen to the planes coming and going. I am going to listen to the waves crashing.

I am going to listen to God's voice speak to me.

Mon / 2021 Nov 15 / My Facebook Post

Lord, it's me again. Thank you for the planet earth. It is majestic. Thank you for the opportunity to travel. Thank you for my ride or die partner. Thank you for the little things like grains of sand between my toes. Thank you for the big things like the ocean and the sky. Thank you for sharing and thank you for caring. Amen.

Wed / 2021 Nov 17 / Journal Entry

"Back to life, back to reality."
Soul II Soul

I worked at Richland, then stopped by O.G. to visit O.G. She doesn't know me. She cannot remember simple things consistently.
Where were you born? What was your daddy's name? What was your momma's name? What about your brothers and sisters? Who was your husband? What were your children's names? What about your grandchildren? What was your address? What is your birthday?

Miss Jacque and the new nurse, Natalia, reported her seizures are more frequent. Bless her heart.

Fri / 2021 Nov 19 / Journal Entry

I had Virtual Virtues on Zoom. Our topic was anxiety. The group validated my anxiety about getting anxious when I do not have anxiety.

Thu / 2021 Nov 25 / Journal Entry

Thanksgiving
780 days of sobriety
622 days of COVID-19
Abuela's birthday
"Let all your thinks be thanks."
W. H. Auden

Fri / 2021 Nov 26 / Journal Entry

Black Friday

As I hung ornaments on our hodgepodge Christmas tree, I unwrapped two 2020 COVID ornaments and a breast cancer ornament. I got all choked up and cried a little. Jose hugged me.

The news reported that some Broadway shows and restaurants in New York City have closed because people are calling in sick from the Omicron variant. Several news sources report the Omicron variant multiplies seventy times faster in the bronchial tubes than the Delta variant. I am worried for Kristi and her daughter who are traveling to New York tomorrow.

COVID-19 news:
- For the first time in eighteen months, travel restrictions have been lifted for travelers to the United States from thirty-three countries with proof of vaccination and a negative COVID-19 test.
- People with prior COVID-19 infections were five-and-a-half percent more likely to be hospitalized with reinfection than those people who had prior infections and were fully vaccinated.
- Eighty percent of American adults and seventy-six percent of Texans have had one dose of the vaccine.

december

Tue / 2021 Dec 7 / Journal Entry

I started the first week of *Waiting for the Savior* Advent study from Biola University. It focused on the family tree of Jesus. It is made of flawed and imperfect people. It also states, "God has always delighted in using flawed, imperfect people for His glorious, good purposes, and He chose the Redeemer to come through a lineage of broken people." That means there is hope for me.

Tue / 2021 Dec 14 / Journal Entry

I woke up at 4:30 a.m. I sent my friend a text to finalize our plans to have holiday tea at the Arboretum. She texted that there were no tickets available. "Bummer" was my reply. I felt appointment disappointment.

I started to cry. It was silly, but I was sad. I felt ridiculous to be crying over something so insignificant given there are people who have suffered real tragedy and loss. I opened two pieces of chocolate because chocolate makes everything better. On the inside of the foil wrapper, one said, "If you are reading this, you are beautiful and worth it!" Alicia C., Texas. The other read, "After every storm there's a rainbow, no matter how long it takes to show up." Grace V., Ohio.

Janet sent me a present today. There were pencils from Good Vibes that had inspirational messages on them:
- Let Go of that #$@&!
- Namaste All Day
- Best Day Ever
- Be a Nice Human
- Good Vibes Only

- Kind People are my Kinda People
- Happy is the New Black.

There was also a box with twelve square stones. Each was engraved with an inspirational word: Dream, Envision, Improvise, Imagine, Create, Move, Believe, Express, Captivate, Inspire, Risk, and Compose. She enclosed a note that said she has a box, too, and she uses the rocks to focus her energy. Maybe I will use them with my new 2022 planner: twelve rocks for twelve months.

While we made dinner, Jose mentioned that it was the sixteenth anniversary of his heart attack. He was thirty-four when it happened.

After dinner we watched the first two episodes of the *Sex and the City* reboot called *And Just Like That*. This show was very important to me when it first aired in 1998. I was thirty-five, moving up in my career, and divorcing my second husband. I related to the characters who lived through many of the same experiences I was living. The show ran for six seasons. The theme song for the series is my ringtone on my cell phone. Now in the new series, the ladies are in their mid-fifties and still navigating life and love.

In the first episode of *And Just Like That*, Carrie's husband, Mr. Big, dies of a heart attack after working out on his Peloton bike. I cried big tears that rolled off my face. As I watched Carrie shop for and plan Mr. Big's funeral, I cried. As I watched Carrie, Charlotte, and Miranda deal with gray hair, allyship, podcasts, teenage, and adult children, LGBTQ issues, and aging husbands, I cried. One of the original cast members, Samantha, is not in the new series. There was some kind of falling out between the friends. When Carrie receives bereavement flowers from Samantha, I cried. I found it highly relatable, and it was a good cry. Today was not what I expected.

Biola University Advent Project

Prayer:
May the Lord bless you and keep you,
May His face shine upon you and be gracious to you.

May the Lord turn his face toward you and give you peace.
May his presence go before you, behind you, and beside you.
He is with you, and He is for you, in all hours and in all seasons.
Lord, we thank you for your faithful promise fulfilled in the gift of your Son, the Christ-child, the ultimate blessing that reverberates to all the families of earth. Amen.

Wed / 2021 Dec 15 / Journal Entry

"Complete" was my focus word for 2021, and I am super excited to "complete" the renovation of my body. I will get my first tattoos which are 3D areola tattoos for women who have had reconstructive surgery after breast cancer. It will transform my Barbie boobs to look more natural and help me feel more like myself.

I decided to confirm my tattoo appointment for next Monday. The office had no record of my appointment which I made in October. The girl said they had tried to call me and left several messages on my cell that they needed to change my appointment. I never received them. The tattoo artist only comes once a month, so my appointment will not be until February. Of course, my deductible will start over, so it is going to cost me twice as much as I had planned. I was overwhelmed with "appointment disappointment."

Fri / 2021 Dec 17 / Journal Entry

This week's study focused on J-O-Y: "Jesus first, Others second, You last." I needed this!

Tue / 2021 Dec 21 / Journal Entry

"Nothing ever seems too bad, too hard, or too sad when you've got a Christmas tree in the living room."
Nora Roberts

I headed to O.G. to drop off more pull-up diapers and adult wipes. It's a good thing I did. She was completely out of both. The aide reported that she had refused her medicine and breakfast. I sat with her in the dining area and made sure she took her medicine and ate some soup. It was slow and arduous. Then it was time for lunch, so I stayed while she slowly ate lunch. Then they brought dessert. She ate all the dessert.

As I helped her walk to her room, she had explosive diarrhea. The other aides were assisting other patients, so I helped her get undressed, cleaned her body, changed her pull up, changed her clothes, and got her settled in her chair. I spoke to the director, Ms. Jacque, and the nurse about her meds, her thermostat, her layers of clothes, her shower schedule, and her shampoo schedule. I left with a shopping list and a heavy heart.

I am depressed. I have so much to be happy about and thankful for: my family, my grandson, my health, my work, and the holidays.

I am sad for O.G. I am mad that people are unvaccinated. I am sad Kristi's trip did not work out. I am sad I will miss Bible study today. I am distracted and having a hard time focusing on the reason for the season. I am sick and tired of this pandemic.

Kristi's husband tested positive for COVID. He had a fever, so he got tested. They postponed their holiday gatherings. Bridget is in Chicago. Chicago officials recommend all visitors self-quarantine for two weeks due to Omicron. Barbara reported her son's girlfriend, who is a pulmonologist, has been exposed to COVID and is waiting for results to see if she tests positive. Barbara was able to locate six at-home rapid tests but said multiple stores are sold out. We joked about the *COVID Chronicles* becoming the *Omicron Odyssey*. We said prayers for health for all.

I was watching TV and saw an interview with Amy Morin, LCSW, who wrote *Thirteen Things Mentally Strong People Don't Do*:
1. They don't waste time feeling sorry for themselves.
2. They don't give away their power.
3. They don't shy away from change.
4. They don't waste energy on things they can't control.
5. They don't fear taking calculated risks.

6. They don't worry about pleasing everyone.
7. They don't dwell on the past.
8. They don't make the same mistakes over and over.
9. They don't resent other people's success.
10. They don't give up after the first failure.
11. They don't fear alone time.
12. They don't feel the world owes them anything.
13. They don't expect immediate results.

Fri / 2021 Dec 24 / Journal Entry

Christmas Eve

We slept late. We went to Flying Fish for lunch since we could order at the counter. We could seat ourselves and fetch our drinks. Many restaurants are short-staffed and lack enough servers for their customers.

We made a Christmas Eve Walmart run. It was crowded, and we got several laughs at last minute shoppers. Some men were looking at the "As Seen On TV" aisle for last-minute gifts for their wives. They will be in trouble. People were panicking in the food aisles because they couldn't find the allspice or vanilla wafers.

We picked up cookies from Crumble Cookies, then went to Spec's Wine, Spirits & Finer Foods to stock the bar for the party. Holy Moly Batman! Specs was super busy! We almost got plowed over in the parking lot by a driver who was not paying attention. The checkout line wound all the way around the store to the back aisle.

It is eighty degrees on Christmas Eve. We put on our Christmas gnome pajamas when we got home, made dinner, and watched *Being the Ricardos* and *It's a Wonderful Life*.

I stayed up and watched midnight mass from the Vatican on TV. Pope Francis delivered a message about "Littleness" and read a letter he wrote called "You Are Christmas."

From Pope Francis, Christmas Eve Mass, 2021:

Today, all is turned upside down. God comes into the world in littleness. This is the challenge of Christmas: God reveals himself, but men and women fail to understand. God lowers himself to be great. Jesus is born in order to serve, and we spend a lifetime pursuing success. God does not seek power and might; he asks for tender love and interior littleness.

Lord, teach us to love littleness. Help us to understand that littleness is the way to authentic greatness.

Tue / 2021 Dec 28 / Journal Entry

"The most wasted day of all is that during which we have not laughed."
Sebastian R.N. Chamfort

I continued to work on de-decorating. It is somewhat depressing, and it made me think about the reason for the season. Does our focus on God and Jesus go away with our decorations? I think for many, the answer is, unfortunately, "Yes." This makes me sad. It also makes me reflect on my own practice, which happens to be my focus word for 2022.

I met virtually with the Bible Chicks. We talked about a phrase presented in the lesson, "Groan with gladness." Bridget is in Chicago, and she is concerned that her flight may be canceled due to rising Omicron cases. Barbara just returned from Oklahoma where she said goodbye to her longtime friend, Jack, who recently passed away. Kristi and her husband are still isolated because he tested positive for COVID. They postponed their Christmas celebrations until January 9th.

I am struggling with my sinus infection and coughing. Major is recovering from pneumonia. We all have things to groan about, but we are all fully aware that God is working in our lives. Kristi mentioned a meme she saw on Facebook, "And just like that… Santa is gone until next year…but Jesus is still here with gifts that never end."

Wed / 2021 Dec 29 / Journal Entry

I slept late because I did not feel well. I had drainage in my throat that caused me to have major bouts of coughing. My whole body ached from severe coughing. I know it is related to my sinus infection because I have dealt with this for years. However, I could not help but wonder if it was COVID-19.

By two p.m. I felt horrible. I decided to try and get an appointment to get medicine before the holiday weekend. I searched for an appointment online at MedPost Sachse. The clinic was closed the rest of the week. I searched for other MedPost locations in Garland, Richardson, and Rockwall. They were completely booked through next week. I tried calling my general practitioner, Dr. Medina. He was booked through January 10th.

It was a perfect storm: people are sick, people have COVID, people are trying to beat the January 1st deductible renewal, and people are looking for COVID tests.

I searched the Baylor Scott & White website for other doctors and clinics and decided to try an e-visit. I answered a long questionnaire, paid forty dollars, and received a text: "You need to be seen in person, and you should probably get a chest x-ray to rule out pneumonia."

They never talked to me online or on the phone. They gave me a phone number to call to get assistance finding an appointment. I called the number and the agent suggested that I call Dr. Medina. I did that. Call MedPost clinics. I did that. Try a CVS Minute Clinic. So I searched online and got an appointment at the Minute Clinic down the street at 4:30 p.m. It was four o'clock.

I drove to the Garland CVS, checked in, and was seen by a physician assistant and nurse. They gave me another prescription for my cough and suggested over the counter Afrin nasal spray and Zyrtec. The shelves were ravaged at the pharmacy, but I was able to get the medicine they prescribed. There were lots of people waiting to get vaccinated. There were no at-home COVID testing kits on the shelves. I felt very lucky to have scored an appointment.

Once I got home, I started feeling worse. I do not have COVID. I do not have pneumonia. I do not have the flu. I have a sinus/upper respiratory issue, and I feel like shit. I know, comparatively speaking, COVID, pneumonia, and the flu are considered life threatening, serious illnesses. Sinus infections are looked upon as minor illnesses—except for people like me who have suffered at least one and up to four infections annually for most of my life. The news reported the United States hit an all-time record of new cases today due to Omicron.

I took my medicine. I took a steam shower. We ate dinner and watched the satirical dramedy, *Don't Look Up*. The plot was strangely similar to our current politics, anti-science mentality, and social media issues.

Fri / 2021 Dec 31 / Journal Entry

Another sucky New Year's Eve

The pandemic seems to be over, even though it continues to make the news.

- The Omicron variant is in the United States.
- People who are fully vaccinated do NOT need to self-quarantine after contact with someone who had COVID-19, unless they have symptoms. They should get tested five-to-seven days after their exposure, even if they do not have symptoms, and wear a mask indoors in public for fouteen days.
- The death rate for fully vaccinated adults is virtually zero.
- People who are not fully vaccinated should stay home for fouteen days after the last contact with a person who has COVID-19. If they exhibit symptoms like fever, cough, shortness of breath, loss of taste and/or smell, they should self-quarantine in a separate room from other household members, if possible.
- President Biden is expanding family vaccination clinics.
- Pfizer and Merck have treatments on the way that will reduce the

seriousness of physical symptoms related to COVID-19. This will in turn reduce mental issues by alleviating the domination of the illness in our daily lives.
- President Biden's administration is buying ten million treatments of Paxlovid, made up of thirty pills for five days, at a cost of $530 each. Americans will probably not pay anything out of pocket for the treatment.
- Mental health issues related to the coronavirus continue for teachers, nurses, and school children.

COVID-19 statistics:
Cases worldwide: 266,423,000
Deaths worldwide: 5,267,169
Cases in the United States: 49,234,572
Deaths in the United States: 788,161

2022

january

Tue / 2022 Jan 4 / Journal Entry

The Bible Chicks discussed the term "God winks." This is a term I had heard while watching the Hallmark channel. God winks are defined as an event or personal experience, often identified as a coincidence, so astonishing it is seen as a sign of divine intervention, especially when perceived as an answer to a prayer. This term is definitely the best one for all those times during the pandemic that I felt like God was speaking to me.

Wed / 2022 Jan 5 / Journal Entry

I stayed home today to give my coworkers a break from my incessant coughing and blowing. Jose called to inquire about travel insurance for our cruise we had rescheduled. I had been bugging him about it because I felt like something could go wrong given the rising cases and my ongoing sinus infection. He was informed the cruise had been suspended, and we would receive a full refund. I think it was a big God wink.

Thu / 2022 Jan 6 / Journal Entry

One year anniversary of the Capitol Attacks

I was supposed to go to a meeting at UT Dallas with my new student teachers, but it was moved to a Zoom meeting since the COVID cases are rising again. UTD will be all virtual until February. The news reported that the number of Texas students and staff who tested positive topped more than 110,000 in one week. School districts are struggling with increased COVID cases in students, teachers, bus drivers, and substitute teachers. Debates continue about mask requirements on campus and in-person versus online learning. A Virginia mother was arrested when she threatened to bring loaded guns to school if her child was required to wear a mask.

Some districts are so desperate, they have asked employees who have tested positive, but are asymptomatic, to report to work. Some districts are closing due to staffing shortages, but then parents are throwing a fit because they don't have daycare for their kids. Hospitals and medical facilities are experiencing the same issue.

I received an email from Raise Your Hand Texas about the annual conference next month.

Dear Kimberly,

In light of the recent surge in COVID cases and the strain it is placing on our districts, campuses, and communities, we have made the difficult decision to postpone the Leadership Symposium scheduled for February 16-18 until later this year.

Thank you for your patience and understanding. More importantly, thank you for the service and support you provide your staff, students, and community.

Sincerely,
Charles Butt
Foundation Team

I attended an all-day training session at Region 10. All the sessions were related to testing and accountability. According to the Texas Education Agency (TEA), the impacts of COVID-19 preliminary STAAR analysis showed a decrease in academic performance with a larger decline in math and reading. Reading achievement went back to 2017 achievement levels, while math regressed back to 2013 achievement levels.

Tue / 2022 Jan 11 / Journal Entry

I led the closing prayer for our study. I incorporated my focus word for 2022. I prayed that we can all "practice" an attitude like Jesus. It may lead to suffering, persecution, and/or death, like Jesus; but we can do it humbly like Jesus. I prayed that we would not grumble. I prayed for our friends, co-workers, and students. I prayed for relief.

Fri / 2022 Jan 14 / Journal Entry

Jose and I stopped at Walgreens and bought four BinaxNOW COVID-19 Antigen Rapid Self-Test At Home Kits. They got a big shipment, and the limit was four kits per customer. Each kit cost $23.99 and contained two tests. I also bought card protectors for our vaccine cards.

Mon / 2022 Jan 24 / Journal Entry

"Sometimes God lets you hit rock bottom, so you discover He is the rock at the bottom."
Unknown

I had follow-up appointments at the Cancer Center. First, I met with Dr. Hughes. She took measurements to detect signs of lymphedema. It is most commonly caused by removal or damage to the lymph nodes during cancer treatment. The main symptom is swelling in an arm or leg. She uses a machine to measure the fluid in the extremities. My reports showed some changes in my right arm but thankfully nothing outside of the normal range and nothing to be concerned about.

She also examined my breasts. She said while I did not need any more mammograms, I still needed to check for lumps and pain. The belly fat they used to reconstruct my breasts can become bumpy from necrosis, which is the death of cells due to disease, injury, or lack of blood supply. So far, so good. She raved about the tattoo artist and was excited for me to finish that part of my journey.

Then, I had a follow-up appointment with my oncologist, Dr. Trumbly. He said my bloodwork was boring, but we discussed a Zometa infusion. The infusion is delivered intravenously once a year. Zometa is used to fight side effects of the anastrozole medication I take, and it helps reduce the risk of skeletal events and postmenopausal osteopenia. In other words, breast cancer can move to the blood and travel to the bone marrow.

My cancer was caught early in stage I, but it could still occur. Thus, follow-up visits and estrogen blocker treatment for five to ten years are still necessary. The estrogen blocker, my age, and post menopause can affect my bone density. Therefore, I will need bone scans and annual infusions. There is a small risk of osteonecrosis of the jaw, and I must notify Dr. Trumbly if I have any dental procedures. There is also a risk of renal (kidney) malfunction with the infusion. I must continue to take calcium and vitamin D supplements. So my diagnosis is not bad, but I am not cured, and I am not out of the woods. I have great doctors, so I feel blessed.

I drove to the Parr Park Painted Rock Trail in Grapevine. The weather was spectacular!

I parked at the Church of the Holy Cross and walked to the trail in ten minutes. The church has a lovely pond with a giant cross that is taller than the highway overpass behind it. It is lovely. A woman was drawing a monarch butterfly out of chalk on the sidewalk at the entrance to the trail. I had the trail essentially to myself. The rocks had been rearranged and cleaned. It was heartwarming to see many of the rocks I had photographed over a year ago were still there. I took more photos, mostly of groups of rocks.

I met one of the founders, and we had a lovely chat. He told me how the trail came to be and showed me the first rock, a flag of Iceland, which is where he was when the pandemic hit in the United States.

We stood among a new installment of yellow heart rocks which was created to honor loved ones lost due to COVID. The Rock Trail recently broke the Guinness World Record for the largest display of painted pebbles at 24,459 rocks. He told me how Guinness required each rock to touch, how a donor had paid the $15,000 fee, and how three weeks before "the count" they had to make 8,000 more rocks to break the record.

I told him about my first painted rock find in Waco weeks before the pandemic. I told him about Woodbridge painted rocks, our faerie doors, the faerie village, and the Woodbridge treasure hunt. A CNN news crew arrived and filmed a story about the park.

Later, I enjoyed listening to songs from my Girlz Playlist. I cranked the music while I drove back and forth to Grapevine and sang at the top of my lungs.

- "Firework" Katy Perry
- "Try" Pink
- "Primitive" Annie Lennox
- "Breathe" Faith Hill
- "Coming Out of the Dark" Gloria Estefan
- "Take a Bow" Madonna
- "San Andreas Fault" Natalie Merchant
- "Dear Mr. President" Pink
- "Kiss of Life" Sade
- "Building a Mystery" Sarah McLachlan
- "I Could Fall in Love" Selena
- "Don't Let Go" En Vogue
- "Creep" TLC
- "White Rabbit" Jefferson Airplane

My throat was sore because it has been so long since I held a little car concert. I stopped at Bahama Bucks and got a black cherry, shaved ice snow cone for me and a sugar-free pina colada snow cone for Jose. When I got home, we sat in our front yard in our Adirondack chairs and enjoyed the warm weather and snow cones in January.

We took the dogs for a walk around rabbit run and dog alley. All the dogs were out and happy to see Dexter and Major. Jose has nicknames for some of the dogs: Sharpie is a Shar Pei, Amazon is a Boxer, and Frankie Sinatra is a blue-eyed mutt.

Our Holly Hills neighbors were out when we got home, so we chatted with them for the first time since the holidays. We also got to Facetime with Kat, Jordan, and Jensen. I felt reconnected today. It felt good.

Tue / 2022 Jan 25 / Journal Entry

One of my former employees is in the hospital with COVID and pneumonia. She needs to be in the ICU, but there are no beds currently available due to staffing shortages at area hospitals. Her family has checked over fifty hospitals, and they are waiting for approval for a hospital in Houston to admit her even though she lives here in the Dallas area. Her family is not allowed to visit.

Wed / 2022 Jan 26 / Journal Entry

I talked to Michael, and he reported that there was a COVID outbreak in Terlingua. Several church members tested positive, and the one and only restaurant had to close because of staff shortages. Oxford Glen called and said it was safe to visit O.G. The quarantine had been lifted. My friend got an ICU bed at Richardson Methodist. Prayers were answered.

Jose spoke to one of his work colleagues. She reported that nine of her family members had passed from COVID this past month.

Thu / 2022 Jan 27 / Journal Entry

I pray on the way to work. I pray while I drive. I talk to God as if He is in the front seat of the car. I begin with gratitude. I thank Him for the day, for opening my eyes, for the opportunities the day brings, and for answered prayers, my family, my friends, my job, and my health. I pray for specific people who are on my mind. I pray for our leaders. I ask God to use me as His vessel and help me practice an attitude like Jesus. I pray to lead, guide, coach, help, and inspire. I pray to pray better and to practice prayer faithfully.

I checked in with Dad, and I told him about my prayer practice. He told me he prays silently in his head every night when he goes to bed. He prays for people and asks God to give them peace—not health, or wealth, or whatever—just peace. Then he told me about Grand Daddy George's funeral in the 1980's. He said the family was seated at the front of the church in Waco. He said he felt like he was having a panic attack. He felt like standing up and screaming. The priest said a prayer for the family to be at peace. Dad said he felt a feeling of calm and peace wash over him at that moment. He prays for other people to experience the same feeling.

We also talked about how Jesus prayed throughout the Bible. Jesus taught the disciples to pray with The Lord's Prayer:

"This, then, is how you should pray: Our Father, who art in heaven, hallowed be thy name; thy kingdom come; thy will be done on earth as it is in heaven. Give us this day our daily bread; and forgive us our trespasses as we forgive those who trespass against us; and lead us not into temptation but deliver us from evil" Amen (Matthew 6:9-13).

Jose made meatloaf, roasted broccoli, and mashed potatoes for dinner. We talked about the strangeness of the pandemic at this time. The world seems to be back to normal, but we hear stories of people we know who have family or friends of friends who are dealing with COVID more than any other time during the pandemic.

As I was writing this, I got a notification on my phone. It was a headline from an ABC news outlet that said, *"Scientists are working toward a universal vaccine that protects against variants as well as some common colds, but experts say it is years away."*

Sat / 2022 Jan 29 / Journal Entry

We purged the filing cabinets of Jose's 2021 records and put them in storage boxes to keep for three years. We cleaned and rearranged the garage. I love having everything neat, clean, organized, and in its place. I thought about the boxes of garage sale stuff I moved today. When I opened the boxes, I realized I didn't even remember what I had put inside. When I saw what used to be treasures inside, I realized I had not even missed them. I felt empowered to let it go, get rid of it, say goodbye, and move on. It was a good reminder that stuff is just stuff!

The news continues to revolve around COVID. At this point there is a general attitude that everyone will get COVID. There are even people who are trying to contract the virus to get it over with. This is NOT being recommended by health officials. Some people are now getting Flurona which is the flu and coronavirus at the same time.

The CDC warns that cloth masks may not be safe enough against the Omicron variant. They may recommend N95 or double masks. 1,700 Americans are still dying every day from COVID. Most of them are unvaccinated. 160,000 people are currently hospitalized due to COVID in the United States. Over 53 million people have visited the free at-home COVID test website. Free N-95 masks have started to be distributed at pharmacies.

The news reported on "The Great Resignation." While hundreds of thousands of people left their jobs, hundreds of thousands of people were hired in new jobs. There is so much movement in the job market that they called it "musical cubicles." The pandemic and working from home have caused many people to redesign their work/life balance.

february

Tue / 2022 Feb 1 / Journal Entry

The sun came out, and the ice continued to melt. We took the dogs on a walk on the trail. We had to watch our step because there were several sections of the icy sidewalk on the trail. It was sunny and cold, with no wind. The trees were glistening from the ice and sunlight. The only sound was ice melting. The dogs were happy to get out and get some fresh air. I snapped some ice pictures on the trail. I posted the pictures with the caption, "Variety is the ice of life."

My neighbor posted pictures of her daughter at The Enchanted Fairies Portrait Studio. I was intrigued, so I investigated it. I decided to make an appointment for myself. The website states that it donates the portrait sitting fee to Kidd's Kids, a local non-profit that supports families who have children facing severe health challenges. "Have a faerie nice day!"

Thu / 2022 Feb 3 / Journal Entry

"A strong woman is like an eagle; against the winds she soars."
Gift Gugu Mona

I drove to White Rock Lake to look for the bald eagles I had seen posted on Facebook. I didn't know where to find them, and their location was not disclosed on Facebook, so I drove around and looked for people who were looking up. Sure enough, I found those people.

The bald eagles, who have been named Nick and Nora, built a huge nest near Buckner Boulevard and Lake Highlands Drive. Nick was perched on the top branch of a tall tree. I watched him for an hour and a half, and he never left. He was too far away to get a good picture on my cell phone, but the sunlight reflected on his white head, and I could visibly see him turning his head from afar.

Then Nora poked her head out of the nest. She hopped out and flew to sit on a branch near Nick. The two sat together, probably watching us watching them. Then Nora took to the skies and soared overhead for quite a while. Sometimes she would get so high, she would disappear from the naked eye.

The weather was lovely, and I enjoyed every minute I spent watching, waiting, and snapping pictures with my phone. I took a few videos that I edited later. I visited with other bird watchers who were geeking-out like me. They were very willing to share their binoculars with me. It was a great day!

Fri / 2022 Feb 4 / Journal Entry

Jose drove me to my appointment for my first Zometa infusion. We had a private room with a recliner and heated blanket for me, a chair for Jose, and a TV in the room. The nurse took blood first and sent it to the lab at the hospital across the street to get my creatinine levels. It took about thirty minutes for the lab results. Jose and I kept busy on our phones. Then the nurse returned with the calculated dosage of Zometa. It took about twenty minutes to receive the infusion, and then I was done.

I couldn't help but wonder about what chemotherapy would have been like. I am so very grateful that I didn't have to endure chemotherapy or radiation. I feel extremely blessed, but at the same time, I feel guilty for dodging that bullet.

Mon / 2022 Feb 7 / Journal Entry

"FEAR has two meanings. Forget Everything and Run, OR Face Everything and Rise."
Zig Ziglar

I woke up and thought about the interesting and happy dream I had just had. I could not remember all the details, but I knew I was out of town and shopping local business shops and boutiques for faerie-related items. I had on a very chic (think *Sex and the City* designer style) cowboy outfit with glamorous cowboy boots. I looked and felt fabulous, and I was surrounded by people who were dressed like me, so I fit in. Then, I woke up.

I dressed in hot pink and black to match my breast cancer mask. I did my hair and applied full makeup, including magnetic false eyelashes. The ritual of getting dressed is an important rite of passage for women, especially for me today.

I arrived at the Skin and Laser Center for my appointment with Marie Sena for my areola tattoos. I was early. I filled out the customary paperwork for a new patient. The brochure states that Marie Sena specializes in creating realistic 3D areola tattoos for women who have had breast reconstruction after breast cancer. This is a highly specialized artistic procedure that focuses on strategic pigmentation of the skin. Marie Sena is an artist, medical illustrator, and professional tattoo artist. She received her master's degree in medical illustration from UT Southwestern Medical Center.

Marie Sena called me back at exactly 9:00 a.m. She was pretty and petite. Her arms, chest, and fingers were covered in tattoos. She was polite and professional. She explained the process of the 3D nipple and areola tattoo in a gentle and reassuring manner. She took vertical and horizontal measurements of my breasts to determine the proper placement of the tattoos. We discussed size and pigment. I laid on a spa table, and she gave me a beautiful, crocheted blanket.

Due to the mastectomy surgery and reconstructive DIEP flap surgery, I had very little feeling when the nine tattoo needles delivered dye to my skin. As she worked, we talked about her background as a tattoo artist and medical illustrator. I shared my cancer-during-COVID journey with her. We talked about her hometown, Sante Fe, New Mexico, and the altitude. We discussed the TV series *Breaking Bad* and how her husband had been a production assistant on the set for several seasons. And just like that, it was done. I no longer have blank Barbie boobs. Now I need ten to fourteen days to heal.

Tue / 2022 Feb 8 / Journal Entry

"You glow differently when you are not hating or hurting, bitter or messy."
Unknown

Today's Bible study lesson was about how we use our words. We must be careful not to use our words to hurt people, then turn right around and praise God. We must be mindful that we do not judge people and talk behind their back and that we do not distort the truth to our own advantage.

This poem by Carol Wimmer has appeared several times in the past week on Facebook. It has been falsely attributed to Maya Angelou. I mentioned it during a conversation with a coworker. Then Barbara sent it to the Bible Chicks today. God wink?

"When I Say I am a Christian" by Carol Wimmer

When I say, "I am a Christian"
I'm not shouting, "I've been saved!"
I'm whispering, "I get lost sometimes
That's why I chose this way"
When I say, "I am a Christian"
I don't speak with human pride
I'm confessing that I stumble—
needing God to be my guide
When I say, "I am a Christian"
I'm not trying to be strong
I'm professing that I'm weak
and pray for strength to carry on
When I say, "I am a Christian"
I'm not bragging of success
I'm admitting that I've failed
and cannot ever pay the debt
When I say, "I am a Christian"
I don't think I know it all
I submit to my confusion
asking humbly to be taught

When I say, "I am a Christian"
I'm not claiming to be perfect
My flaws are far too visible
but God believes I'm worth it
When I say, "I am a Christian"
I still feel the sting of pain
I have my share of heartache
which is why I seek God's name
When I say, "I am a Christian"
I do not wish to judge
I have no authority
I only know I'm loved

Fri / 2022 Feb 11 / Journal Entry

A Day Without a Mask

"Morning is God's way of saying one more time, go make a difference, touch a heart, encourage a mind, inspire a soul, and enjoy the day."
Unknown

I arrived at "The Enchanted Fairy Portrait Studio" at Willow Bend Mall with my wedding dress in hand. Two girls helped me dress and took photos. They gave me a crown and wings, dusted me with fairy glitter, and started the photo shoot. They had three scenes: a mushroom forest, a unicorn, and a mirror pond. They also had props including a lighted sphere, gilded birdcage, treasure chest, bow and arrow, bunny family, frog prince, magic wand, and butterfly. We took photos for about thirty minutes.

Afterward, I walked around Willow Bend Mall. Half of the stores were closed. Hardly anyone was there, but it brought back a nostalgic feeling of so many days that I spent at the Galleria, Valley View, Collin Creek, NorthPark, and Prestonwood malls. Malls are rare now. I miss them. Again, it's been about thirty years since I "hung out" at a mall. I wandered into SkyPony Gallery to look around. The artwork was eclectic and very cool. I found a tray of painted rocks and chatted with one of the artists about my fascination with them. She was very much like me—my age, stature, style, and hair. She was very interested in the Parr Park Trail. I purchased three painted rocks that said "Faith," "Love," and "Hope." I added them to my rock garden on the back porch.

I sat in the Adirondack chairs in the front yard and enjoyed the sunny, warm afternoon weather. Life is grand!

Tue / 2022 Feb 15 / Journal Entry

"To be alive is to be vulnerable."
Madeleine L'Engle

The ten o'clock news reported the eagles' nest was blown down due to the high winds today. One egg did not survive. I was heartbroken. I lay in bed and tossed and turned for over an hour. I felt grief for so many things, and I could not get the image of the eagles circling and crying over their nest out of my mind.

The nest that fell was three feet wide and weighed 100 pounds. They had built it on an unstable dead cottonwood branch. The eagles are relatively young, maybe three or four years old. Biologists believe it was their first attempt to build a nest and mate, so they are hopeful the pair will try again. I am too. I started reflecting on some of the events that have been bothering me, and I started going into a dark hole of sadness and despair.

I didn't like that train of thought, so I started thinking about O.G.'s house and her stuff. I started to feel anxious about her estate and what would be involved in dealing with it when the time comes. I started to feel guilty that I had not been to see her for Valentine's Day, even though she does not seem to know the difference.

I started thinking about aging and being out of touch with things like TikTok, crypto currency, and 90's rappers who performed at the Super Bowl halftime show. I started thinking about how I had prayed for the eagles and the animals this morning, and then the nest fell, and I questioned God, man, and my faith. Then I felt bad for showing attitudes of compromise and losing my sense of faithfulness.

I said a prayer.

I continued to toss and turn. I thought about my friends: Bridget, who has been so strong and worked so hard and is sick again. I feel like she cannot catch a break. Kristi, who is bothered by things that are happening at the school where we both used to work. I hated leaving that campus. I felt a wave of grief wash over me because I do not think I ever allowed myself to grieve leaving something I had worked so hard to build.

I tried to think of pleasant things like pretty dresses and the joy I felt at the Enchanted Fairy photo shoot. I thought about faeries, wings, butterflies, treasure chests, glitter, and the Pegasus...and then, I felt sad. I miss the faerie village and the Woodbridge treasure hunt. I miss the painted rocks. I miss the magic and feeling of community. I miss the time the pandemic lock down provided me to reflect, explore, create, and grow. I miss it, and I have been searching for something to replace those adventures.

I miss indoor shopping malls. I miss going to the mall with my mom. I miss my mom. I thought about how these things making me sad were also part of *The COVID Chronicles*. I wondered if we were close to an end of the pandemic and if I was close to the end of this project. I got sad. I got anxious. I felt like I was on the last leg of a vacation when you do not want it to end and you know you have to return to real life soon.

I had a conversation with Chris at work today. We discussed minimalism and "stuff." I thought about letting go of my Barbie ornaments, my Madame Alexander dolls, and some of my china and crystal in the next garage sale. It needs to happen. It makes me sad to sell these things that are valuable to me for $1.00—but honestly, nobody will pay more. Then I started to think about all the other stuff we have that is sentimental to me but essentially worthless to everyone else. It made me even more sad.

So many things that were once considered rare, expensive, and valuable become obsolete and worthless. Maybe that is why we save things—so we can be reminded of our own worth and not have to face the fact that we, too, may become obsolete.

I prayed for faithfulness. I prayed for it all.

Wed / 2022 Feb 16 / Journal Entry

800th Inspirational Quote of the Day:

"The moments between your milestones are not filler."
Nelou Keramati

I woke up determined NOT to be in a funk. I prayed on the way to work for everything I had thought about last night. I could not help myself, because misery loves company, so I searched for stories about the eagles, Nick and Nora. Lo and behold, there were several reports that they were still in the White Rock area. They were spotted in an abandoned hawk's nest, which is common eagle behavior.

Work went by quickly. I went by Oxford Glen to check on O.G. on the way home. She was sitting in her room. The thermostat was set at eigthty-five degrees. She was happy as a clam. I gave her a little heart-shaped box of five Valentine's chocolates. We went out to the living area, and she and another resident, Miss Judy, played a competitive game of bean bag toss. The nurse, Natalia, put orders in for hospice care.

Sat / 2022 Feb 19 / Journal Entry

"Choice by choice, moment by moment, I build the necklace of my day, stringing together the choices that form artful living."
Julia Cameron

I spent the day in the guest bedroom cleaning out bookshelves. I went through all the hardcover books and novels I had and moved over thirty out to the garage to sell in April. I also sorted through old school files and threw away at least half of the pile. It took all day. I also found a spiral of poems I wrote when I was a teenager full of angst. I kept them for now. I found a folder of poems I wrote for Jose when we first met. I kept them, too.

I hardly made a dent, but it was a start.

I started tackling photo albums. My goal was to minimize the number of albums I have from thirty to less than thirty. I painstakingly went through the first three photo albums. I made stacks of photos I wanted to scan and store digitally. I made stacks of photos for each kid and family member to give to them at Christmas. If they want to keep them, they can; if they do not want them, they can throw them away. I threw away a bunch of old photos that were faded, duplicates, or just bad photographs.

It made me think of the time Michelle and I went through the closet of photos at my parents' house after mom died. It is hard to throw away pictures of people. It does not feel right at the time, but then life goes on and those guilty, sad feelings go away. I thought about the time and work I was saving Jose and the kids from having to do someday, and it made me feel good that I love them enough to do it for them.

Sun / 2022 Feb 20 / Journal Entry

Jose and I worked in the office today. He needed to organize his workspace, so I helped him purge old files, office supplies, and a box of all kinds of cords. We created another pile of trash and garage sale goods. It took several hours even though we are clean and organized people to start with.

Mon / 2022 Feb 21 / Journal Entry

"Be like a train; go in the rain, go in the sun, go in the storm, go in the dark tunnels! Be like a train; concentrate on your road and go with no hesitation."
Mehmet Murat İldan

My first project today was to update The Lozada Contact list with new addresses and share the file with Jose. The second project was to update our password list and share it with Jose.

Those little projects may seem insignificant, but they serve several purposes. One, they help me and Jose feel organized and less anxious. Two, they serve as a treasure map, of sorts, for our family, if something happened to us. Three, they force us to review our "stuff" and delete old stuff and reflect on whether we need the stuff we have or not. I feel like I have "practiced" minimalism all weekend.

Wed / 2022 Feb 23 / Journal Entry

Another day without a mask

"Very often a change of self is needed more than a change of scene."
A. C. Benson

I eliminated half of a banker's box of education materials I had saved. It included notes in spirals and three ring binders from Harvard: The Art of Leadership conference, The National Principals Leadership Institute in New York City, and Raise Your Hand Texas leadership conferences. I found notes from my time as principal at Memorial Pathway Academy and the Garland Alternative Education Center. It was time well spent.

I purged all my files at work. I continue to purge photos and school files. The more I work on it, the easier it gets to throw things away. I am getting more comfortable with shutting certain chapters of my life for good.

Posted on Facebook:
Pope Francis: "Do you want to fast this Lent?"
Fast from saying hurtful words and say kind words.
Fast from sadness and be filled with gratitude.
Fast from anger and be filled with patience.
Fast from pessimism and be filled with hope.
Fast from worries and trust in God.

Fast from complaints and contemplate simplicity.
Fast from pressures and be prayerful.
Fast from bitterness and fill your heart with joy.
Fast from selfishness and be compassionate.
Fast from grudge and be reconciled.
Fast from words. Be silent and listen.

Thu / 2022 Feb 24 / Journal Entry

Another day without a mask

Memories on my Facebook timeline popped up about the Cousins Trip to Waco, the Museum of Illusions, and the Leaning Tower of Dallas. It's where these chronicles began two years ago.

Sat / 2022 Feb 26 / Journal Entry

"When admiring other people's gardens, don't forget to tend to your own flowers."
Sanober Khan

Kat was at our house by 8:00 a.m. with Jensen. We got to keep him overnight for the first time! He is starting to clap and bang his hands like he is playing the drums, eating baby food, crawling, and pulling up to a standing position. He loves his new baby cell phone and watching YouTube *Cocomelon* nursery rhyme videos. He likes to play with his image in the mirror. He likes to play on the floor with Pop and crawl all over him. He likes to look at books with Lolli.

I love watching Jose interact with him. It is enough to make my heart explode. When we put him to bed between us, we both lie there and cannot take our eyes off of our precious boy. I get choked up and cry because my heart is so full. I never knew how much I missed out on motherhood and raising a child with the love of my life, but today I got my chance.

God has blessed us more than I can describe. I thought back to Kat and Jordan getting married at the beginning of the pandemic. I thought about Jensen being born during the pandemic. I thought about our blessings. We watched several episodes of *Love is Blind*. Love truly is blind when it comes to Gummy Bear.

COVID is still in the news every day, but it is no longer the leading story. Deaths related to COVID worldwide are over 5.8 million people. Over 900,000 of those people have been Americans. The CDC eased masking recommendations for seventy percent of the country, including schools. Factors that helped the decision to ease masking recommendations include the total numbers of infections, hospitalizations, and hospital capacity. Masks on public transportation will continue until March 18th.

Is the pandemic over? Is it going to be an actual event—like a declaration? Or better yet, will it be a celebration? Or will it just simply fade away with no significant moment in time? Will everything simply slip back to normalcy?

march

Sun / 2022 Mar 6 / Journal Entry

There's always light after the dark. You have to go through that dark place to get to it, but it's there, waiting for you. It's like riding on a train through a dark tunnel. If you get so scared you jump off in the middle of the ride, then you're there, in the tunnel, stuck in the dark. You have to ride the train all the way to the end of the ride.
Han Nolan

I did not read today's Lenten study until Monday. It describes exactly what I have been feeling. I feel sick and tired. I am sick and tired of feeling sick and tired. I have not been focusing on God, or really anything, because I have no energy. I feel guilty asking for healing for Major and me because I don't feel worthy. There are so many bigger issues God must deal with right now with Russia and Ukraine.

Mon / 2022 Mar 7 / Journal Entry

Biola University Lent Project:
Answer me speedily, O Lord;
My spirit fails!
Do not hide your face from me,
Lest I be like those who go down into the pit.
Psalms 143:7-8

I have been in a funky funk. I would like to blame it on my allergies, the Russian invasion of Ukraine, the not-so-clear end to the pandemic, and other things. I have felt particularly funky about my lack of direction and creativity the past few weeks. It is disheartening that the topic for Oprah's journal is "Connection." I feel anything but connected. I feel very disconnected. My Rock in the Box word is "Express," and my 2022 word is "Practice." I would like to practice expressing my frustration with not feeling connected this week.

When I look at the Lenten study, I see one common theme. God is always there. I can always be connected to God. God wants to be connected with me. I think about how God must feel when He does all the work to prove his faithfulness, and sinners like me do not appreciate it. Instead of being frustrated with other people in my life who I feel are falling short of their friend and family duties to me, I need to focus on my behaviors toward God.

Tue / 2022 Mar 8 / Journal Entry

"I prefer to sail in a bad ship with a good captain rather than sail in a good ship with a bad captain."
Mehmet Murat İldan

I met with Bridget and Barbara for Bible study. Kristi is in Italy. We discussed the "Tree of Life" lesson and analyzed the fruits of the tree of life (the Spirit), and the fruits of the tree of knowledge (the flesh). According to Galatians 5:16-25, the fruits of the spirit include: love, joy, peace, patience, kindness, goodness, faithfulness, gentleness, and self-control. Those sound good to me. The fruits of the flesh include: immorality, impurity, sensuality, idolatry, sorcery, strife, jealousy, anger, disputes, envy, and drunkenness. Those are no bueno.

Wed / 2022 Mar 9 / Journal Entry

"She was a wild wicked slip of a girl. She burned too bright for this world."
Emily Bronte

I did not sleep well, but I got up and went to work. By the time I drove home, I felt awful. I did not go to O.G. to check on O.G. I could not sit in her room with the heater blazing on eighty-five degrees. I got home and went to bed. I could not get comfortable. I could not breathe except through my mouth. My mouth and tongue were so dry they felt like sand. I could not quit blowing my nose or coughing. My muscles already hurt; my brain felt like it was going to explode. I even pulled a muscle while coughing. I peed and peed some more when I coughed. I started crying.

I called for Jose, and I dumped all my emotions on him for at least thirty minutes. I am so tired of this chronic illness. I have suffered since I was a little girl. I know it is not as bad as many diseases, and people certainly do not consider allergies that serious, but honestly— and I said it to Jose out loud in my rant—it felt worse than my cancer.

I had stage one cancer. I had three surgeries. I recovered from my surgeries. This torture with allergies and bronchitis has been recurring two or three times a year throughout my life. It affects me every day. It determines my daily activities. I have to decide if I am willing to risk getting sick every single time I do any outdoor activity. I watch the news constantly to be apprised of pollen counts and wind direction.

I cannot describe how much sucking up, gutting up, pretending, apologizing, and suffering I have done throughout my life and career because of my allergies. Do I feel bad and guilty for feeling bad? Yes, more than anyone knows. Do I feel like a wuss because I want to complain and cry today? Of course I do.

I am so depressed and frustrated. I have not been myself since I got sick around Thanksgiving. I told Jose that I often wish I could go to sleep and die because I can't get any relief. This is true. This is how I feel.

I cried and ranted. I ranted about my depression. My patio plants have dried up and died because I haven't cared for them. I do not feel like traveling because I do not care. I do not want to take photos and create memories for people because they really do not care. I just want to get my finances in order so I can leave Jose money. I do not want to leave him a mess. He has put up with so much, and he deserves so much more.

I just let everything I felt come rushing out, unedited, and Jose listened. The more I cried, the less I could breathe. I felt like my faith was at rock bottom, and all I could do was apologize, wipe my tears, blow my nose, and ask God for mercy.

I felt bad for feeling bad. I felt even worse that I felt all these feelings and wanted to die after being fortunate not to have ever had COVID. I felt disgusted with myself for losing my faith and having a pity party when I have not experienced a personal loss of a loved one from COVID. I felt like shit mentally, physically, and spiritually.

When you pass through the waters, I will be with you; and when you pass through the rivers, they will not sweep over you. When you walk through the fire, you will not be burned; the flames will not set you ablaze. (Isaiah 43:2)

We ordered pizza, and I went to bed.

Thu / 2022 Mar 10 / Journal Entry

727 days of COVID

Two years ago, I packed up my files at RCHS in case spring break was extended due to COVID-19. When I arrived at work today, I saw a momma goose nestling a newborn gosling under her wing. It is a sign of spring and new birth.

I attended the groundbreaking ceremony for Red River Hall. There were speeches by the President of Dallas College Richland campus, the Chair of the Dallas College Board of Trustees, the new Chancellor of Dallas College and others. The architect also spoke and said, "This building will outlive us." This is true.

Red River Hall will house 2400 early college students from Richland Collegiate High School, J.J. Pearce, Lake Highlands, Rowlett, Naaman Forest, Conrad, and Hillcrest. On the two-year anniversary of the beginning of the pandemic, it is a sign of hope and the future.

Fri / 2022 Mar 11 / Journal Entry

A cold front blew through, and it was a day to stay inside. I still feel yucky. I made an appointment with an ear, nose, and throat doctor for Monday afternoon.

Sat / 2022 Mar 12 / Journal Entry

Ten Year Anniversary

I love hiking in the California hills in early springtime and watching the green creep over the brown of the landscape and the flowers bloom and spread—orange, pink, purple, blue, yellow—carpeting what was once dry and seemingly dead. They remind me of God's goodness as well as of the reality of Christ's resurrection.
Dr. Alicia M. Dewey

Today was our ten-year wedding anniversary. We were married on March 12, 2012, at 12:00 p.m. near hole 12 on the Muddy Creek Trail. We walked the entire trail and enjoyed the fresh air and sunshine.

I found two painted rocks. One had a heart and arrow on it. Happy Anniversary! We didn't exchange gifts—we always do something traditional. The traditional gift for ten years is tin or aluminum. We decided to count our new roof fascia board as our gift. How romantic!

We ordered Dinner for Two from Chili's and watched the new *West Side Story* movie. As I listened to "Somewhere," I thought about our world coming out of the pandemic. I thought about my lovely life with Jose.

"Somewhere" by Leonard Bernstein and Stephen Sondheim

There's a place for us,
Somewhere a place for us.
Peace and quiet and open air
Wait for us,
Somewhere.
There's a time for us,
Someday a time for us,
Time together with time to spare,
Time to learn,
Time to care.

Someday, somewhere,
We'll find a new way of living,
We'll find there's a way of forgiving.
Somewhere,
There's a place for us,
A time and a place for us.
Hold my hand and we're halfway there.
Hold my hand
And I'll take you there.
Somehow
Someday, somewhere!

When the movie was over, I gave Jose an envelope with the two portraits from Enchanted Fairy. I enclosed a note that said:

Jose,
Happy 10th Anniversary!
You make my life like a fairytale, and you make me feel like a princess. Thanks for making my dreams come true.
Forever,
Kim

It was midnight—time to move the clocks forward for Daylight Savings Time and fall asleep to *Sex and the City*.

Mon / 2022 Mar 14 / Journal Entry

I had an appointment with Dr. Frank, an ear, nose, and throat doctor to get help with my chronic sinus illness. He ordered blood work, allergy testing, and a CAT scan of my sinuses.

Praise the Lord, my soul; all my inmost being, raise his holy name. Praise the Lord, my soul, and forget not his benefits - who forgives all your sins and heals all your diseases; who redeems your life from the pit and crowns you with love and compassion; who satisfies your desires with good things so that your youth is renewed like the eagle's. The Lord works for righteousness and justice for all the oppressed. (Psalms 103:1-6)

Tues / 2022 Mar 15 / Journal Entry

We rearranged the garage and purged enough files to eliminate a filing cabinet!

Wed / 2022 Mar 16 / Journal Entry

"Live a life that one day you can look back on it and smile."
Unknown

I spent all day on the photo project. I organized family photos of Jose and my relatives and ancestors. I tackled kid photos. I made stacks for Christian, Kat, and Kyla that I am giving to them at Christmas. I eliminated seven scrapbooks of photos. I removed photos I liked so I could scan and store them digitally. It felt good to get rid of stuff and to revisit old memories.

Thu / 2022 Mar 17 / Journal Entry

"Hope you wake up feeling like a blank canvas, paint yourself beautiful today."
Unknown

We loaded all our camping stuff in Jose's truck to give to Kat and Jordan. We rearranged the garage shelves. We washed the trucks. Jose cleaned the bathrooms, ceiling fans, and air filters. I dusted the furniture.

I gathered my collections of teacups and snow globes and set them aside for the next neighborhood garage sale. I am tired of dusting them.

I retrieved my grandfather, Papal's, World War II cassettes from the attic, so I can get them digitized before they deteriorate. I made an appointment with a furrier to sell my full-length mink and full-length sheared beaver fur coats that I have not worn in thirty-five years.

I threw away storage bins of Tae Kwon Do memorabilia, twenty years of greeting cards, and old recognition plaques and certificates.

Tue / 2022 Mar 22 / Journal Entry

Today's Bible study was on the topic of "Exile." I loved it! At first the word "exile" sounds ominous and depressing, but the lesson, as usual, was timely and full of hope. We watched a video that began by stating, "There's something about being home where everything's just right. We're surrounded by people we love and trust. There is a feeling of stability and safety." I thought about the eagles in their nest near White Rock Lake. I thought about Jose and me during COVID.

The video continued, "Others might even be forced to leave their home and go live in a foreign land. We call this going into exile." I thought about the Ukrainians being forced from their homes due to the Russian invasion. I thought about people who self-quarantine to prevent spreading COVID to their family, friends, neighbors, and colleagues. As the video continued, it asked, "Is there any hope of going home?" I thought about O.G. leaving her home and her lifetime of memories to live in a state of dementia at Oxford Glen.

The Bible Project states: *"Exile is a human condition. It's that feeling of alienation and longing for something more, no matter where you live. It doesn't matter where you live, we are all longing for a better home."*

I think this sums up how I have been feeling as we come out of the global pandemic. I have felt disconnected from my pandemic routine while I search to create a new post-pandemic routine that is fulfilling and creative.

The lesson continued to talk about Jesus and how "he wandered about with no home." If we can develop the purging skill, we could actually free ourselves of so much that weighs us down. We would be better able to spend time, effort, and money on making us better people. What a gift that would be to the ones we love and care about. To become unselfish and relinquish all that we value and hold dear. To be able to fly free like the monarch butterfly, or walk freely, like Jesus, without the burden of possessions.

I thought about my efforts to minimize, and that when we focus on Jesus, we cannot focus on other things. When we commit to following Jesus, we discover a new way of being human. That sums it up nicely. I think my biggest "aha moment" of the entire pandemic was a new way of thinking, living, and loving.

Thu / 2022 Mar 24 / Journal Entry

"Life is not fair, but God is good."
Dr. Dianne Collard

I went to Dr. Frank's for a follow-up appointment. I do not need allergy shots or drops. I do need endoscopic sinus surgery (ESS) in May.

Sun / 2022 Mar 27 / Journal Entry

"The best way to keep your friends is to not give them away."
Unknown

I removed all the dolls from my doll cabinet and carefully wrapped and labeled each one for the garage sale. This was one task I have been dreading. It was difficult to decide to part with a lifetime of collectibles and memories. We took the dogs on a walk halfway through the project so I could take a mental break. I decided to keep my Malibu Barbie, my breast cancer Barbie, the Bride and Frankenstein Madame Alexander dolls (which remind me of Halloween and our wedding), and the Annabelle doll. She is a replica of my grandmother in Waco. All the others will go in the garage sale for $1.00 each.

COVID-19 updates:
There are currently four ways to treat the virus:
1. Antiviral pills developed by Pfizer and Merck
2. Monoclonal antibodies for high-risk patients
3. Remdesivir for patients twelve years old and older who are admitted to the hospital
4. Convalescent plasma therapy.

The news reported that there are currently less than 40,000 COVID related hospitalizations in the United States. That number is down from 160,000 hospitalizations in January.

Over 975,000 people have died from COVID in the United States.

The New York Times reports the four best ways to reduce COVID that have small costs and large benefits:
1. More booster shots. Currently twenty-five percent of Americans are unvaccinated, twenty-five percent are vaccinated but not boosted, and forty-seven percent are boosted.
2. Evusheld is a treatment for people who are immunocompromised and are exposed to COVID.
3. Paxlovid is a treatment for people who have been infected with the coronavirus.
4. Masks can be worn when there is an outbreak for anyone who wants to protect themselves.

The CDC approved a second booster. President Biden got his second booster. He stated the pandemic is not over, but it is not controlling our lives.

My liberal friends post about the humanitarian crisis in Ukraine. My conservative friends post about the cost of gas. Life is basically back to normal.

april

Fri / 2022 Apr 1 / Journal Entry

Barbara sent me a link to a KERA Public Radio interview with Matt Paxton, author of *Keep the Memories and Lose the Stuff: Declutter, Downsize and Move Forward with Your Life*. These are some takeaways from the interview:
- Most people spend between $500,000 and $1,000,000 filling their house with stuff during their lifetime. The average estate sale brings in maybe $8,000.
- We hang on to stuff, not because of the stuff, but because of the people attached to the stuff.
- Stuff tells stories. We all have stories. We need to get the stories down to something people can actually consume.

Tue / 2022 Apr 5 / Journal Entry

"Be present."
Unknown

I felt pretty good today, until the afternoon. My cough would not stop. By the time I got to Bible study, I was exhausted from another marathon bout of hacking, coughing, and choking. I opened the Zoom meeting, and when Kristi joined, she found me sobbing. I managed to make it through Bible study, but as the night progressed, things went from miserable to worse.

Hear my prayer, O Lord and let my cry come to you. Do not hide your face from me on the day of my trouble. Incline your ear to me. On the day that I call, answer me speedily. For my days vanish like smoke; my bones burn like glowing embers. My heart is stricken and withered like grass so that I forget to eat my bread because of the sound of my groaning. My bones cling to my skin. I am like a pelican of the wilderness. I am like an owl in the desert. I lie awake, and I am alone like a sparrow on

the rooftop.
(Psalms 102: 1-11)

Wed / 2022 Apr 6 / Journal Entry

I woke up at 3 a.m. and coughed non-stop for four hours. I considered going to the emergency room. I had another meltdown, went into a very dark place, and thought about dying. I prayed, I coughed, I cried, I prayed some more. Finally, I fell asleep around 7:30 a.m.

I called Dr. Frank, and he prescribed another cough medicine. By the time I waited in line at the pharmacy and coughed up my lungs in my truck, it was too much. I got soup from Chiloso and Big Gulp Mountain Dew from 7-Eleven. The soup, liquids, and cough syrup helped me take a much-needed nap. I hate being sick. I feel disconnected, unorganized, and out of control. It is unnerving.

"In Jesus we have a Savior who intimately knows our suffering and despair because He 'dwelt among us'. Jesus models the way to handle suffering by seeking His Father. We are not meant to walk alone in our pain and suffering. We were created to seek Him in our time of need."
Dr. Penny Bacon

Fri / 2022 Apr 8 / Journal Entry

I met with the Virtual Virtues on Zoom. The topic was "Empathy". We had a Holly Hills Hangout. Life seems back to normal.

Sat / 2022 Apr 9 / Journal Entry

"Spring is the time for plans and projects."
Unknown

I did laundry. I washed all the blankets, sheets, and comforters. I sprayed Lysol on every surface in an attempt to kill the coughing germs. I ate a half sandwich. The antibiotics are wreaking havoc on my appetite. I have no energy. The wind continues to blow forty to fifty miles per hour. Will it ever stop?

Have mercy on me, O Lord, for I am in trouble;
My eye wastes away with grief,
Yes, my soul and my body!
For my life is spent with grief,
And my years with sighing;
My strength fails because of my iniquity,
And my bones waste away.
I am a reproach among all my enemies,
But especially among my neighbors,
And am repulsive to my acquaintances;
Those who see me outside flee from me.
I am forgotten like a dead man, out of mind;
I am like a broken vessel.
For I hear the slander of many;
Fear is on every side;
While they take counsel together against me,
They scheme to take away my life.
But as for me, I trust in You, O Lord;
I say, "You are my God."
My times are in Your hand;
Deliver me from the hand of my enemies,
And from those who persecute me.
Make Your face shine upon Your servant;
Save me for Your mercies' sake.
(Psalms 31: 9-16)

Sun / 2022 Apr 10 / Journal Entry

Palm Sunday

"Let us reflect on where our hope lies, and in whom our hope lies."
Dr. Lindsey Huang

Today was not a good day. I did not eat. I felt depressed. I cried. I have no energy. Jose felt bad for me. I went back to bed around three o'clock. I decided to text the Bible Chicks that I was not going to make it to see *Jesus Christ Superstar* at Fair Park Music Hall Tuesday night. It makes me sad, but I am relieved. I do not have the energy to begin to pretend like I am having a good time. I know that I would cough all the way through the musical, and that would make me a disrespectful audience member. Everyone would stare at me and think I have COVID. I needed to let it go. I hope they can find someone to use my ticket.

Biola University Lent Project Day 41

Prayer
Dear Lord Jesus,
You are not a far off, impersonal God unconcerned and unfamiliar with our seasons of suffering or the worries of our daily lives. Thank you for being a Savior that cares about our physical and spiritual condition. Give us a spirit of humility as we rely on your Holy Spirit to cultivate hope within us. May this hope result in praise and honor to you, and a desire to share this hope with others. As we await your return, may we continue to put our hope in you, following you faithfully no matter our earthly circumstances.
Amen

Mon / 2022 Apr 11 / Journal Entry

"As long as you are breathing, there is more right with you than wrong with you, no matter what is wrong."
Jon Kabat-Zinn

I made myself get up and get dressed. I insisted that Jose and I go out for breakfast. We needed to get out of the house. We needed to eat. The wind has subsided, and it smells like rain. Finally, there is moisture in the air. Blue jays, cardinals, yellow waxwings, doves, sparrows, and grackles were eating at the bird feeder this morning.

The dove continues to sit on her nest despite the hurricane force winds of the past week. I spotted a monarch butterfly today. There is a new chameleon living outside the bathroom window. He has been hanging out all weekend. The salvia has sprouted. There are signs of hyacinth and zinnia sprouts, too.

Biola University Lent Project Day 42

"For now, more often than not, we take up our crosses daily, and perhaps more often than not, its accompanying afflictions. For in this too, the Lord is good."
Dr. Adam Johnson

Prayer
Father, in the midst of the fear, anxiety and real suffering,
We await, we long for, the power of your resurrection.
Come soon, Lord. Come soon.
Amen

Wed / 2022 Apr 13 / Journal Entry

Create in me a pure heart, O God, and renew a steadfast spirit within me.
(Psalms 51: 10)

I had a follow-up appointment with Dr. Lemmon. He graduated me, so I do not have to return to his office unless I develop some sort of issue with my reconstruction.

Biola University Lent Project Day 43

Prayer
Dear Lord, as we continue the journey through Holy Week, help me to trust you more fully and live in your forgiveness, healing, and wholeness. Remind me that you will not leave me, and in the process, renew my heart.

Take away that which is within me that does not bring you glory so I may abide in you and bear fruit in your name. Give me a heart for those around me to share the gospel of Jesus, full of truth and love.

Father, I pray all these things in the authoritative name of Jesus and the power of the Holy Spirit, Amen.

Thu / 2022 Apr 14 / Journal Entry

"The day the Lord created hope was probably the same day He created spring."
Bernard Williams

- It is a beautiful spring morning.
- 920 days of sobriety.
- 762 days since March 13, 2020, when it all began.
- The mask mandate for public transportation was supposed to expire, but it has been extended for two weeks due to additional surges in COVID cases.
- The COVID case numbers are not being tracked since so many people have home testing kits now.
- Variant surges continue. Very few people are wearing masks. I am keeping one in the car, one at work, and one on my person, just in case.

Biola University Lent Project Day 44:
"We would do well to contemplate how the sufferings of Christ are a proclamation of the goodness of God and how trials in life do not obviate God's trustworthiness. Christ is present with us, not, perhaps, to alleviate our suffering, but instead to fellowship with us and sustain us through it."
Kevin Greiner

Fri / 2022 Apr 15 / Journal Entry

Good Friday

Count your rainbows, not your thunderstorms."
Unknown

We took the dogs for a walk on the Muddy Creek Trail. The woods were green; the birds and squirrels were active. The bluebonnets are large and lush this year. We saw Frazier Crane. The dogs, Jose, and I enjoyed the quiet, long walk.

Jose wrote me a note and asked if I wanted to go out to dinner. I checked "Yes."

Sat / 2022 Apr 17 / Journal Entry

Let everything you do be done in love.
(I Cor. 16:14)

We sold the couch, recliners, bench, cedar chest, curio cabinet, and glass side table, thanks to the Woodbridge Resident page. Let the minimalism journey continue! Everything else is ready for the garage sale next weekend. Jose and I washed all the window screens and cleaned all the window glass inside and out. We can see clearly now.

Sun / 2022 Apr 18 / Journal Entry

Easter

God must've had a blast painting the stripes on the zebra, hanging the stars in the sky, putting the gold in the sunset. What creativity! Stretching the neck of the giraffe, putting the flutter in the mockingbird's wings, planting the giggle in the hyena. And then, as a finale to a brilliant performance, He made a human who had the unique honor to bear the stamp, 'In His Image.'"
Max Lucado

A beautiful rainbow came out over the house. The Holly Hills neighbors gathered outside to admire it.

acknowledgments

I am deeply indebted to and forever thankful for the individuals who were part of my pandemic experience. Thank you for sharing and caring.

Family: Jose, Christian, Kyla, Kat, Jordan, Taylor, Jensen, Dad, Rosie, Michelle, Nicole, Jim, Angela, Shelley, Lisa, Michael, Mamal (Miss Gladys/O.G.), Papal, Grand Daddy and Annabelle

Bible Chicks: Kristi, Bridget, and Barbara

Bible Resouces: The Bible Project and Biola University's Lent Project and Advent Project

Educators: Colleague and friend Chris, staff and students at Richland Collegiate High School, staff and student teachers at UTeach, University of Texas at Dallas, Raise Your Hand Texas and Charles Butt Scholar mentees

Creatives: Christine Nicolette-Gonzalez and Janis Dworkis of Laureate Life Press, Leslie, and Michelle—authors, publishers and proofreaders.

Wood Biscuit: Kenny Newell
Woodbridge Treasure Hunt: Brad Holley
Pinot's Palette
Parr Park Painted Rock Trail
Woodbridge Residents: chalk art, window posts, faerie village, painted rocks

Holly Hills Hangout Crew and East Side Pink Ladies

Parallel Universe Pal: Janet

Members of 2020 Vision / Ama21ing Poissibilities Facebook group

Health Care Heroes: Dr. Tang, Dr. Lemmon, Dr. Hughes, Dr. Trumbly,

Dr. Frank, Nurse Navigator Amy, Marie Sena, nurses, medical professionals, dentists, chiropractors, vaccinators, nursing home staff, and claims specialists.

Contractor and Crew: Blake, Niko, Paolo, and Juan

Critter Crew: Dexter, Major, Arnold, Fred and Ethel, Manny, Frasier, Rocky, Rita, Rudy, Moana, Merida, Mulan, and Mufasa, Mo and The Governor, Nick and Nora, Sharpie, Amazon, and Frankie Sinatra.

Essential workers

GOD

journal prompts and discussion questions

Historical/Hysterical Journey
1. What was your first memory of the pandemic being a pandemic?
2. At the beginning of the pandemic, everyone had to "shelter at home." How did this impact you?
3. As you read the COVID statistics, how did it make you feel?
4. The United States accounted for ¼ of the worldwide deaths due to COVID. What are your thoughts and feelings about this?
5. What were your primary news sources during the pandemic?
6. How did your opinion of the media shift during the pandemic? Why?

A Spiritual Journey
1. What role did religion play in your life during the pandemic?
2. What is your personal relationship with organized religion?
3. What is your personal relationship with God?
4. How did you feel when you read about the author's spiritual journey?

A Renovation
1. Describe your personal health journey during the pandemic.
2. How did your schedule change during the pandemic?
3. How did your workspace change during the pandemic?
4. How did your living space change during the pandemic?
5. Did you experience personal loss because of the pandemic (job, social interaction, friends, family, school, health, wealth, security, etc.)
6. How did your personal celebrations transform during the pandemic (birthdays, graduations, anniversaries, birth of babies, deaths of loved ones, etc.)
7. How did your holidays transform during the pandemic (Spring Break, Mother's Day, Memorial Day, Father's Day, 4th of July, Labor Day, Halloween, Thanksgiving, Hanukkah, Ramadan, Christmas, Easter, New Year's Eve, and other holidays you celebrate)?

The Nature of Things
1. Describe the role the outdoors played for you during the pandemic.
2. What was your relationship with plants during the pandemic?
3. How did animals play a part in your pandemic story?
4. How did you witness the importance of nature during the pandemic?

A Creative Excursion
1. Describe how meal planning, shopping, prepping and cooking challenged you during the pandemic.
2. How did you occupy your free time during the pandemic?
3. What are some examples of creative problem solving you witnessed during the pandemic?
4. In what ways did your personal creative juices flow during the pandemic?
5. How was entertainment transformed for you during the pandemic?
6. How did your use of technology evolve during the pandemic?
7. What were your favorite things to watch, read or listen to during the pandemic?

A Political Perspective
1. How did your involvement in politics transform during the pandemic?
2. How did George Floyd's murder affect you?
3. Did you vote in the presidential election? Why or why not?
4. How did the January 6th attack on the Capitol affect you?
5. In many instances, states could make their own rules during the pandemic. How did you feel about different rules for different counties, states, etc.?
6. Did you experience any political division in your personal life?
7. In your opinion, how would you evaluate President Trump's handling of the pandemic?
8. In your opinion, how would you evaluate President Biden's handling of the pandemic?
9. Do you trust the CDC? Why or why not?

The Evolution of Education
1. What was your personal experience with school during the pandemic?
2. How do you feel about the Class of 2020 missing out on normal senior activities?

3. What do you think about online education?
4. How has your perception of teachers and educators transformed since the pandemic?
5. How has your opinion of public education changed since the pandemic?

Community and Communication
1. What role did social media play for you during the pandemic?
2. How has the way you communicate with your friends, family, neighbors, and co-workers transformed since the pandemic?
3. Did you witness or participate in any community building activities during the pandemic?
4. Do you think the pandemic resulted in unity or division of your community? Why?
5. How did you keep connected to friends and family during the pandemic?

SNOWVID and Caregiving
1. Did you have any bad weather or natural disaster experiences during the pandemic?
2. If you were in the Texas area during SNOWVID, how were you affected by the storm?
3. Were you responsible for caregiving during the pandemic?
4. Did you worry about any of your loved ones during the pandemic? In what way?
5. Did you catch COVID? How? What happened? What were your symptoms?
6. Did you wear masks? Why or why not?
7. Did you self-isolate?
8. Did you take COVID tests?
9. Did you take COVID medicine?

Deconstruction
1. Did you organize or clean out anything during the pandemic?
2. How do you feel about getting rid of stuff?
3. What role did alcohol or other substances play in your family during the pandemic?
4. How do you feel about making your end-of-life arrangements?

The Treasures
1. What were the positive outcomes of the pandemic for you and/or your family?
2. How did you find positivity during the pandemic?
3. Do you believe in God winks? How? Why?
4. Did you see evidence of God winks in the book?
5. What is your best memory during the pandemic?
6. Did any of the quotes in the book speak to you? Which ones? In what way?

Personal Reflections
1. What do you miss about the pandemic?
2. Who do you miss?
3. What did you learn about yourself as a result of the pandemic?
4. What do you wish for yourself? Your family? Your community? Your nation? The world?
5. Did you cancel anything or anybody during the pandemic?
6. Did you go on any travel adventures during the pandemic?
7. How was your experience traveling affected by the pandemic?
8. What scared you the most during the pandemic?
9. What surprised you the most during the pandemic?
10. Did the book remind you of anything you had forgotten?
11. What will you never forget about the pandemic?

references and resources
(in order of appearance)

A-Z Quotes (Introduction)
https://www.azquotes.com/

Stephen Covey, *The 7 Habits of Highly Effective People* (Introduction)
https://www.franklincovey.com/the-7-habits/

2020 Vision/2021/Ama21ng Po22ibilities/To Be in 23/Un4gettable in 2024 (Introduction)
https://www.facebook.com/groups/496287444564162

The Bible Project (3/26/2020)
https://bibleproject.com/

Socrates Café/Virtual Virtues (4/17/2020)
https://www.facebook.com/groups/1945762662407251

Obama Foundation (5/16/2020)
https://www.obama.org/stories/president-obamas-graduation-message-class-2020/

Carry the Load (5/25/2020)
https://www.carrytheload.org/dallas-memorial-march/

Jane Elliott's "Blue Eyes/Brown Eyes" Anti-Racism Exercise (6/3/2020)
https://www.youtube.com/watch?v=ebPoSMULI5U

Emmanuel Acho, *Uncomfortable Conversations with a Black Man* (6/3/2020)
https://www.youtube.com/channel/UC3DoYiL7X_N1Ta1o4HE9Mlg

Robin DiAngelo, *White Fragility* (6/3/2020)
https://www.robindiangelo.com/

Martin Luther King, Jr., *The King Philosophy* – Nonviolence365 (6/3/2020)
Social Inequalities Explained in a $100 Race 6/4/2020)
https://www.youtube.com/watch?v=4K5fbQ1-zps

La Familia de Esperanza (6/29/2020)
https://www.lafamiliadeesperanza.org/

5 Loaves Food Pantry (6/29/2020)
https://5loavesfoodpantry.org/
The New International Version Bible (7/6/2020)
https://www.biblegateway.com/versions/New-International-Version-NIV-Bible/

Dr. Hue Tang, MD (8/11/2020)
https://www.methodisthealthsystem.org/doctors/hue-m-tang-md/
Methodist Medical Center, Richardson, Texas (8/13/2020)
https://www.methodisthealthsystem.org/methodist-richardson-medical-center/

Zach Williams and Dolly Parton, "There Was Jesus," YouTube Video with Lyrics (8/14/2020)
https://www.youtube.com/watch?v=F_cXBD1LkrI

Dr. Jenevieve Hughes, MD (8/24/2020)
https://www.methodisthealthsystem.org/methodist-richardson-breast-surgeons-mg/

Dr. Alan R. Trumbly, DO (8/28/2020)
https://www.methodisthealthsystem.org/doctors/alan-r-trumbly-do/?utm_source=local-listing&utm_medium=organic&utm_campaign=website-link

Dr. Joshua A. Lemmon, MD (9/16/2020)
https://www.regionalplasticsurgery.com/plastic-surgeon/dr-lemmon-dallas-tx/

Parr Park Art Rock Trail (10/23/2020)
https://www.facebook.com/parrparkrockarttrail/

Advent-ure Challenge (11/4/2020)
https://www.theadventurechallenge.com/collections/all

Delish.com, Thanksgiving for Two (11/22/2020)
https://www.delish.com/holiday-recipes/thanksgiving/g1312/thanksgiving-for-two/

Amanda Gorman's Inaugural Poem, "The Hill We Climb" Full Text (1/20/2021)
https://www.cnbc.com/2021/01/20/amanda-gormans-inaugural-poem-the-hill-we-climb-full-text.html

President Biden's Speech on the anniversary of the COVID-19 Shutdown 3/13/2021)
https://www.whitehouse.gov/briefing-room/speeches-remarks/2021/03/11/remarks-by-president-biden-on-the-anniversary-of-the-covid-19-shutdown/

Oxford Glen Memory Care Residence at Sachse (6/24/2021)
https://www.oxfordseniorliving.com/senior-living/tx/sachse/bunker-hill-road/?utm_source=GBP&utm_medium=organic

Biola University Advent Project (12/14/2021)
https://ccca.biola.edu/advent/

Amy Morin, LSCW, *13 Things Mentally Strong People Don't Do* (12/21/2021)
https://amymorinlcsw.com/mentally-strong-people/

As Seen on TV 12/24/2021)
https://asseenontv.com/

Pope Francis, Christmas Eve Mass, 2021 (12/24/2021)
https://www.vatican.va/content/francesco/en/homilies/2020/documents/papa-francesco_20201224_omelia-natale.html

Enchanted Fairies Portrait Studio for Kids, Plano, Texas (2/1/2022)
https://enchanted-fairies.com/plano-tx/?location=plano-tx

Kidd's Kids (2/1/2022)
https://www.kiddskids.org/

White Rock Lake Bald Eagles Fans (2/3/2022)
https://www.facebook.com/WRLBaldEagles/

Marie Sena Restorative Tattooing (2/7/2022)
https://www.restorativetattooing.com/

Biola University Lent Project (3/7/2022)
https://ccca.biola.edu/lent/

Leonard Bernstein and Stephen Sondheim, *West Side Story*, "Somewhere" – lyrics (3/11/2022)
https://www.westsidestory.com/somewhere

Dr. Thomas C. Frank, MD (retired) (3/14/2022)
https://www.tomfrankmd.com/

KERA Interview, Matt Paxton, *Keep the Memories, Lose the Stuff* (4/1/2022)
https://think.kera.org/2022/03/31/decluttering-is-hard-but-it-teaches-you-a-lot-about-yourself/

Made in the USA
Columbia, SC
11 January 2025